WORLD EMPLOYMENT REPORT 2004-05
EMPLOYMENT, PRODUCTIVITY AND POVERTY REDUCTION

WORLD EMPLOYMENT REPORT 2004-05

EMPLOYMENT, PRODUCTIVITY AND POVERTY REDUCTION

International Labour Office   Geneva

World Employment Report 2004-05: Employment, productivity and poverty reduction
Geneva, ILO, 2005

References

ISBN 92-2-114813-0 (92-2-116360-1 (web pdf))

CORPORATE AUTHOR(S): International Labour Office, Employment Strategy Department

ILO DESCRIPTORS: employment, employment creation, poverty alleviation, labour productivity, developed country, developing country

ILO FACET: 13.01.3

Also published in French: *Rapport sur l'emploi dans le monde 2004-05: Emploi, productivité et réduction de la pauvreté* (ISBN 92-2-216360-5 (web pdf)), Geneva, 2005; and in Spanish: *Informe sobre el empleo en el mundo 2004-05: Empleo, productividad y reducción de la pobreza* (ISBN 92-2-316360-9 (web pdf)), Geneva, 2005.

ILO Cataloguing in Publication Data

Page-setting by the International Labour Office (DTP), Geneva
Printed in Switzerland   ATA

Preface

Productive employment is the economic foundation of decent work. Laying this foundation is the central challenge we now face. Decent and productive employment remains only an aspiration for many hundreds of millions of people, frustrated by a reality of rising unemployment or employment that does not provide the chance to escape poverty.

Access to productive work that provides an adequate income for working women and men and their families is the surest route out of poverty. The slowdown in the rate of poverty reduction since 1990 bears witness to the fact that much more needs to be done to meet the widespread call to "give workers a fair chance at a decent job". A rapid fall in the numbers living in absolute poverty in China and other Asian countries in the 1980s gave way to a slower pace of poverty reduction in the latter part of the 1990s. Throughout this period poverty has continued at very high levels in large parts of Africa.

Increased focus on the generation of decent work opportunities is central to achieving the goals established by the United Nations Millennium Summit. The Millennium Development Goals underscore the need for "decent, productive employment" for young people, echoing the call for the promotion of "freely chosen, productive employment" in the ILO's Convention concerning Employment Policy (No. 122).

In most of the developing world, "employment" and "unemployment" are crude measures of the state of people's livelihoods and life chances. More than three times the number of unemployed people in the world are indeed "employed", but under conditions so poorly remunerated as to prevent them and their families from earning more than US$1 a day per person. "Unemployment" as such is thus only the tip of the iceberg of the decent work deficit. We need not just more, but better jobs.

Thus, a major policy priority, as articulated in the recent report of the World Commission on the Social Dimension of Globalization, is to make "decent and productive employment" a central, rather than residual, objective of macroeconomic and social policies for a fair globalization.[1]

This *World Employment Report* takes as its starting point that, in today's world of widening inequality, productivity performance is a central issue for all policy-makers concerned with a more equitable, pro-poor pattern of world development. Productivity growth, after all, is the engine of economic growth, and it is only through increases in productivity that economies are able to sustain the levels of economic growth needed to increase opportunities for decent and productive work.

The *World Employment Report 2004-05* brings together three linked themes: employment, productivity and poverty reduction. Investing in improvements in

---

[1] The report of the Commission, *A fair globalization: Creating opportunities for all*, was published in February 2004 and is available at www.ilo.org/public/english/fairglobalization/report/index.htm

productivity enables working men and women to obtain income and assets to lift themselves out of poverty. With decent and productive jobs, workers can invest in the health and education of their children, and thus in the future of the economy as a whole.

The main aim of this Report is to explore the evidence regarding the impact of productivity performance on both employment growth and poverty reduction. The Report finds that there are tradeoffs to be made in striking the right policy balance between employment and income growth, and between productivity growth and poverty reduction. The Report tackles four questions central to narrowing the decent work deficit in the world.

- How do we ensure that we get the right balance between productivity growth and job creation for each country?

- Since agriculture remains a major part of the economy in most developing countries and employs a very large number of the world's poorest people, what are the most appropriate rural development policies for the improvement of productivity, the generation of decent work opportunities and for fostering poverty-reducing growth?

- Productivity growth depends on both worker and capital mobility between firms and sectors and also on employment stability to ensure continuous quality improvement in successful enterprises. How do we balance flexibility and security in the labour market to promote economy-wide productivity growth?

- Productivity performance varies widely between firms, with larger, more heavily invested companies generally having higher levels of performance than smaller firms. Policies which enable smaller firms to close this productivity gap will have a big impact on a country's economic performance. Which policies work best for small and medium-sized enterprises?

The Report concludes that bridging the "global productivity divide" is an important channel towards achieving the "fair globalization" called for by the World Commission on the Social Dimension of Globalization, as well as the chief means towards the reduction of poverty. The Report argues that the focus needs to be on the parts of the economy where the majority of people work – such as in agriculture, small-scale activities in the urban and rural informal economy, and in services as well as manufacturing.

Increasing opportunities for decent work is central to shaping a fair globalization and creating an enabling environment for the achievement of the goals of the Millennium Declaration. This will entail crucial choices about the pattern of development. Dialogue, involving trade unions, employers' organizations and others, is vital to finding the right balance of policies for employment creation, productivity growth, and poverty reduction. This Report will help inform and enrich that dialogue.

Juan Somavia
Director-General
November 2004

Acknowledgements

The *World Employment Report 2004-05* was produced by a team under the guidance of Lawrence Jeffrey Johnson and Duncan Campbell. The team comprised Marva Corley and Dorothea Schmidt, who were involved in the overall preparation of the Report, along with Janine Berg, Sara Elder, Steven Kapsos, Nomaan Majid and Naren Prasad. In addition, Claire Harasty, Christian Kingombe and Isabelle Guillet assisted during various stages of the development of the Report. Research assistance was provided by Francesco Paolini, Kalina Popova, Harnik Deol, and Harvey Clavien. Administrative and secretarial support was provided by Christine Sutton, Julia Lee-Sukmana and Lynda Pond. Geraldeen Fitzgerald edited the English version of the Report, and Alan Wittrup was responsible for the database and design of the CD-ROM and Internet site.

The team would like to acknowledge Göran Hultin's support and valuable contributions from colleagues within the Employment Sector who provided comments and suggestions for the Report, in particular, Rashid Amjad, Peter Auer, Christoph Ernst, Ajit Ghose, Michael Henriques, Riswanul Islam, Muhammed Muqtada, Anne Posthuma, Trevor Riordan, Arturo Tolentino and Paul Vandenberg. The team also received valuable contributions and comments from Stephen Pursey, Gerry Rodgers, Jim Baker, Jean-François Retournard, David Kucera, Umit Efendioglu, Oliver Landmann, Jean Majeres, Andrew Sharpe and Marco Vivarelli.

The team would also like to thank our colleagues in the Printing Section who were responsible for overseeing the production of the printed Report, the Desktop Publishing/Graphic Arts Unit who designed the cover layout and completed the pagesetting, and the Proofreading/Quality Control Unit who provided the proofreading of the Report.

Background papers used in the Report were prepared by experts in the field of labour markets, productivity analysis and poverty, from within and outside the ILO. Excerpts from some of these papers are incorporated in the Report and hyperlinks exist to most of the complete papers, which can be found on the CD-ROM. Within the ILO, papers were prepared by Peter Auer, Janine Berg, Ibrahima Coulibaly, Steven Kapsos, Nomaan Majid, Emily Sims, Paul Vandenberg, Dominique Gross, Bernd Balkenhol and Juergen Schwettmann. Outside the ILO, papers were prepared by Gustavo Crespi Tarantino, Aziz Kahn, John Logue, Jacquelyn Yates, Oliver Landmann, Dipak Mazumdar, Rajneesh Narula, Prasado Rao, Andrew Sharpe, Bart van Ark, Hedwig Duteweerd and Ewout Frankema. Country case studies were prepared by Juan Chacaltana on Latin American economies, Eliano Franco on Argentina, and Zoltán Román on Hungary.

The team would also like to express their continued appreciation to those individuals who were directly responsible for the collection, analysis and dissemination of labour market information within the ILO Bureau of Statistics, ILO regional offices, and national ministries of labour and statistical offices. Support and assistance was also provided by the ILO regional and subregional offices, in particular the Budapest and Lima Subregional Offices. The team is particularly grateful for the fruitful exchanges with participants during the World Employment Report seminars held jointly with the Ministry of Labour, Hungary, in Budapest and the Ministry of Labour, South Africa, in Pretoria.

Contents

Tables

Figures

Boxes

Overview and main policy messages

Dismal chances for decent employment are as unsustainable as they are widespread in today's interdependent world economy and underscore the imperative of promoting decent work as the central aim of development. For the ILO, this implies the need for the world community to coalesce around two basic aims. The first of these, as articulated in the report of the World Commission on the Social Dimension of Globalization[1] is that of making employment a central objective of macroeconomic and social policies – rather than a hoped-for outcome of policies that, more often than not, do not directly address the employment challenge. The Commission report's conclusion is predicated on the observation that rising economic interdependence has neither been inclusive nor uniformly beneficial.

The second shared objective is that of poverty reduction, with a focus on the fundamental role that employment plays in attaining that objective. For a variety of reasons – a context of inadequate global economic growth among them – the 1990s largely saw a slowdown in the rate of poverty reduction. This, in turn, reinforces the need for policies to focus on "working out of poverty", a theme broadly explored at the International Labour Conference in 2003.

Employment creation and poverty reduction have long been mainstays of ILO research, policy advice and technical cooperation. Their need to remain so is again reinforced in an environment in which economic interdependence is coinciding with imbalances, asymmetries and inequality in the world. Less common is the association of employment and poverty reduction with the third theme of this Report, productivity.

Why a focus on productivity?

The fundamental reason for addressing the three issues together is based on the simple observation that a substantial share of poor people in the world is already at work: it is not the absence of economic activity that is the source of their poverty, but the less productive nature of that activity. In purely empirical terms, the link between work of low productivity and poverty is starkly clear. It is a straightforward proposition that if people – in particular, the 550 million people working in poverty – were able to earn more from their work, then poverty would decline. It is not just any work that can raise people out of poverty; what is needed is productive work. The ILO Employment Policy Convention, 1964 (No. 122), promotes freely chosen, "productive" employment. The Millennium Development Goals articulate the objective of decent, "productive" employment for young people.

---

[1] World Commission on the Social Dimension of Globalization: *A fair globalization: Creating opportunities for all* (Geneva, ILO, 2004).

The indications of a decent work deficit in the global labour market, from the absence of social protection to the absence of basic rights at work, are many. A key *economic* indicator of that deficit is whether men and women earn enough from their work to lift themselves and their families out of poverty. It is here where productivity matters most. It is through productivity that a material link exists between employment of any sort and decent work. This, by implication, suggests that a narrow focus on "unemployment" and "employment" as a means of describing labour market conditions is, in fact, a sorely inadequate gauge for most countries of the world.

The main policy messages of the *World Employment Report 2004-05* are laid out in this overview. It is useful to begin, however, with a brief discussion of the importance of productivity in the creation of decent jobs and poverty reduction.

The benefits of productivity gains

The pursuit of productivity gains is essential for increasing standards of living, for it is through this approach that rising levels of wealth are generated. The beneficial effects of productivity gains can be evaluated at the level of the individual worker or enterprise, as well as at the macroeconomic level at large. For workers, an increase in productivity ideally leads to higher wages, allowing them to take home higher pay or to reduce their working time, or both. For the enterprise, productivity gains result in lower unit costs of production and thus higher profits that can be reinvested and also distributed to workers in the form of higher wages or more jobs, as well as to shareholders in the form of increased dividends. Producing more with less also allows enterprises in competitive markets to lower their prices, and is thus a chief means by which enterprises shore up their competitiveness (and can, at the same time, make other firms relatively less competitive).

There are also important macroeconomic benefits arising from productivity gains. Aggregate demand both fuels productivity growth and is bolstered by it, both directly and indirectly. As to the latter, the direct stimulus comes from workers who are also consumers with higher disposable income to spend as a result of wage gains arising from improvements in their productivity. The indirect stimulus to consumption arises through the price channel: lower prices resulting from improved productivity are the equivalent of an increase in real incomes for people. Productivity contributes to a country's standard of living, as the most fundamental barometer of living standards is the earnings that people make, and the determinant of those earnings is the productivity with which people work.

Simple theories, but complex realities

The benefits of improving productivity seem straightforward, but a thorough understanding of productivity would fill (and has filled) volumes as, rather unhelpfully, just about "everything" matters. Indeed, a truly thorough excavation of the topic would entail an unpacking of all the determinants of growth and development. For example, the prime source of productivity growth is technological change. Technological change, in turn, relies on innovation, which itself is influenced by an array of institutions, the quality of the supply of human capital, competitive market dynamics, spending on research and development (R&D), and investment in general. These in turn depend upon the strength and stability of aggregate demand, and thus on the macroeconomic framework. Investment is a catalyst for innovation, but the reverse is also true: innovation spurs investment. The determinants of productivity growth cannot be thoroughly fathomed without consideration, not only of the supply side, but also of the demand side components.

But sources of productivity growth also depend on macroeconomic institutional and regulatory factors. Changes in the organization of work and production have a profound influence on productivity, and one long acknowledged – from Adam Smith's depiction 250 years ago of the birth of the factory system with its ever more minute division of labour, to contemporary discussions of the "knowledge economy" and "high performance work systems", both of which underscore the salience of human capital and its organization as a source of productivity growth and competitive advantage.

Commercial regulations, for example the ease or difficulty with which new businesses can start up, can either facilitate or frustrate the entry into new, higher value-added activities. More fundamentally still, basic property rights and enforcement of contracts also play a role in productivity dynamics:

> Strengthening property rights over land appears to be an important element. For example, the 1978 rural reforms in China, which entailed a shift from collective to household farming, are credited with engendering increases in agricultural productivity and an explosion in town and village enterprises which have been the engine of growth in China up to the mid-1990s. In a similar vein a government program which increased tenurial security in West Bengal had a large positive effect on agricultural productivity. Issuance of property titles to urban households in Peru led to an increase in labor hours and a shift in labor supply from work at home to work in the outside market. Land reform acts passed in Indian states account for about ten per cent of the overall fall in poverty across the 1958-1992 period.[2]

Basic infrastructure also matters. An adequate transportation system lowers costs and improves market access, for example. So does a good communications infrastructure. Well-developed health-care and education systems are part of the social infrastructure which, among their other benefits, also improve productivity, since a healthy person is more productive, as is an educated one.

For the obvious reason of the breadth of the topic, the present Report is not intended to be a historical review of growth and development with productivity as its cornerstone. Rather, its ambition is more circumscribed. The Report takes as its starting point the stark observation that, in today's world of widening inequality, differences in productivity performance emerge as an important policy

---

[2] Robin Burgess and Anthony Venables: *Towards a microeconomics of growth* (World Bank Policy Research Working Paper 3257, April 2004), p. 13.

factor to which attention needs to be devoted, particularly towards the goal of creating the conditions for decent work and poverty reduction.

The challenge can be visualized in figure 1 below, which shows the 20-year average annual growth of labour productivity, 1980-2000, in several countries, benchmarked against their per capita national income in 1980. The implication is that some countries that were relatively poor in 1980 became substantially wealthier because they were able to sustain strong growth in productivity, while others that were relatively poor in 1980 are, in relative terms, poorer still today, as productivity growth lagged.

In particular, many developing countries in the upper left of the figure (e.g. Singapore, the Republic of Korea) sustained substantial growth in labour productivity and were in consequence able to follow the path of income conver-

Figure 1.   Annual growth in labour productivity between 1980 and 2000 vs. GDP per capita in 1980 (US dollars, PPP)

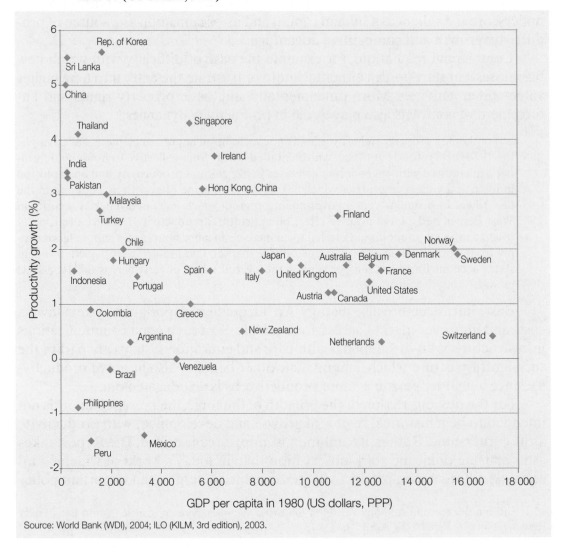

Source: World Bank (WDI), 2004; ILO (KILM, 3rd edition), 2003.

gence with the wealthier countries; that is, they would have moved substantially to the right of the figure if their per capita income were shown for the year 2000, rather than 1980. The fact that many highly developed economies, such as Switzerland, show low annual productivity growth rates does not indicate that later on in the development process productivity growth no longer matters. The relatively low growth rates only indicate that at later states of development the levels of productivity are so high that further productivity growth slows down compared to earlier stages.

In contrast, developing countries in the lower left of the figure trailed behind in productivity growth over the 20-year period, the result being a greater gulf between them and the "high productivity performers" in per capita wealth. Again, decent work has many components; the fundamentally economic component is access to a level of income adequate to escape from poverty, which ultimately must come from growth – growth in output, growth in productivity, and growth in jobs.

A controversial topic? A simple understanding of productivity

If the beneficial outcomes of productivity improvements are so important in both theory and fact, why does the topic elicit such a broad spectrum of views: from those who single-mindedly view productivity gains as the panacea for economic growth, to those who are considerably warier? The answer is simply that productivity increases and jobs can be, and often are, inversely related – jobs can be lost as a result of improvements in productivity. The conditions under which this occurs beg the question of how productivity improvements themselves occur. And to understand that requires a simple definition of productivity.

Productivity is a relationship between outputs and inputs. It rises when an increase in output occurs with a less than proportionate increase in inputs, or when the same output is produced with fewer inputs. For example, a garment worker's productivity could be understood as how many shirts she is able to stitch in one hour. Let us assume that she can produce two. If new capital investment – a new sewing machine, say – allows her to complete three shirts in one hour rather than the two she had been producing, then this would be a 50 per cent increase in her productivity – perhaps attributable in part to new skills she has acquired, and in part to "new technology".

Yet productivity can be understood in terms of *value* as well as *volume*. For example, if for whatever reason the value of the final product increases (an increase in its price with no increase in the cost of inputs), this in money terms is an increase in productivity. It can even be imagined that productivity could increase in *volume* terms, (e.g. more coffee beans picked with the same number of workers), but decline in *value* terms through plummeting market prices, as has indeed happened in the case of coffee. Thus, higher physical productivity can result in lower earnings and incomes rather than higher ones.

When productivity growth is the outcome of the expansion of output with existing or even more "inputs", such as labour, then this can lead to a situation in which everyone benefits. As a simple arithmetic proposition, however, if output growth trails the growth in productivity, then fewer inputs, such as labour, are required to produce a given level of output. This downside of productivity growth is historically commonplace. Labour-saving technological change often allows firms to produce the same or greater output with less labour input. Indeed, at least since the Luddite protest of two centuries ago in England,[3] the central concern of workers has been that gains in productivity brought about by new machines result in job losses. In an immediate sense, their concerns were indeed justified. In a longer term, aggregate sense, they were not; the Industrial Revolution was associated with substantial employment growth.[4]

The loss of a job is one matter. But potential adverse consequences of productivity gains are not limited to job loss alone. What if, for example, higher productivity is reflected solely in higher profits, rather than higher wages, perhaps because workers have little bargaining power? Or take, for example, the worker who is wary of productivity increases because, for him, it translates into working harder (more intensively) or longer hours for the same pay. Productivity has increased (through what amounts to a reduction in the cost of labour input) without any direct benefit to the worker whose effort was responsible for it. Indeed, the latter case has a contemporary resonance in Europe in recent months, as some companies on the grounds of remaining cost-competitive have sought to expand working time with no change in the level of remuneration.

In short, wariness over the impact of productivity growth is roundly justified, and the concern is even greater in today's world of growing economic interdependence. For example, the search for any one company's productivity improvements is less and less confined to national boundaries. The three-year recovery from the recent recession in the United States was characterized both by substantial gains in productivity and the longest period of "jobless growth" in post-war history. While their claims are overstated, as the Report's second chapter will discuss, critics of the relatively poor employment performance in the United States in that period attribute this to the outsourcing of jobs formerly in the United States to foreign locations – "jobless" in one location but "job-creating" in another in the broader geography of global competition.

The longer-term impacts of productivity growth

In the long term, there is no necessary trade-off between the growth of productivity and that of employment. And the evidence broadly corroborates this. Eco-

---

[3] In 1811, a group of workers in England formed a secret organization to fight against what was in their view the outcome of the Industrial Revolution. Their targets were the wide-frame stocking machines which were causing falling wages and unemployment in the Midlands. Letters were sent to factory owners, demanding the removal of the machines and workers broke into factories to destroy the new machines that the employers were using.

[4] At the time, however, employment growth had a further, defining characteristic: the master craftsman embodying all the skills needed to produce a product that was replaced by a greater number of workers with a lower level of skill.

nomic history shows that, in the long run, the growth of output, employment and productivity proceed in the same, positive direction. This is not, however, to say that the trends in each variable are either linear or homogeneous across countries. Indeed, a stagnation or decline in productivity characterizes some countries in the world well beyond the short term.

Of course, to the worker who loses his or her job as a result of productivity gains unmatched by an expansion in output, the notion that this is an "adjustment cost in the short term" is of little consolation. The fact that job losses will occur is an argument in favour of institutional and policy preparedness on both the supply side and the demand side of the labour market. The former, for example, would rely on efficient mechanisms for labour market intermediation through public and private employment services. It would also rely upon mechanisms for training and skill development in the event that a new job relies on a different set of skills from those needed for the old one it is replacing. Support to the demand side is also essential, which is why many countries engage in counter-cyclical spending or adjustments in monetary policy over the business cycle as a means of curbing the decline in aggregate demand and encouraging investment. Simply stated, costs in the short term can be mitigated by appropriate labour and macroeconomic policies and institutions.

The focus on job losses arising from the growth of productivity is typically a microeconomic perspective. As such, it is a partial view, trained on an individual company or sector, a particular location, and at a particular point in time. In consequence, it misses how economies adjust to productivity changes happening in any one sector.

Productivity gains work their way through the macroeconomy

People benefit from the reduction in costs that productivity gains elsewhere in the economy provide, even if those gains result in employment loss in the sector of their origin. The impact of productivity growth in any one sector of the economy depends upon the existence of "compensatory mechanisms" through which the economy adjusts. As such, productivity changes at the microeconomic level have important macroeconomic ramifications – two in particular. One is when technological innovation in any one sector finds cost-reducing and efficiency-enhancing applications in others; for example, the widespread application of information and communication technologies (ICT) has been a boon for productivity growth economy-wide, whether in traditional industries, such as garments, or in accelerating the growth of industries at the forefront, such as biotechnology. The other is through changes in relative prices. In competitive markets, an increase in productivity will result in a decline in the price of the product in which productivity gains have occurred. This might or might not result in a "net" increase in demand for that product. But this, too, does not tell the full story; a decline in relative prices is equivalent to an increase in real income for consumers, who, with their increased income, may then stimulate demand for other products or services in other sectors of the economy. In other

Figure 2. Productivity growth rate and unemployment rate in the United States, selected periods

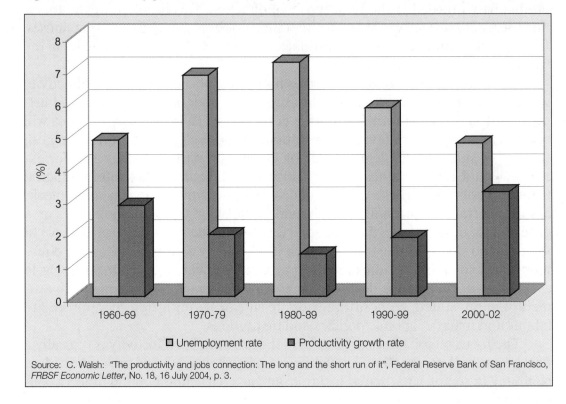

Source: C. Walsh: "The productivity and jobs connection: The long and the short run of it", Federal Reserve Bank of San Francisco, *FRBSF Economic Letter*, No. 18, 16 July 2004, p. 3.

words, productivity increases in one sector could shift the composition of consumer demand economy-wide. One consequence is aggregate employment growth, although not necessarily in the sector in which the positive productivity dynamics have occurred. Evidence of this is suggested in figure 2, which shows the inverse relationship between productivity growth and unemployment in the United States in the aggregate.

The trade-off between productivity and employment growth as part of development

A single-minded focus on the inverse relationship between employment and productivity growth is too narrow. This is hardly surprising, and much wisdom, theory and evidence confirm this. In fact, the loss of jobs attendant upon productivity growth is just what is "supposed to happen" in the course of development. A long-standing assumption of development thinking is that of a country's gradual transformation out of relatively low value-adding agriculture and into higher value-adding manufacturing. Such structural transformation raises productivity overall, as productivity is higher in the newer sector, manufacturing, while the employment decline in agriculture is the result of achieving higher productivity in that sector as well.

At any level of development, productivity growth is pushing the structural transformation of economies. It is also a channel through which poverty reduction can occur. The Report presents evidence that when productivity and employment growth occur in the sectors in which poverty is heavily concentrated, the effect on poverty reduction is the strongest.

Main policy messages of the *World Employment Report 2004-05*

What, then, are the most important questions to address on the linkages between employment creation, productivity growth, and poverty reduction? The Report argues that there are four of particular relevance if the ultimate aim is not just employment but decent work and poverty reduction. The questions can be simply stated, as is done below. Their answers are more detailed, as the Report elaborates.

- What are the conditions under which employment and productivity growth can advance in tandem, creating an expanding "virtuous circle" of decent and productive employment opportunities?

- From the traditional standpoint of development economics, structural transformation out of agriculture and into industry and services has been the long-accepted path. But since most of the world's poorest people continue to depend on the land for their livelihoods, is it not the case that agricultural productivity is central to pro-poor growth? But is agriculture itself still relevant to development?

- A certain degree of labour and capital mobility is no doubt good for productivity growth – indeed, this is what structural transformation is all about – but is a certain degree of employment stability also important?

- If small firms and small-scale activities generally have lower levels of productivity than large firms, what can be done to overcome the potential of a "productivity divide" between large-scale and small-scale activities?

The Report's main messages address these questions.

1. Productivity and employment growth: Trade-offs and complementarities

That productivity and employment stand at times in inverse relation to one another is, as mentioned, a partial view based on enterprise-level considerations and specific time-frames. The latter is most apparent over the business cycle, although it is also true that this inverse relationship can be rather durable over time. For example, ever higher productivity and less employment describe the secular trend in agriculture and, in many countries, manufacturing as well.

It was noted above that adjustment at the macroeconomic level to gains in productivity wherever they originate can indeed be employment-enhancing. Two qualifications might potentially challenge this benign outcome, however. The first is whether, in view of rising economic interdependence and the technology-induced greater mobility of production factors, the positive link between employment and productivity growth – at least at any particular national level –

has undergone qualitative change. Much of the contemporary popular debate in the United States, for example, is on the ICT-induced surge in outsourcing attending the recent years of economic recovery. This was in turn reflected in substantial productivity gains and, until recently, anaemic employment growth in the country. A plausible claim can be made that ICT has been a catalyst in reshaping an international division of labour in which service-sector work that can be "digitalized", e.g. data processing, or software development, can be located in areas that enjoy comparative cost advantages.

It is also the case that, whereas the outsourcing of lower skilled, less well paid jobs is not a new phenomenon, increasing educational and skill levels in developing countries enjoying labour cost advantages, India and China predominant among them, may be attracting jobs once thought relatively immune to relocation. While the concept of such a "qualitative" change in the international division of labour has a certain logical appeal, the data to date are both incomplete and inconclusive. For example, in value terms, the United States, in fact, " insources" more jobs than it outsources. Nor, moreover, do most forecasts of the outsourcing of digitalized work from the United States suggest a substantial magnitude relative to the overall pattern of job creation and job destruction in the country.

It can also be argued that there are net benefits of outsourcing (or "offshoring") arising from the various compensatory mechanisms referred to earlier, such as reduced costs, repatriated profits, and new markets for home-country goods and services. According to one study, for every dollar spent on outsourcing, the United States domestic economy gains US$1.12-US$1.14, while the foreign host country receives US$0.33.[5]

> It is institutions that make the difference in promoting the virtuous circle of productivity and employment growth.

To the worker who loses his or her job or fails to find one, however, these putative gains are rather abstract. Also, it would be premature to measure just how much developed country labour markets are in the throes of permanent, fundamental change.

In policy terms, it is safer to argue in favour of renovating labour market institutions so that they are equipped to keep pace with today's more rapid structural dynamics in the economy, characterized in some instances by an unusually high rate of permanent separations and a disproportionate loss of high-paying jobs. This underscores the need for a focus on "supply-side preparedness", with a particular emphasis on providing access to skills relevant to the future demand for labour.

A further qualification relates to whether differences in an economy's stage of development alter in any way the analysis of the macroeconomic advantages

---

[5] McKinsey Global Institute: *Offshoring: Is it a win-win game?*, August 2003 (www.mckinsey.com/knowledge/mgi/offshore).

of productivity growth. Here, two issues are noteworthy. The first arises from the observation that the mutually supportive, positive gains of productivity, employment, and output growth have eluded some regions in the world. Nor can the barriers to creation of a virtuous circle be described as "short-term". The reasons for the stalled trajectories are manifold and would involve a case-by-case review of markets, policies, governance, and institutions.

> *The central point is that the failure to reap the macroeconomic gains of employment and productivity growth is attributable to inadequacies in the markets, governance mechanisms, conditions and institutions through which such gains ought to occur.*

Promoting productivity and employment growth together applies to countries at any level of economic development.

The second issue, a more general one, is whether an argument in favour of a strong policy focus on productivity can be made in the context of the widespread unemployment or underemployment that is characteristic of developing countries. In short, is there a policy choice between favouring employment and favouring productivity growth?

> *The answer must be that there is no such "either/or" choice: both employment and productivity growth must be jointly pursued – and this, for several reasons. As noted at the very outset, the problem often is not the absence of work, but of work that is sufficiently productive to yield a decent income. A focus on improving the productivity of the informal economy ought to be a priority policy concern.*

It is also the case that, for companies that compete in global markets from any location in the world, a focus on productivity is essential, irrespective of its employment consequences, and a prescription to forego productivity improvements in favour of employment would not be sustainable.

> *The assumption that, in conditions of unused or under-used labour, employment of any type ought to take precedence over productivity improvements is unsound. In fact, it could carry with it the implication of widening inequality, since at higher levels of economic growth, it is productivity growth that contributes the major share.*

In this context, it is useful to note that a labour-intensive development strategy is not necessarily a low-productivity strategy. Both theory and evidence – in particular, from the successful Asian economies – permit the conclusion that countries are well advised to emphasize the "factor" in which they have comparative advantage – and the availability of low-cost labour is a common such factor in the developing world.

Wage employment in the labour-intensive modern sector is more productive than the alternative it replaces. Focusing on the abundant factor, labour, can thus be an employment-rich, as well as a productivity-enhancing strategy.

Finally, and again a hallmark of the development model of several Asian countries, a focus on continuous productivity improvement as a catalyst for industrial upgrading is one that acknowledges the transitory nature of competitive advantage, and therefore allows enterprises to secure ever more stable niches in global markets.

In the priority interest of providing income-generating work for their citizens, many developing countries opt for "employment-intensive" infrastructure building and maintenance projects over "equipment-intensive" methods of production. Here, too, it would seem that this reflects a conscious choice to maximize employment rather than productivity. Such a conclusion would be misleading, however. One reason is the same as that offered above; participants in "labour-based" production are likely to be employed at a higher level of productivity than their alternative work and earnings opportunities provided. There is also a second reason, as follows:

Evidence shows that the direct and indirect employment and economic effects of labour-based projects can often be superior to those of equipment-based projects. While this is self-evident in terms of employment outcomes, beneficial effects are further expanded indirectly, as income earners have more to spend in the local economy.

A focus on where people really work is as important as a focus on emerging, dynamic sectors.

There is widespread agreement that economic growth is the outcome of the shift of resources out of declining activities and into emerging, higher value-added ones. And much has been written on the historically unprecedented, "textbook" demonstration of rapid structural transformation in many East Asian countries. No doubt there is much still to learn from them. But emulation is difficult.

A sensible approach to addressing decent work deficits in the more immediate term is to focus on where labour actually works. In so doing, the focus shifts to the informal economy, on the one hand, and to the growing service sector, on the other.

A "stylized fact" of post-war development is the growth of the service sector in industrialized countries, as well as in the developing world. The term "service sector" disguises the considerable heterogeneity of employment in this sector. Service-sector jobs can be found at both ends of the decent work spectrum; the growth of the service economy is strongly correlated with wealth, as higher disposable incomes allow for the purchase of services previously "unconsumed" or delivered through non-commercial means as household activity – cooking at home, rather than eating out, for example. At the other extreme, the often burgeoning growth of the urban informal service economy in cities in developing countries is a reflection of underemployment in the rural economy and an insufficient rate of employment creation elsewhere in the economy.

> *The service sector has been characterized as technologically non-progressive and unavailing of opportunities for productivity growth. This depiction, however, is incorrect. The sector in fact runs the gamut from low-productivity activities in the informal economy to some of the most productive occupations at the technological forefront of the modern economy.*

The transformation of the banking and financial services industries, wrought by the diffusion of information and communication technologies, is a case in point.

> For structural transformation to occur, a range of well-functioning institutions in the labour market, as well as other markets, is essential.

The evidence shows convincingly that the positive relation between productivity growth and employment growth in the service sector is not limited to the most advanced service activities of the wealthiest countries. The growth of India's software industry is a well-known case in point, but the evidence is more general still.

> *An analysis of 15 countries for which there are data shows convincingly that transportation and communication, a major share of service-sector employment, demonstrate higher than average productivity gains – that is, they contribute disproportionately to aggregate productivity growth – and, in most instances, to employment growth as well.*

A final point can be made on linking the dynamic sectors of the economy to those where most of the jobs currently are.

> *A strategy for increasing productivity and employment over the long run should have dual components: investing in the dynamically growing sectors of the economy, while building capacity in sectors where the majority of labour is employed. Establishing linkages in the supply chain between the two is one mechanism.*

2. Agriculture: What role in development?

Structural transformation is once again the implicit point of reference for the Report's third chapter. The observation was made earlier that the decline in agricultural employment arising from productivity increases has been the classic path to economic development. Indeed, the point at which countries experience an absolute decline in agricultural employment has long been regarded as the "turning point" in development.

Agriculture should not be ignored if the focus is on poverty reduction.

A major part of the characteristics of the productivity/employment relationship in the agricultural sector arises from the nature of agricultural production itself; as standards of living rise, people tend to spend a proportionately lower share of their income on food. Known as "Engel's Law", the main implication is that an expansion in output made possible by improvements in agricultural productivity is often not met by an equal expansion in demand, and employment in the sector declines as a result.

But 75 per cent of the world's poor live in rural areas where agriculture is the mainstay of the economy. In fact, the agricultural sector employs 40 per cent of developing countries' workforces and contributes over 20 per cent of their GDP. The United Nations family has set itself the ambitious aim of halving the numbers of those in extreme poverty by 2015. Any serious effort to do so must acknowledge that there is both a geographical and sectoral component to address. In particular, the bulk of the world's extreme poor live in rural Asia and sub-Saharan Africa. And most of their economic activity is in agriculture.

There is extensive literature in economics on employment and poverty reduction. The literature on productivity and employment is equally extensive. However, considerably less attention has been paid to the direct linkage between productivity and poverty reduction. To the extent that it is low productivity, and thus low incomes, that underpin the phenomenon of rural poverty, a direct relationship between productivity increases in agriculture and poverty reduction ought to be apparent.

In a longer time frame, for economic development to occur, underpinned by the migration from low-productivity to high-productivity sectors, the policy framework – including investment, education, skills, and infrastructure policies – needs to play a strong, supportive role. While such a role is essential, a prescription for rapid structural transformation would seem, in purely empirical terms, easier said than done. Without a convergence of many factors, or "cumulative causation", sustained productivity growth in agriculture could merely result in employment displacement, rural-to-urban migration, and the replacement of rural poverty with the poverty of the urban informal economy.

Neglecting the agricultural sector during the process of industrialization can constrain the development process. While economic development needs industrialization, in many economies industrialization also requires the development of the agricultural sector. The policy challenge is to find the right balance in fostering the development process in all three sectors – agriculture, industry, and service – simultaneously.

It is in this context that two points are of particular interest. First, there are many developing countries in which both productivity *and* employment have increased in the agricultural sector.

Rather than considering agriculture as a mere way station on the road to economic development, it should be considered an essential part of that road – and one of continued relevance. This is especially true as the evidence shows convincingly that it is in those countries in which productivity and employment in agriculture have both grown where extreme poverty has declined the most. More specifically still, the growth of agricultural productivity is the strongest predictor of the reduction of extreme poverty.

China is a good case in point: while rapidly becoming the "world's manufacturing base", it is also a country in which agricultural output and employment have both risen, and poverty has fallen substantially.

> Return the focus to agriculture for promoting decent work: if agriculture has lagged behind, this is a symptom of a coordination failure involving the retreat of public policies.

The second point is that it is widely acknowledged that since the "green revolution" of the 1970s and 1980s, rural development and the agricultural sector in many developing countries fell victim to an era of policy neglect in the 1990s. The neglect, moreover, has occurred both at the national policy level as well as within the multilateral system. While the point cannot be unequivocally made, it is perhaps no mere coincidence that the decade of rural policy neglect of the 1990s also witnessed a pronounced slowdown in the rate of poverty reduction in the developing world.

For many although not all developing countries, it makes sense to promote the growth of productivity and employment in the agricultural sector. To do so requires:

- A focus on food price development. It is important that food prices in the poorest parts of the world do not rise to levels that could harm the poor and thereby undermine poverty reduction. At the same time, prices have to be high enough to ensure that food-exporting countries can foster an attractive investment environment and earn enough foreign exchange to meet domestic development objectives.

- A focus on income distribution, particularly a better distribution of land ownership in agriculture, both to facilitate output growth and accelerate poverty reduction.

- Investment in water supply, infrastructure, health, education, agricultural research and development, and other institutional reforms, even though the impacts of these kinds of investments have a relatively long gestation period.

- That non-farm activities should be fostered as an additional source of employment creation, adding further to the poverty reduction potential of the agricultural sector.

> Agricultural productivity growth depends on social rather than private investment alone, e.g. in water management, communications, skill development, land reform, etc.

It ought finally to be noted that whether a focus on agricultural productivity and employment growth makes sense for a country depends on that country's stage in the development process, and the potential of its agricultural sector in terms of natural resources and human resources. Nor is national action alone adequate.

The vitality of the agricultural sector depends upon international commodity prices, product niches, and market access. As such, success at any national level depends critically on the behaviour of the world community and the achievement of the Doha round of trade negotiations within the World Trade Organization, without which steps towards fairer globalization – one of greater inclusion and less poverty – cannot be made.

3. Workforce mobility, workplace stability: How does each relate to productivity?

If economic development is enabled by structural transformation out of lower to higher valued-added activities, it stands to reason that a certain amount of capital and labour mobility is necessary for this inter-sectoral transition to occur. Capital mobility is present when adequate savings, whether domestic or foreign, are available for investment in new growth sectors in a context of macroeconomic stability and sufficient demand. Labour mobility relies in turn on the availability of workers with appropriate skills or the ability to acquire them with relative ease.

> Employment "stability" is not "labour immobility": jobs and skill requirements can change for the same person working for the same firm.

But the evidence shows that, however important the mobility of capital and labour might be for higher productivity, a certain amount of stability is just as important. The measure of stability used is average employment tenure, or the amount of time a worker stays with his or her present enterprise. A useful distinction to make at the outset is that "stability" is not a synonym for "immobility", since employment tenure is not the same thing as job tenure; an employee can remain in long-term employment with an individual enterprise but undertake new jobs and assignments over the course of his or her tenure with the firm.

Why, then, is such employment stability important for high levels of productivity? The most convincing answer lies in human capital theory.

Much of how workers learn to do their jobs better comes from formal training and the training they receive on the job from more experienced workers, as well as from simply learning by doing. Employers have no incentive to invest in their employees' training if they believe that their employees will leave the enterprise before the gains of that investment can be realized. Employees, on the other hand, have no incentive for acquiring new, more productive ways of doing things if, in the absence of some employment security, they fear they will "work themselves out of a job".

There are, moreover, significant feedback mechanisms: for example, the high level of productivity that employment stability brings shores up the competitiveness of the enterprise and thus its ability to provide employment security to its workforce.

Employment stability promotes productivity growth, but the reverse is also true: productivity growth promotes employment stability.

There are considerable differences in the length of average aggregate tenure across countries, sectors, and occupations. Many factors account for these differences. In purely arithmetic terms, for example, a country in which output is growing faster than in another will have lower average tenure as more new jobs are being created, bringing down the average tenure duration. Countries that have younger workforces, such as those in the developing world, will also have lower average tenure than those in which the workforce is older, and consequently has been on the job longer and is likely to be less mobile. Countries or industries characterized by a high share of small firms are also likely to be ones in which average tenure is lower, as small firms enter and exit the market more frequently than do large firms. Despite these and other factors explaining differences in tenure, however, evidence suggests that these differences are quite stable over time: for example, average aggregate tenure is substantially lower in the United States than in many European countries, but this has been the case for two decades and in a proportion that is roughly the same now as it was then.

Economies change. Labour laws and institutions often need to change, too. But they are often more consistent with, rather than counter to, economic incentives and market forces – that is, employment stability laws exist, but there are powerful economic incentives for stability to occur.

Apart from the raw economics of an industry or demographics of a country, institutional differences have an important role to play in explaining differences in average tenure. For example, a labour market institution such as employment protection legislation can make an enterprise's ability to engage in economic dismissals either more or less difficult. There is, in fact, a strong and convincing correlation between average tenure and the "stringency" of employment protection legislation in regulating economic dismissals. On the one hand, many have argued that employment protection legislation needs to be reformed with a view to providing greater "flexibility" at the micro level. There may well be instances in which this is called for. On the other hand, however, it is noteworthy that the *legislated* promotion of an appropriate level of employment stability is consistent with, rather than counter to, the purely *economic* incentives for employment stability on both the supply and demand sides of the labour market. In short, it makes economic sense for employers to seek to retain their workforce.

For all policy environments, the question is how best to obtain the greatest benefits from the mobility of capital and labour, and the productivity-enhancing inter-sectoral transformation that they support, while at the same time providing adequate employment stability at the micro-level in the interests of promoting high levels of productivity.

There are no easy answers to obtaining this policy and institutional balance. In view of the intensification of product market competition arising from globalization and rapid technological change, it is indeed possible that product market regulation will need to be made more compatible with more rapid adjustments to change.

A prescription for the full-scale reform of product market regulation would be difficult to identify. This, however, does not preclude the identification of some common areas of change. For example, reducing the regulatory and/or cost burdens often facing new business start-ups makes good sense.

The regulatory/institutional challenge for most countries is to define a concept of "protected mobility" for ensuring economic as well as social efficiency, allowing flexibility for the firm and protection for the worker.

It may be that labour market institutions and regulations are in need of adjustment. The evidence now weighs in favour of new regulations or re-regulation, rather than a focus on deregulation that has dogged the debate on labour market flexibility for a quarter of a century. And two pieces of that evidence are particularly convincing.

There is a strong and positive correlation between a country's openness to trade, a measure of its globalization, and how much that country spends on active labour market policies as a percentage of GDP.

There is a strong and positive correlation between spending on active labour market policies and workers' perceptions of their employment security.

Some countries appear to have a workable balance between the amount of micro-level flexibility the regulatory system affords, and workers' perceptions of their own employment security.

What appears to matter is whether workers feel that, if they lose their current job, they will be able to make the transition smoothly into one of equal or better quality. This in turn implies an effective (and productive) means of dealing with the changes wrought by globalization in an institutional environment that promotes an appropriate level of micro-level flexibility, backed up by a strong guarantee at the macro level of labour market security.

Different countries will approach the challenge of adjustment in different ways. A concept of "protected mobility", or the promotion of both flexibility and security, would appear to make sense. An appropriate level of employment stability is important to this. Finally, employment stability is also important at the macroeconomic level; working men and women who feel secure in their jobs or in their ability to find acceptable alternative employment provide a stimulus to aggregate demand, whereas employment insecurity can weaken aggregate demand.

4. The small-scale/large-scale productivity difference

An empirical regularity of most countries' economic structures is the predominance of small relative to large enterprises as a share of total enterprises, and as a significant share of total employment as well. In definitional terms, the small and medium-sized enterprise (SME) sector typically refers to enterprises in the formal economy. But, relative to industrialized countries, developing countries are characterized by a higher share of a range of small-scale activities of many types, such as self-employment, and small enterprises and micro-enterprises, operating in both the formal and informal economies. These latter small-scale activities usually operate at lower levels of productivity than do large firms.

A key challenge for improving standards of living in developing countries is therefore to improve productivity in small firms and in small-scale activities generally. The challenge is all the more important in view of the productivity differential between small and large firms and, thus, the implication that inequality in the form of a "productivity divide" can have structural roots.

Small firms have their own survival strategies based on the segmentation of markets.

In view of their productivity disadvantage, one question is why small firms are not driven out of competitive markets. Evidence does suggest a higher degree of volatility in the small-firm environment, with a higher rate of start-ups and failures. This notwithstanding, the question is how, with a lower level of productivity, small firms manage to survive in competitive markets.

Small firm survival appears to hinge on the fact that small firms compete in different markets from the markets in which large firms compete, even when small firms are ostensibly producing the same product as large firms.

On the one hand, the shelter of non-competitive markets (markets that may not be fully exposed to trade liberalization or markets that are in fact multiple for ostensibly the same product) is useful, as it provides at least some security for the jobs that small firms create. In some instances, of course, the route to productivity improvement could be at the expense of employment creation. On the other hand, however, the jobs are often of lower quality and less well remunerated than those in the more competitive, modern sector of the economy; that is, there are substantial decent work deficits in the range of small-scale, informal activities.

> While the growth of large firms is not to be discouraged, there are ways of overcoming the disadvantage of small firms; collective action by small firms themselves, assisted by local authorities and other actors can boost productivity and market access.

Experiences in some countries have shown that the productivity disadvantage of small firms is not necessarily an intractable problem. Despite relatively high wages, for example, small firms in northern Italy have been able to overcome their size disadvantage by being part of a dense network that blends competition with cooperation. The productivity advantages can once again be expressed in simple terms.

Through cooperation, such as the collective purchase of raw materials or the joint sponsorship of industry training, input costs can be lowered. Similarly, through the collective sharing of orders too large for any one small firm to fulfil, market share can be expanded.

As such, some models of small-firm cooperation can promote both improved productivity and employment growth, as input costs are lowered and output is expanded. Such models are not an enclave, but fully integrated into the global economy. They can also be successful in the perpetuation of local "social capital", or trust. Indeed, a considerable advantage of building cooperative links among small firms is that, in so doing, greater social cohesion can be generated as well as a shared commitment to local development.

Developing countries can promote the integration of their small firms into the broader economy and thereby overcome the inequality inherent in their "dualistic" economic structures characterized by unintegrated markets, a small modern economy and a much larger informal economy. The upgrading of existing clusters of small firms, the development of efficient cooperatives, access to commercial credit, and the collective provision of missing business services are ways in which developing countries such as Brazil, India and Indonesia are attempting to address the challenge of integrating their small firms in wider markets. By implication, this too is a strategy for improving productivity in the informal economy, and for building bridges between the formal and informal economies.

The main messages of the Report can, of course, neither be prescriptive nor lend themselves to identical policy changes in a diverse world. The search for answers to all of the four main questions elaborated in the chapters of the Report can nevertheless make a fundamental contribution to the promotion of decent work, the economic underpinning of which is productive employment.

1. Global trends in employment, productivity and poverty

1.1. Recent global developments

"Employment, productivity and poverty reduction" is the title of the *World Employment Report 2004-05*. This topic was chosen based on the strong conviction and empirical evidence that creating decent employment opportunities is the best way to take people out of poverty. In addition there is a strong link between productivity[1] and decent work – work that not only provides a sufficient level of income but also ensures social security, good working conditions and a voice at work. This link needs to be investigated to help identify the best development strategies for the less developed economies in the world.[2]

Rather than discussing poverty in general (table 1.1), this analysis of labour market trends centres on poverty among the world's workers (table 1.2) — or "working poverty". The concept of the working poor in the developing world adds a new dimension to the study of labour markets by placing decent and productive employment at the forefront of the poverty discussion. In fact, the

**Table 1.1.   US$1 a day and US$2 a day poverty shares
(world and regions, selected years, percentage)**

Region	US$1 a day total poverty				US$2 a day total poverty			
	1980	1990	2003[a]	2015[b]	1980	1990	2003[a]	2015[b]
World	39.7	27.0	19.5	13.2	65.7	59.8	51.2	40.5
Latin America and the Caribbean	11.3	12.1	10.4	8.9	29.9	29.6	25.4	22.2
East Asia	61.6	31.2	14.9	5.7	85.3	68.8	43.2	22.4
South-East Asia	31.4	16.6	9.3	6.0	69.2	59.3	47.8	39.0
South Asia	52.3	40.9	28.4	14.4	89.0	85.4	75.7	60.1
Middle East and North Africa	3.2	2.5	2.0	1.7	26.5	21.8	20.8	17.3
Sub-Saharan Africa	42.6	44.1	45.7	44.6	73.0	75.8	76.4	75.5
Transition economies	1.2	1.5	3.9	1.6	1.5	4.5	17.9	7.5

Note: Proportion of population below US$1 (2) a day is the percentage of the population living on less than US$1.08 (2.16) a day at 1993 international prices. The US$1 (2) a day poverty line is compared to consumption or income per person and includes consumption from own production and income in kind. It is based on purchasing power parties (PPP), indicating that people would be able to purchase the same quantity of goods in any country for a given sum of money. That is, the comparison is based on the notion that the standardized dollar should buy the same amount in all countries.

[a] Estimates.   [b] Projections.

Source: Calculations based on World Bank, 2004a.

---

[1] In this and the following chapters the focus is on labour productivity, which is calculated as output per person employed. The expressions labour productivity, productivity, output per worker, output per person employed and GDP per person employed are all used as synonyms, following the common practice in the literature on this topic.

[2] By choosing these indicators many other important labour market indicators are not directly considered in the analysis, but of course indirectly influence labour markets. For example, changes in labour market institutions do have an impact on productivity and employment creation.

Table 1.2.   US$1 a day and US$2 a day working poverty shares in total employment (world and regions, selected years, percentage)

Region	US$1 a day working poverty share				US$2 a day working poverty share			
	1980	1990	2003[a]	2015[b]	1980	1990	2003[a]	2015[b]
World	40.3	27.5	19.7	13.1	59.8	57.2	49.7	40.8
Latin America and the Caribbean	15.6	16.1	13.5	11.5	41.2	39.3	33.1	28.8
East Asia	71.1	35.9	17.0	6.5	92.0	79.1	49.2	25.8
South-East Asia	37.6	19.9	11.3	7.3	73.4	69.1	58.8	47.7
South Asia	64.7	53.0	38.1	19.3	95.5	93.1	87.5	77.4
Middle East & North Africa	5.0	3.9	2.9	2.3	40.3	33.9	30.4	24.9
Sub-Saharan Africa	53.4	55.8	55.8	54.0	85.5	89.1	89.0	87.6
Transition economies	1.6	1.7	5.2	2.1	1.7	5.0	23.6	9.8

[a] Estimates.   [b] Projections.
Source: Kapsos, 2004.

majority of the poor of working age receive inadequate incomes from their labour, which leaves them and their families below the poverty line. In addition, they usually do not benefit from other aspects of decent work.

Current estimates for 2003 show that 1.39 billion people in the world work but are still unable to lift themselves and their families above the US$2 a day poverty line. Among them, 550 million cannot even lift themselves and their families above the extreme US$1 a day poverty threshold.[3] Expressed in shares this means that 49.7 per cent of the world's workers (and over 58.7 per cent of the developing world's workers) are not earning enough to lift themselves and their families above the US$2 a day poverty line, and that 19.7 per cent of the employed persons in the world (and therefore over 23.3 per cent of the developing world's workers) are currently living on less than US$1 a day (table 1.2). It is expected that the trends in total number and in shares will decrease in 2004.

Unemployment and employment trends

On top of the need to create 1.39 billion decent jobs for those people who work but still live with their families below the US$2 a day poverty line, account has to be taken of the number of people who were looking for work but could not find any employment opportunity to get an idea of the size of the employment component of the decent work deficit in the world. In 2003 there were 185.9 million people in the world who were unemployed, despite the recovery from the economic slowdown in 2001 and 2002. While more people were employed in 2003 than during the years of the economic downturn, the overall growth in the labour force meant that job creation could only just keep up with the growing number of people who wanted to work. This is why the unemployment rate for

---

[3] In the following text "extreme poverty/extreme working poverty" is sometimes used as a synonym for the US$1 a day poverty/working poverty threshold and "moderate poverty/moderate working poverty" is sometimes used as a synonym for the US$2 a day poverty/working poverty threshold.

the world showed almost no change, from 6.3 per cent in 2002 to 6.2 per cent in 2003. Box 1.1 discusses the limitation of unemployment figures.

This relative stagnation in unemployment rates between 2002 and 2003 was found in most regions: East Asia moved from 3.1 per cent to 3.3 per cent, South Asia remained at 4.8 per cent, the Middle East and North Africa rose from 11.9 per cent to 12.2 per cent, sub-Saharan Africa moved from 10.8 per cent to 10.9 per cent, the transition economies decreased from 9.4 per cent to 9.2 per cent and the industrialized economies remained at 6.8 per cent. The only regions showing a significant change were South-East Asia where the unemployment rate dropped from 7.1 to 6.3 per cent, and Latin America and the Caribbean where the rate decreased from 9.0 to 8.0 per cent. Over the past ten-year period, the industrialized economies were the only region that experienced falling unemployment rates, while rates in all other regions either remained stable or increased (table 1.3). The transition economies saw a sharp increase from 6.3 to 9.2 per cent, and unemployment in South-East Asia increased from 3.9 to 6.3 per cent.

Employment-to-population ratios, the share of people with work amongst the working age population, did not move considerably in most regions. Should this ratio increase? As a matter of fact stable or even decreasing employment-to-population ratios can indicate that there is no demand for additional employment as people prefer not to work. The existence of unemployment, however, shows that people are actively looking for work and cannot find work. Therefore an increase in employment-to-population ratios is needed to meet the demand of these people to work. In addition, in most developing economies only very few people can afford voluntarily to stay out of the labour market. If they do so it might be because they have simply given up hope. Therefore a rise in the employment-to-population ratio could demonstrate that employment opportunities are being generated and those without work should not necessarily give up hope. Importantly, however, this indicator does not give a clear picture of the quality of the jobs being created – that is, whether additional decent and productive jobs have become available.

Only the industrialized economies and the Middle East and North Africa witnessed a notable increase in the employment-to-population ratio over the last ten years (table 1.3). In the latter case this was mainly due to the increasing participation of women in the labour markets in the region. Despite this increase, women in this region have by far the lowest labour force participation rates in the world (for more details, see ILO, 2004a, 2004b). The most drastic change was observed in the transition economies where the employment-to-population ratio dropped from 58.8 in 1993 to 53.5 in 2003. Even though a decrease in employment-to-population ratios often reflects an increase of people staying in education for longer periods, in the case of the transition economies only part of the difference can be explained in that way. In addition, as a result of the shocks associated with the transition process, considerably fewer employment opportunities were created and people were thereby "forced" to stay out of labour markets.

Box 1.1. Additional labour market indicators: looking beyond employment and unemployment

When a person reaches working age, he or she does not necessarily enter the labour market. The person can stay outside the labour market and would then be called inactive. This inactivity can be voluntary – the person prefers to stay at home or to begin or continue education – or involuntary, where the person would prefer to work but is discouraged and has given up hope of finding work. If the person enters the labour market, he or she can either be employed or unemployed. The number of people employed or unemployed within an economy are very important indicators, but they do not provide a complete understanding of labour markets.

Unemployment and employment

A person is only counted as unemployed if he or she is without a job and is actually looking for work.[1] Pure unemployment numbers mask information on the composition of the jobless population and therefore miss out on important particularities of the unemployed, such as socio-economic background, ethnic origin, and duration of unemployment. In developing countries, which often lack effective unemployment insurance mechanisms, concentrating on unemployment runs the further risk of excluding from the analysis the less privileged population who simply cannot afford to be unemployed. The problem in developing economies is therefore not so much unemployment, but rather the conditions of work of those who are employed.

Within the group of those who are employed, people can be employed full-time or part-time, underemployed, or even over-employed. As mentioned above, belonging to the employed population does not imply anything about the quality of the job or about wages and earnings. An employed person may work in the informal economy under poor conditions, with no contract and a low salary.

Working poverty

As working under such conditions is not at all what would be called a "decent job", the ILO developed the concept of working poverty to cover those people who work but do not earn enough to lift themselves and their families above the US$1 or 2 a day poverty line. There is a very high likelihood that people who constitute the working poor work in the informal economy (whereas the reverse is not necessarily the case – people who work in the informal economy are not necessarily working poor). For this reason the estimate of working poor can be interpreted as a first approximation of people who work in the informal economy with very low earnings.

It is important to note that, by definition, a person is counted as working poor only if that person is unable to lift himself or herself *and his or her family* above the poverty threshold. This means that somebody who earns only 50 cents a day would not be considered as working poor if somebody else in the family earns enough to make sure that each family member lives on more than US$1 a day. Conversely, somebody might earn as much as, for example, US$5 a day but with a family consisting of, say, 10 members (9 of them not working) each member would be living on less than US$1 a day. Such a person would still be counted as working poor. Finally, including the whole family in the concept of working poverty ensures that a rich young person in the developing world who has just started work life and works without remuneration in order to gain work experience is not considered to be working poor.

Given the limitations of pure employment and unemployment figures, this chapter pays greater attention to two indicators more pertinent to the developing world: trends in working poverty, and trends in labour productivity. These indicators are important in their contributions to determining wages and incomes. In conjunction with unemployment, the working poor and productivity figures give a first good indication of the magnitude, distribution and depth of decent work deficits around the world. To find out more about these deficits, subsequent ILO work on this subject will incorporate additional labour market indicators, including *status in employment* and *employment by sector*. Employment status categorizes workers into the major groups of wage employment, self-employment and unpaid family workers (also termed contributing family workers), according to the international classification.[2] These indicators are particularly relevant for developing regions because they give an idea of progress in development, by looking at trends in the number of people in wage employment and in sectors that may be dominated by informal employment and unpaid family work.

[1] For a precise definition of unemployment see: http://www.ilo.org/public/english/bureau/stat/download/res/ecacpop.pdf

[2] Resolution concerning the international classification of status in employment, adopted by the 15th International Conference of Labour Statisticians, Geneva, 1993 (available at: http://www.ilo.org/public/english/bureau/stat/download/res/icse.pdf).

Table 1.3. Labour market and economic indicators
(world and regions, selected years, percentage)

Region	Unemployment rate			Employment-to-population ratio		Percentage change in labour productivity	Annual labour productivity growth rate	Annual labour force growth rate	Annual GDP growth rate
	1993	2002	2003	1993	2003	1993-2003	1993-2003	1993-2003	1993-2003
World	5.6	6.3	6.2	63.3	62.5	10.9	1.0	1.8	3.5
Latin America and the Caribbean	6.9	9.0	8.0	59.3	59.3	1.2	0.1	2.3	2.6
East Asia	2.4	3.1	3.3	78.1	76.6	75.0	5.8	1.3	8.3
South-East Asia	3.9	7.1	6.3	68.0	67.1	21.6	2.0	2.4	4.4
South Asia	4.8	4.8	4.8	57.0	57.0	37.9	3.3	2.3	5.5
Middle East and North Africa	12.1	11.9	12.2	45.4	46.4	0.9	0.1	3.3	3.5
Sub-Saharan Africa	11.0	10.8	10.9	65.6	66.0	–1.5	–0.2	2.8	2.9
Transition economies	6.3	9.4	9.2	58.8	53.5	25.4	2.3	–0.1	0.2
Industrialized economies	8.0	6.8	6.8	55.4	56.1	14.9	1.4	0.8	2.5

Source: ILO, 2003b; ILO, 2003c; IMF, 2003; see also ILO, 2004a, technical note.

Productivity and GDP

Over the past decade, labour productivity (see box 1.2 for an explanation of labour productivity) in the world increased by almost 11 per cent. This was mainly driven by the impressive growth in labour productivity in East Asia (75 per cent between 1993 and 2003), but also in South Asia and South-East Asia, which have experienced considerable increases in their labour productivity levels (37.9 and 21.6 per cent, respectively). Labour productivity growth in the industrialized economies also surpassed world productivity growth with an increase of 14.9 per cent. Even though this is less than in the Asian regions, it is worth bearing in mind that Asia started from low levels of productivity, thereby

Box 1.2. What is labour productivity?

Productivity in general measures how efficiently resources are used. The basic definition of labour productivity is output, or value added, divided by the amount of labour used to generate the output. While labour productivity is sometimes defined as output per hour worked, the present chapter instead uses annual output per person employed; not only are better data available for the latter indicator, but also there is a stronger linkage to the human component of productivity. Labour productivity differs from total factor productivity, which accounts for sources of productivity beyond the basic measures of labour such as management quality, technological progress, impacts of disease, crime levels, and systems of government, among others.

Despite its name, labour productivity increases when value added rises through the better use, coordination, etc. of *all* factors of production. Value added may increase when labour is working smarter, harder, faster or with better skills, but it also increases with the use of more or better machinery, the reduction in the waste of input materials or the introduction of technical innovations. Indeed, any non-labour factor that raises value added will raise labour productivity. Take, for example, an improvement in product quality that allows a good to be sold for a higher price, even if there is no change in the number of the good produced. The term labour productivity is therefore correct in that any non-labour change that increases value added makes workers more productive, but it is slightly misleading in that it denotes productivity in general and not that which specifically involves workers. For example, a farmer's access to training can improve his or her productivity. But a farmer's access to a newly built road that facilitates travel to the market (or a buyer's travel to the farm) can do the same.

There is wide variation in labour productivity among different countries in the world owing to a host of factors, most of which are directly and positively related to the level of economic development of the countries concerned. It is important to underscore the fact that differences in labour productivity levels have essentially nothing to do with differences in how hard workers work – on the contrary they often indicate differences in working conditions. A poor worker in a developing economy can work long hours, strenuously, under bad physical conditions, but yet have low labour productivity and therefore receive a low income because he or she lacks access to technology, education, or other factors needed to raise productivity. Similarly a worker in a highly developed economy may have high labour productivity despite working relatively fewer hours.

facilitating gains. In addition, overall improvements in employment creation and the reduction in average unemployment rates in the industrialized economies indicate that at a more advanced stage of economic development – often characterized among other things by lower labour force growth rates – the productivity growth rates needed to have a positive impact on labour markets are typically lower than in earlier stages of development. The transition economies have experienced impressive labour productivity growth rates since 1999 and have thereby contributed to the world's recent growth in productivity. Over the past ten-year period labour productivity grew by 25.4 per cent in that region. In Latin America and the Caribbean, the economic crises that took place at the beginning of the new millennium had a dampening effect on the already slow rise in labour productivity, resulting in a productivity increase of just above 1 per cent over 10 years (or 0.1 per cent per year). Also in the Middle East and North Africa, productivity levels are still close to those in the region ten years earlier, while sub-Saharan Africa experienced declining productivity on average.

A comparison with the GDP growth rate trends over the past ten years makes it clear that GDP growth is not identical with growth in labour productivity, but that the trends in these indictors usually move in the same direction. East Asia had impressive average GDP growth rates of 8.3 per cent annually, followed by South Asia (5.5 per cent per annum) and South-East Asia (4.4 per cent per annum). GDP growth in Latin America and the Caribbean recovered only recently, again in parallel with a recovery in productivity growth. On average over the past ten years GDP grew by 2.6 per cent per year. The 2.9 per cent annual growth for sub-Saharan Africa – a rather low rate of GDP growth for a developing region – was matched by the decrease in productivity growth in the region. Finally, the industrialized economies saw GDP growth in tandem with productivity growth and even though growth was lower than in some developing regions, this again must be considered in the context of the industrialized economies' higher initial GDP levels.

There are two regions that seem to go against the trend of GDP and labour productivity moving in the same direction: the transition economies, and the Middle East and North Africa. The transition economies have witnessed 2.3 per cent annual growth in labour productivity, but annual GDP growth of only of 0.2 per cent between 1993 and 2003. The Middle East and North Africa have had only 0.1 per cent of labour productivity growth per year, but annual GDP growth in the region has been as high as 3.5 per cent during the ten-year period.

In the transition economies this is still the result of the ongoing structural dynamics. In the first phase of the transition many old firms had to close, which not only destroyed the region's potential to create GDP but also destroyed many jobs. In addition, the increase in unemployment and underemployment combined with the rising feeling of insecurity for many people put a constraint on GDP growth from the demand side. With GDP growth rates decreasing at a similar speed as employment, labour productivity (GDP divided by the number of people employed) stayed stagnant. In phase two, once all the uncompetitive firms had left the market, those that had survived tried to increase their competitiveness through capital investment and further shedding of labour, while increasing their output, which caused labour productivity to increase dramatically.

The Middle East and North Africa reflects the diversified picture of the oil-producing versus the non-oil-producing economies in the region. Overall the GDP-creating effect of the oil-producing economies – as a result of the increases in demand for oil and overall price increases for oil – went in parallel with employment growth in the non-oil-producing economies, leading to high GDP growth rates accompanied by stagnant productivity. Does this indicate that employment creation hinders productivity growth? Yes, if the jobs created are not decent and productive, providing an insufficient income for the employees, and making it impossible for them to have an impact on the demand side of the economy. In fact the case of the Middle East and North Africa should not be taken as a case against employment creation but rather as a perfect example of why in the longer run decent employment creation and productivity growth have to go hand in hand with GDP growth. Only then will economic growth lead to poverty reduction.

Poverty and working poverty

Taking the labour market trends together with trends in GDP and productivity growth, it can be seen that the working poverty picture (table 1.2) as well as the total poverty picture (table 1.1) in the world is the clear outcome of the inter-relation of these indicators. Reducing poverty and working poverty requires both productivity growth and employment creation. East Asia and South Asia are good examples that underscore this point: the two regions saw the highest productivity growth rates over the last ten years. At the same time, unemployment rates stayed at low levels. This, in combination with the reasonably stable employment-to-population ratios, indicates that productivity gains did not lead to job shedding. As a result the proportion of US$1 a day working poverty and overall poverty has been decreasing in these regions. This positive trend went in tandem with considerable decreases in the share of informal employment. In South-East Asia (with high productivity and GDP growth rates but also increasing unemployment rates), US$1 a day working poverty and total poverty have decreased but at a lower rate than in the rest of Asia. In Latin America and the Caribbean (with almost no productivity growth, below average GDP growth, high unemployment rates and stagnant employment-to-population ratios), there is very little change in US$1 a day working poverty and total poverty. In sub-Saharan Africa (with negative productivity growth rates, low GDP growth rates, high unemployment rates and almost stagnant employment-to-population ratios), US$1 a day working poverty stayed the same and total poverty even increased. The same is true for the poorer economies in the Middle East and North Africa, despite the fact that their employment-to-population ratio has increased (but mainly for lower quality jobs as discussed above).

In terms of US$2 a day working poverty and total poverty, the picture looks similar for those economies in East Asia that managed to get into the virtuous cycle of productivity growth, employment generation and GDP growth. Here the decrease in both poverty measures has been the highest. But why is it then that the proportion of US$2 a day working poverty only decreased slightly since the beginning of the 1990s? In fact, it is expected that in 2015 the bulk of the world's US$2 a day working poverty will be in South Asia, and the region will account for a full 40 per cent of the world's US$2 a day working poor. Given the trend in robust productivity growth in this very poor region, the gains from this growth will be enough to lift the people out of extreme poverty but not yet enough to lift them above the US$2 a day poverty threshold. This on the one hand indicates that the employment opportunities created are often of low productivity and therefore low earnings, and on the other hand it is partly also the result of the high labour force growth rates and the lack of jobs for those wanting to work. The problem is similar in South-East Asia and the poorer economies in the Middle East and North Africa. In Latin America and the Caribbean, US$2 a day working poverty declined slightly, indicating that some of the jobs created were of high enough quality to let people work themselves and their families out of poverty. Finally, the transition economies have seen a dramatic increase in US$2 a day working poverty and total poverty, mainly for reasons discussed above. There is reason to hope that the high productivity growth rates achieved in recent years will finally lead to GDP growth and employment growth, ultimately reducing working poverty. Some economies in the region have already entered this stage.

How likely is it that the world will halve working poverty by 2015?

The analysis of labour productivity trends, labour market trends, and trends in working poverty and total poverty shows that those regions that have managed to increase productivity levels in the longer run *and* have managed to create employment opportunities for their growing labour forces have best managed to reduce working poverty and overall poverty. As a result, they are well on track to reach Target 1 set forth in the first Millennium Development Goal of halving the proportion of people living on less than US$1 by 2015 (for details on the Millennium Development Goals, see box 3.1 in Chapter 3 of this Report).

These results are underlined by estimates presented in table 1.4, taking the IMF GDP growth rates of the developing world for the period 1995 to 2005 and projecting this trend to 2015. There is a chance to halve the global proportion of US$1 a day working poverty by 2015. The growth rate needed would be 4.7 per cent, less than the 5 per cent projected between 1995 and 2005. But by taking East Asia – and above all China – out of the picture, the forecast looks less robust. Only South-East Asia, South Asia, the transition economies and the Middle East and North Africa are currently on track to meet the goal. For the latter two regions this is the result of the low levels of extreme working poverty. The region of Latin America and the Caribbean is slightly off track, while sub-Saharan Africa is significantly off track, with a GDP growth rate of over 8 per

**Table 1.4.   GDP growth rates required to halve working poverty by 2015
and IMF average GDP growth rates 1995-2005**

	GDP growth required to meet objectives		IMF average GDP growth rates
	Halve US$1 a day working poverty	Halve US$2 a day working poverty	1995-2005
World except industrialized economies	4.7%	Over 10%	5.0%
World except East Asia and except industrialized economies	5.3%	Over 10%	3.8%
Transition economies	4% to 5%	8% to 10%	3.3%
East Asia	3% to 4%	6% to 8%	7.9%
South-East Asia	4% to 5%	Over 10%	4.1%
South Asia	5% to 6%	Over 10%	5.8%
Latin America and the Caribbean	3% to 4%	4% to 6%	2.4%
Middle East and North Africa	4% to 5%	8% to 10%	4.0%
Sub-Saharan Africa	Over 8 %	Over 10%	3.7%

Note: These calculations are based on the assumption that the growth needed to reduce working poverty by 1 per cent will be the same as it was in the past. If this ratio changes because of changes in policies or institutional arrangements, this would have major impacts on the GDP growth rates needed.
Source: Kapsos, 2004.

cent needed to halve US$1 a day working poverty by 2015. Of course it has to be borne in mind that halving working poverty in this region was an even bigger challenge from the outset than in other regions.

The outlook becomes even bleaker when the goal is to halve US$2 a day working poverty. Only East Asia has a realistic chance, whereas none of the other regions will succeed unless their GDP growth rates increase considerably. Given these estimates, it is important to keep in mind that growth alone is not enough. It is the decent employment content of growth that really matters if economies want to tackle working poverty along with unemployment. Total poverty will decrease only if progress in these two areas can be achieved. And in the longer run, GDP growth will occur only in the presence of increases in productivity and decent employment creation. Only with productive jobs where workers can use their potential, and only with decent employment opportunities, will people permanently stay out of poverty. In short, workers need to be in a position to stimulate demand through their consumption and invest in themselves and the future of their children. In addition, decent employment opportunities not only address the income component of poverty but also the humanity component by giving people the chance to voice their concerns, to participate more fully in decisions in the world of work and to be respected for their work. This in turn can help the economy as a whole to develop further.

In the light of the persistently high number of working poor, together with the over 185 million people currently unemployed and the uncertain number of people who remain outside the labour force for involuntary reasons, it is clear that there is a large and persistent decent work deficit in the world – one that poses a great challenge in the fight against poverty.

1.2. Regional trends[4]

Latin America and the Caribbean

According to the United Nations, the region of Latin America and the Caribbean[5] is struggling to reach Target 1 of the first Millennium Development Goal of halving the proportion of people living on less than US$1 a day by 2015. A closer look at some labour market indicators in this region gives a first indication as to why it is unlikely that poverty will be halved by 2015. For the past ten years, there has been a slight decline in the region's employment-to-population ratio, indicating that there has been employment creation but that it has not been sufficient to absorb the growing labour force (table 1.3). One explanation for this trend could be that people decide to stay in education or otherwise freely decide to remain outside the labour force. But with stagnant educational indicators (see ILO, 2003a) and persistently high shares of poverty in the region (a quarter of the population lives below the US$2 a day poverty line, table 1.2), this explanation appears suspect. Also, the unemployment rate increased from 6.9 per cent in 1993 to 8.0 per cent in 2003 (for additional information and the correct interpretation of these numbers, see box 1.3). Given the trends in these two labour market indicators, it becomes clear that the region as a whole has been unable to make better use of its labour potential in order to boost economic growth.

Although productivity growth has varied throughout the region (figures 1.1a and 1.1b), overall labour productivity growth in the region was only 1.2 per cent between 1993 and 2003. The annual average growth in productivity was only 0.1 per cent (table 1.3). There are exceptions such as Chile, which has seen impressive and consistent increases in labour productivity. Chile now has the highest productivity level of all economies in the region for which internationally comparable data are available (figure 1.1b). At the same time Chile is one of the few economies in the region that has seen a significant increase in its employment-to-population ratio since 1980; in 1980 it was 42.4 per cent, in 2001 it was 49.1 per cent. Most other economies have higher productivity levels than in 1993 but lower levels than in the 1980s (figure 1.1a). Besides Chile, Argentina saw promising development in productivity growth after 1993, but this trend

---

[4] The groupings of economies are adapted from those in *Key Indicators of the Labour Market (KILM)*, 3rd edition (ILO). There are six major groupings in KILM, based on a combination of level of development and geography. It is important to note that the groupings developed for KILM are intended exclusively for analytical convenience and are not intended to express judgement or appraisal as to a given economy's current stage in the development process. There are two developmental groupings: developed (industrialized) economies and transition economies; and four geographic groupings: Asia and the Pacific, Latin America and the Caribbean, sub-Saharan Africa, and the Middle East and North Africa. Each economy appears in only one major grouping; for example, Japan is included in the developed (industrialized) economies grouping and is therefore excluded from Asia and the Pacific. In the present chapter the KILM Asia and the Pacific region is broken down into East Asia and South-East Asia groupings.

[5] The Latin America and the Caribbean region comprises the subregions of **the Caribbean** (Anguilla, Antigua and Barbuda, Aruba, Bahamas, Barbados, Bermuda, British Virgin Islands, Cayman Islands, Cuba, Dominica, Dominican Republic, Grenada, Guadeloupe, Guyana, Haiti, Jamaica, Martinique, Montserrat, Netherlands Antilles, Puerto Rico, Saint Kitts and Nevis, Saint Lucia, Saint Vincent and the Grenadines, Suriname, Trinidad and Tobago, Turks and Caicos Islands, United States Virgin Islands), **Central America** (Belize, Costa Rica, El Salvador, Guatemala, Honduras, Mexico, Nicaragua, Panama), and **South America** (Argentina, Bolivia, Brazil, Chile, Colombia, Ecuador, Falkland Islands (Malvinas), French Guiana, Paraguay, Peru, Uruguay, Venezuela).

Box 1.3.   Urban versus rural labour market information

The ILO has two major publications on regional labour market trends in Latin America and the Caribbean: *Panorama Laboral*, published by the ILO Office in Lima, and the section on Latin America and the Caribbean in Chapter 1, *Global Employment Trends*, published at headquarters in Geneva. Even though these reports focus on the same region, the coverage of the two publications is different. Whereas *Panorama Laboral* focuses on urban area labour market development, *Global Employment Trends* covers urban as well as rural areas. The differences become clear when looking at the unemployment rates. Whereas *Panorama Laboral* estimates a regional unemployment rate of around 10 per cent, *Global Employment Trends* estimates around 8 per cent for 2003. And whereas *Panorama Laboral* reported almost no change between 2002 and 2003, *Global Employment Trends* shows a decline of one percentage point.

Even though urban labour market data are often more reliable than rural labour market data, it is important to make an attempt to focus not only on urban data, especially in economies where the agricultural sector is the main employer. The obvious differences in results therefore reflect an attempt to give the full picture using all the information available. The higher and stagnant urban rates are indicative of some of the challenges associated with the process of urbanization taking place in many countries in the region.

Source: ILO, 2003b and ILO, 2004d.

---

came to a turning point after 1998 and fell sharply with the 2001 economic crisis. Peru also witnessed high productivity growth rates between 1993 and 1997 but this trend came to a halt afterwards. Other economies have either seen only slight increases in productivity over the past ten years (this is the case for Brazil, Colombia, Guatemala and Mexico), yet others (namely Ecuador and Venezuela) have witnessed a decrease.

Agriculture[6] plays an important role in many economies in the region (figure 1.2), thus it is worthwhile to look at productivity trends in this sector. Once again the picture is very diverse: Haiti, with agriculture accounting for over 50 per cent of the economy's employment, saw a tremendous decrease in agricultural productivity of 24.5 per cent between 1993 and 2001,[7] whereas Brazil at the other extreme with a share of agricultural employment of only 20.6 per cent, saw an increase of its agricultural productivity of 65.3 per cent (table 1.5). As can be seen from the table some economies saw increases in both productivity and employment in agriculture between 1993 and the latest year available.

---

[6] The data on agriculture in this chapter include agriculture, forestry and fisheries.

[7] The reasons for this are manifold, including a combination of a lack of investment in the sector, a continuing fragmentation of landholdings and insecure land tenure, high commodity taxes, the low productivity of the often undernourished rural population and declining environmental quality resulting from extreme deforestation, soil erosion, droughts and flooding (US Library of Congress, 2004; FAO, 2004).

Figure 1.1a. **Growth in output per person employed in Latin America and the Caribbean (total economy, selected economies, index 1993=100, 1980 to latest year)**

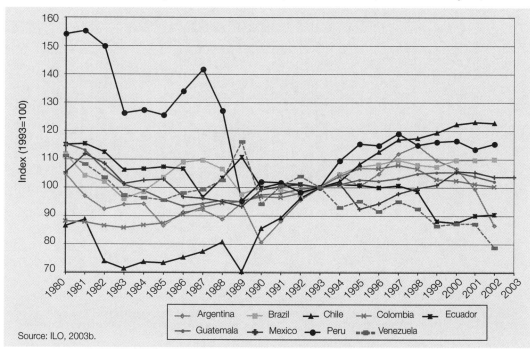

Source: ILO, 2003b.

Figure 1.1b. **Output per person employed in Latin America and the Caribbean (total economy, selected economies, selected years)**

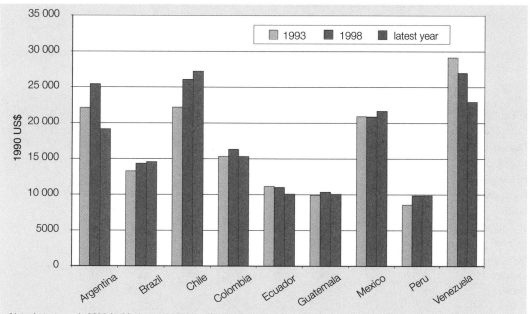

Note: Latest year is 2003 for Mexico and 2002 for all other countries. Figure 1.1a shows trends in labour productivity growth; it does not say anything about the levels. Levels are shown in figure 1.1b. An economy can have higher growth rates over time than other economies but still have lower levels of labour productivity. To make the changes comparable, figure 1.1a uses an index in which 1993 is the base year. This, in effect, puts all economies on a comparable labour productivity scale, whereby all economies have equal values in 1993. The highest line in years following 1993 thereby shows the economy with the fastest growth in labour productivity since 1993.

Source: ILO, 2003b.

**Figure 1.2.   Employment shares by sector in Latin America and the Caribbean
(selected economies, latest year available, percentage)**

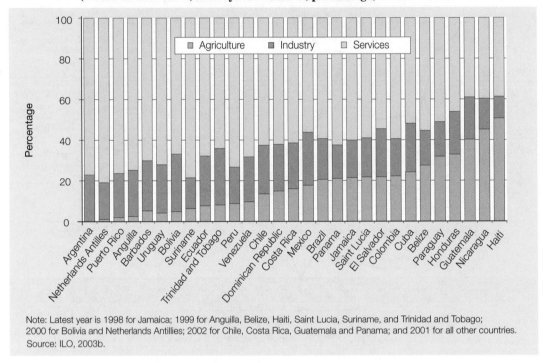

Note: Latest year is 1998 for Jamaica; 1999 for Anguilla, Belize, Haiti, Saint Lucia, Suriname, and Trinidad and Tobago;
2000 for Bolivia and Netherlands Antillies; 2002 for Chile, Costa Rica, Guatemala and Panama; and 2001 for all other countries.
Source: ILO, 2003b.

**Table 1.5.   Selected agricultural indicators in Latin America and the Caribbean
(1993 and latest year available)**

	Change in output per person employed in agriculture between 1993 and latest year available (%)	Change in employment between 1993 and latest year available (%)
Argentina	25.9	–13.1
Brazil	65.3	–14.9
Chile	16.1	–9.5
Colombia	10.1	8.1
Costa Rica	35.3	1.5
Dominican Republic	5.4	16.5
Ecuador	6.9	45.4
El Salvador	–2.7	–2.2*
Guatemala	4.9	29.0**
Haiti	–24.5	n.a
Honduras	–8.8	21.6
Mexico	39.6	–16.7
Nicaragua	16.2	68.9
Panama	39.6	24.7
Paraguay	8.8	24.5
Peru	43.7	82.2
Uruguay	42.2	0.4
Venezuela	–0.6	16.7

Notes: Latest year is 2001 for Brazil and Dominican Republic, 1999 for Paraguay, and 2002 for all other countries. *1994 to latest
year;   **1998 to latest year.
Source: ILO, 2003b.

Figure 1.3. US$1 and US$2 a day working poverty trends in Latin America and the Caribbean (1990-2015, percentage)

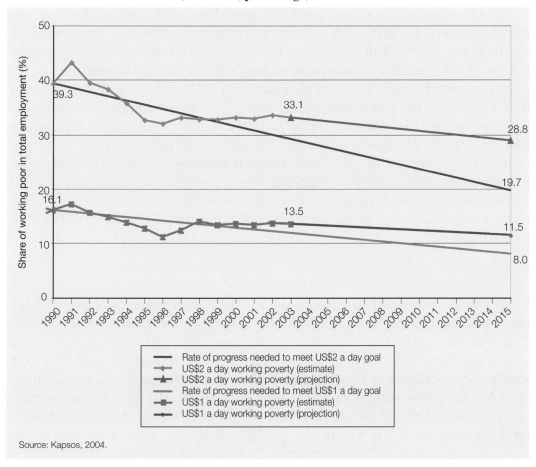

Source: Kapsos, 2004.

Given the very slow development in productivity, the stagnation in terms of employment creation and increasing unemployment rates in most economies in total employment has not improved much since 1990 (figure 1.3). The total number of people working but not earning enough to lift themselves and their families above the US$1 a day poverty line reached 30 million for the first time in 2003 despite the overall economic recovery. In relative terms, however, the US$1 a day working poverty share slightly decreased between 2002 and 2003 from 13.7 per cent to 13.5 per cent. In terms of US$2 a day working poverty, the region saw a more impressive decline in the early 1990s. But after 1996 the share increased and stayed at levels above 32 per cent. The region has to deal with two problems through the creation of decent and productive employment. First, decent employment opportunities are needed to give those who work but are still poor a chance to work themselves and their families out of poverty. At the same time decent and productive jobs are needed to reduce unemployment. If both goals are not tackled effectively, Latin America and the

Caribbean will get even further off track from reaching the Millennium Development Goals.

ILO estimates show that the GDP growth needed to halve US$1 a day working poverty by 2015 is 3.5 per cent per year, more than the region has seen for the past ten years. But at the same time there are strong signs that the region is back on a more solid growth path, making a 3.5 per cent rate possible.

Besides the challenge to create additional GDP growth and to make sure that it would be translated into decent and productive employment opportunities, high levels of income inequality (with the richest 5 per cent of the population receiving 25 per cent of income, as compared to 13 per cent in the developed economies), decreases in public investment (especially in education) and in foreign direct investment in the region, the strong dependence on external markets and the relatively poor quality of the institutional environment have been identified as core issues to be tackled by policy-makers (ILO, 2004d; IMF, 2004; ECLAC, 2004).

East Asia

Economic development in East Asia[8] has been impressive over the past ten years, with an average annual GDP growth rate of 8.3 per cent since 1993 (table 1.3), and this is expected to continue in the near term.[9] This progress is driven mostly by China, the largest economy in the region, but with support also from smaller economies such as Mongolia.[10] The strong growth in the region, however, has not been equally matched by job creation. Although the unemployment rate was only 3.3 per cent for the region in 2003, this represents a slight increase from the 3.1 per cent rate in 2002. Mongolia is the exception in the region, where registered unemployment has been steadily declining in recent years, from 4.6 per cent in 2000 to 3.4 per cent in 2002, following strong growth in GDP.[11]

Unemployment has continued to climb in China and the Republic of Korea, where echoes of "jobless growth" are being heard. In the Republic of Korea, in particular, this is raising concerns of a "hollowing out" of the manufacturing sector, as labour-intensive industries are facing stiff competition from China where many companies are relocating in order to take advantage of lower labour costs

---

[8] The East Asia region comprises China, Democratic People's Republic of Korea, Hong Kong (China), Macau (China), Mongolia, Republic of Korea, and Taiwan (China).

[9] According to the International Energy Agency some dampening effect to GDP and employment could arise in the latter part of 2004, particularly if oil prices remain high. The region's strong reliance on oil for continued growth has created a double-edged sword, by driving the price of oil upwards through strong demand and consequently forcing the region to bear the brunt of higher prices. The impact of higher oil prices will be most severe in oil-importing developing economies such as China, not only because of its dependency on oil, but also because of its less efficient use of oil. On average, oil-importing developing countries use more than twice as much oil per unit of production as OECD countries. Because of this, the impact of a sustained increase in the price of oil is expected to reduce China's GDP by 0.8 per cent and raise inflation by almost 1 per cent in 2004 (International Energy Agency, 2004).

[10] Asian Development Bank, 2004.

[11] However, it should be noted that unemployment in Mongolia may be significantly underestimated as a result of low registration of the unemployed (Asian Development Bank, 2004).

(Xie and Lam, 2004). At the same time China's manufacturing employment has decreased considerably in the past decade as a result of employment releases from state-owned enterprises. The Government of the Republic of Korea has recently taken measures to address the employment issue through the implementation of the Social Pact for Job Creation (see box 1.4).

The strong development in the region is also indicated by the region's performance vis-à-vis labour productivity. Between 1993 and 2003 labour productivity in the region increased by 75 per cent, giving an annual growth rate of 5.8 per cent. Figure 1.4a shows labour productivity growth in those East Asian economies where internationally comparable data are currently available. The figure shows strong productivity growth in the region since 1993 for China, Taiwan (China) and the Republic of Korea and to a lesser extent in Hong Kong (China). All economies in the region were on more or less equal growth paths until 1993, at which point China's productivity growth accelerated at a more rapid pace. More recently, growth has decelerated in Hong Kong (China), Taiwan (China) and to a lesser extent in the Republic of Korea, but it has continued to accelerate in China. It should be borne in mind that stronger growth in China's labour productivity is in part a result of the relatively lower initial level of China's labour productivity in comparison to that in Hong Kong (China), Taiwan (China) and the Republic of Korea – meaning that much of the accelerated growth in China can be attributed to "catching-up" with the other economies in the region (figure 1.4b).

In 1993, productivity levels in the Republic of Korea and Hong Kong (China) were, respectively, more than five times and almost ten times that of China. In 2003, the difference between the Republic of Korea and China had declined to four times and the difference between China and Hong Kong (China) is now just above six times. Output per person employed in China was US$4,463 in 1993, and by 2002 it had increased to US$7,704, meaning that productivity grew by an impressive 6.3 per cent per year over the past decade. Growth in Hong Kong (China), the Republic of Korea and Taiwan (China) during the same period was less per year, at 1.7 per cent for Hong Kong (China), 4.3 per cent for the Republic of Korea and 3.6 per cent for Taiwan (China).

Because of the strong growth in the region and relatively low unemployment rates, East Asia is on track to achieve the Millennium Development Goal of halving the share of people living on less than US$1 per day by 2015. In fact, China has already achieved the goal. Additionally, because China's workforce represents 95 per cent of the labour force in the region, the region has also halved the number of working poor since 1990. The absolute number of workers unable to lift themselves and their families above the US$1 a day poverty threshold fell from 242 million in 1990 to 139 million in 2003, a reduction of 43 per cent. If growth continues on its current path it is expected that the region will more than halve the share of US$1 and 2 a day working poverty by 2015 (figure 1.5 and table 1.1).

Box 1.4.   The Social Pact for Job Creation in the Republic of Korea

The economy of the Republic of Korea has not completely recovered from the financial crisis of the late 1990s. Economic growth has been held back by declining agricultural production and retail services, as well as slowing growth in manufacturing. In 2003, value added in the manufacturing sector increased by 4.8 per cent compared to 6.3 per cent in 2002 (Asian Development Bank, 2003). At the same time, there has been a constant increase in productivity and real wage levels suggesting some trade-off between productivity and job creation, although the rise in real wages since 1998 has been accompanied by growth in productivity. Labour compensation (which includes hourly direct pay plus employer social insurance expenditures and other labour taxes) has been increasing at a faster pace, which has had an important impact on the industry's wage competitiveness.

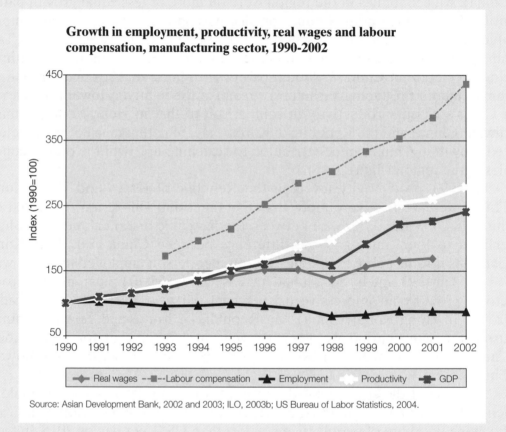

Growth in employment, productivity, real wages and labour compensation, manufacturing sector, 1990-2002

Source: Asian Development Bank, 2002 and 2003; ILO, 2003b; US Bureau of Labor Statistics, 2004.

Identifying job creation and the advancement of industrial relations as its main priorities, a tripartite commission, comprising workers' representatives, employers and the Government, designed the Social Pact for Job Creation in February 2004. The purpose of the pact is to improve the labour situation in the country through tripartite dialogue and to:

• address the persistent problems of employment insecurity, especially rising youth unemployment;

• ease the incorporation of women and old workers into the labour market;

- ensure a more cooperative system of industrial relations by specifying the role of each economic participant;
- provide wage competitiveness while taking into consideration the interests of all parties involved (workers, employers and the Government).

The Government of the Republic of Korea sees the Social Pact for Job Creation as an important step towards constructive collaboration between workers, employers and the Government. It is expected that the adoption of labour legislation, clearly defining the rights and responsibilities of all parties involved, will contribute to a better investment climate in the country and will lead to more investments and the creation of job opportunities.

Source: Republic of Korea Ministry of Labor, 2004; Asian Development Bank, 2002, 2003, 2004.

It should be noted, however, that the decline in the absolute number of working poor in China was among other things the result of positive rural development. This trend has slowed since 2000, and many of the country's current working poor remain in remote, rural areas with degraded land (Asian Development Bank, 2004). Thus, further improved strategies for addressing the special needs of the rural poor are necessary in order to ensure reaching the poverty reduction target (see Chapter 3 of this Report).

**Figure 1.4a.   Growth in output per person employed in East Asia
(total economy, selected economies, index 1993=100, 1980 to latest year)**

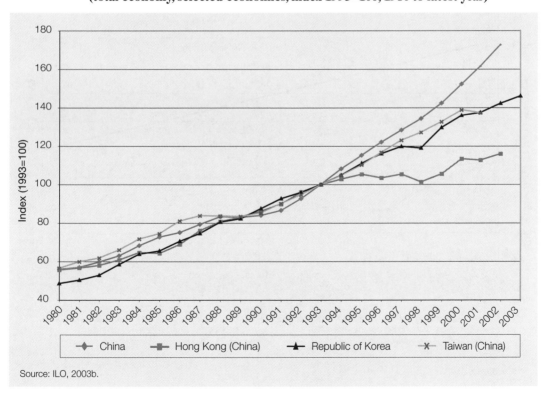

Source: ILO, 2003b.

Figure 1.4b. Output per person employed in East Asia (total economy, selected economies and years)

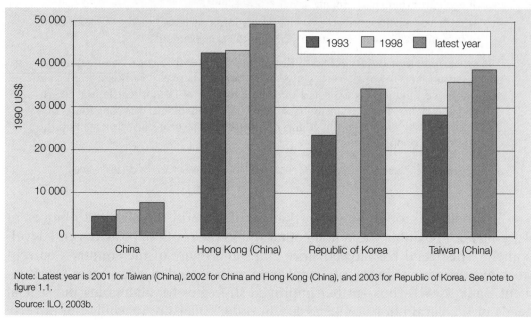

Note: Latest year is 2001 for Taiwan (China), 2002 for China and Hong Kong (China), and 2003 for Republic of Korea. See note to figure 1.1.

Source: ILO, 2003b.

Figure 1.5. US$1 and US$2 a day working poverty trends in East Asia (1990-2015, percentage)

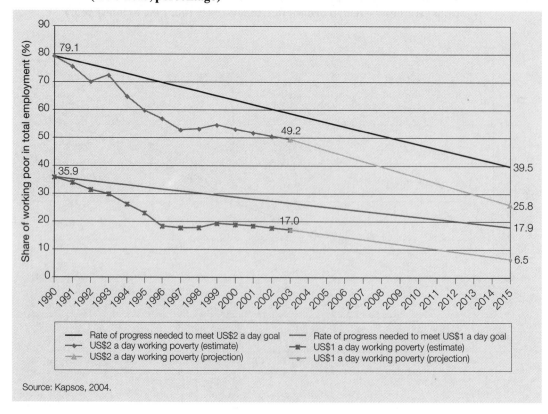

Source: Kapsos, 2004.

In economies such as the Republic of Korea where, as a result of the economic development in the past, US$1 a day poverty is no longer a primary issue, the major concern has been the historical rise in youth unemployment. Recently, more young people have been entering the labour market, but at the same time fewer job opportunities exist because of sluggish job creation (ILO, 2004c). Another particular challenge for the Republic of Korea is to address the competitiveness of its manufacturing sector, while fostering growth, productivity improvements and employment expansion in service industries, particularly in retail trade.

South-East Asia and the Pacific

Overall labour market indicators for the South-East Asia and the Pacific [12] region have deteriorated over the past ten years, although some improvements have been observed recently. Unemployment rates are over two percentage points higher than ten years ago (at 6.3 per cent in 2003) and the employment-to-population ratio is lower than it was ten years ago. The latter partly reflects a growing trend in education; people are not actually looking for work, as they stay in education for a longer period. But at the same time rising unemployment rates indicate that not enough employment opportunities exist. The region's high annual labour force growth rate of 2.4 per cent (table 1.3), resulting from high population growth rates and growing labour force participation rates, contributes to this fact. Another reason for the adverse labour market trends over the past ten years is that some economies still have not recovered from the Asian crisis. This is specifically true for Indonesia, the biggest economy in the region (for details, see box 1.5). Finally, state-owned enterprises in Cambodia and Viet Nam are still releasing a great number of workers.

There has been an upward trend in productivity since 1993 that was much slower than in other Asian subregions but higher than in most other developing regions. Per annum labour productivity grew by 2 per cent lifting the 2003 labour productivity level 21.6 per cent above the level in 1993. A more robust upward trend was interrupted by the Asian crisis in 1997/1998. On the one hand, the crisis did not greatly affect the productivity levels of the less advanced economies such as Myanmar, the Philippines and Viet Nam. On the other hand, the more affected economies in the region have only recently recovered to their pre-crisis productivity levels (figures 1.6a and 1.6b). Myanmar and Viet Nam have seen the highest growth in productivity, signalling a convergence among productivity levels in the region. But the gap remains wide. Figure 1.6b shows the wide range in total output per person employed for those economies where internationally comparable estimates are available. Myanmar's value added per worker is still

---

[12] The South-East Asia and the Pacific region comprises American Samoa, Brunei Darussalam, Cambodia, Cook Islands, Democratic Republic of Timor-Leste, Fiji, French Polynesia, Guam, Indonesia, Kiribati, Lao People's Democratic Republic, Malaysia, Myanmar, New Caledonia, Northern Mariana Islands, Pacific Islands (Trust Territory), Papua New Guinea, Philippines, Samoa, Singapore, Solomon Islands, Thailand, Tonga, Tuvalu and Viet Nam.

one-tenth that of Singapore. Even in Malaysia – one of the more advanced economies in the region – value added per worker is only about one-third of that in
Singapore. Of course this difference is not due to the people's capabilities or
willingness to work – in fact a person working in Myanmar might work longer
hours and physically much harder than somebody in Singapore – but, as a result
of differences in sectoral activities, potentially lower skill levels and less
advanced technologies, their labour input does not translate into the same
amount of output compared with a worker in Singapore.

The range is even greater in agricultural productivity. For example, even
though Viet Nam has experienced an increase in output per person employed
in agriculture of 30 per cent since 1980, Malaysia still produces 80 times more
per person employed in agriculture (in terms of value added) than Viet Nam
(ILO, 2003b), once again not as a result of people's willingness to work but possibly as a result of the lack of technology and training. In terms of having

Box 1.5.   Indonesia: Why institutions matter

From 1967 to 1997, during Suharto's New Order regime, Indonesia's GDP grew by
an average of 7 per cent per annum. Rapid growth – mainly caused by high rates of
labour-intensive exports – was accompanied by a significant reduction in poverty,
along with a diversification of the economy away from agriculture. This development was built on strong macroeconomic policies and was supported by increasingly
liberal trade and foreign investment policies, as well as financial sector policies. But
at the same time, Indonesia's underlying social, financial, legal, and political institutions did not develop accordingly. This lack of functioning institutions, combined
with high levels of corruption under the Suharto regime, made the country vulnerable to shocks. When the Asian financial crisis hit in 1997, the absence of strong
institutions and social consensus as well as the considerable damage caused by corruption made managing the crisis and recovering from it more difficult and more
costly for Indonesia than for other crisis-affected countries. This is reflected in the
productivity performance in all sectors. Whereas some of the other economies in the
region managed to quickly recover to their pre-crisis productivity growth paths,
Indonesia's productivity in all four industries for which data are available has not yet
reached pre-crisis levels (figure 2 below). This is also reflected in stagnating shifts in
employment shares. Until the crisis, Indonesia had reduced the share of employment in agriculture relative to the employment shares in industry and services. After
the crisis this trend came to a halt (figure 1 below), partly because people moved
back to rural areas as they could no longer find employment opportunities in the cities and had no social security to fall back on. This can be taken as a serious sign of
delay in the development process, caused by the fact that social institutions were not
in place. In addition, unemployment rates, which were around 4 per cent before the
crisis, subsequently went up to and remained at over 6 per cent. Finally, the informal
economy increased after the crisis (reflected in the sharp rise of US$1 and 2 a day
working poverty after 1996 in figure 4 below). US$2 a day working poverty has not
yet recovered to pre-crisis levels. All these developments led to stagnation in both
GDP per capita (figure 3 below) and poverty reduction.

1. Employment shares (percentages, index 1997=100, 1985-2001)

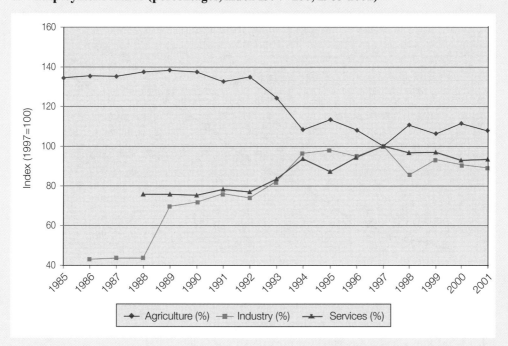

2. Output per person employed (selected industries, index 1997=100, 1980-2001)

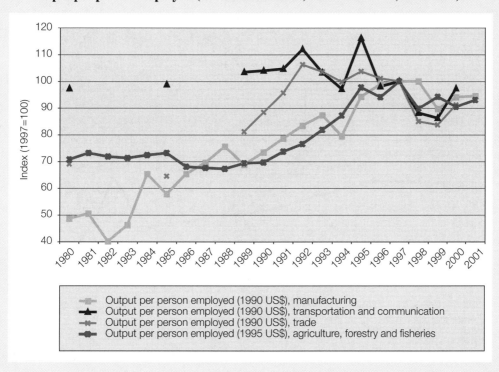

3. GDP per capita in PPPs (1980-2001)

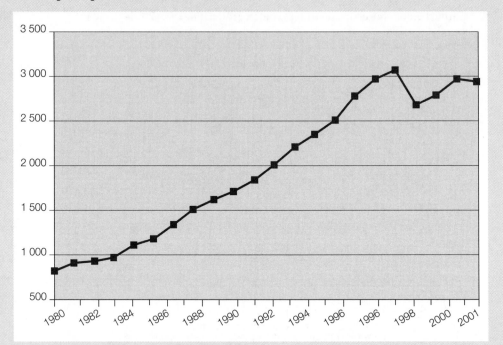

4. US$1 and US$2 a day working poverty trends (1980-2003)

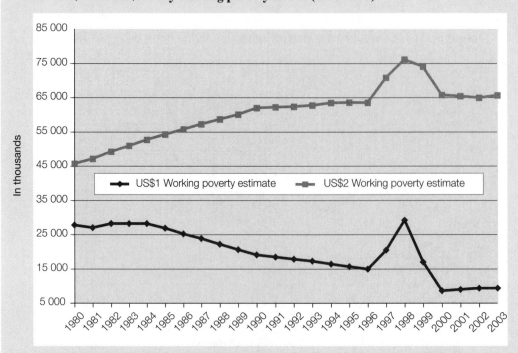

Note: Sectoral productivity data have different groupings from sectoral employment data: agriculture is the same for both, manufacturing and industry are roughly comparable, and communication and transportation can by used as an indicator of the service sector.
Source: ILO, 2003b; World Bank, 2004a, 2004b; Kapsos, 2004; calculations based on these data; World Bank, 2004b; Amjad, 2004.

Figure 1.6a.   Growth in output per person employed in South-East Asia
(total economy, selected economies, index 1993=100, 1980 to latest year)

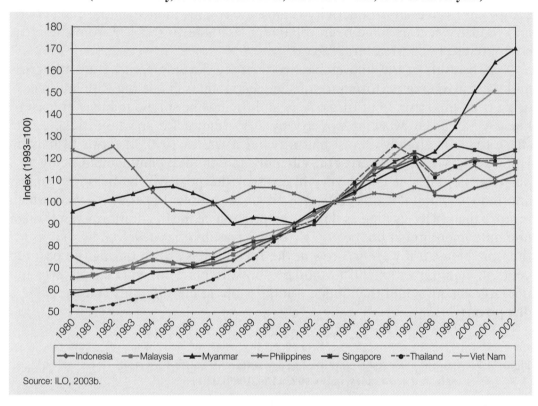

Source: ILO, 2003b.

Figure 1.6b.   Output per person employed in South-East Asia
(total economy, selected economies and years)

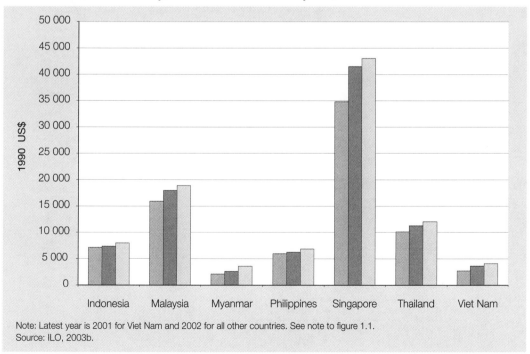

Note: Latest year is 2001 for Viet Nam and 2002 for all other countries. See note to figure 1.1.
Source: ILO, 2003b.

reached pre-crisis productivity levels in this sector, more countries have managed to get back on their agricultural productivity growth path (figure 1.7) compared to overall productivity (figure 1.6a). This indicates that the service and industry sectors have been relatively less able to recover from the crisis compared to the agricultural sector.

As a result of the impressive productivity development before the crisis and the convincing performance of some economies in dealing with and recovering from the crisis, South-East Asia and the Pacific should manage at least to halve US$1 a day working poverty by 2015 (figure 1.8 and table 1.2), as the share today is already almost half of what it was in 1990. In terms of halving US$2 a day working poverty (the current share in total employment being 58.8 per cent in 2003), it is not very likely that the goal will be achieved unless another Asian miracle lifts GDP growth rates to above 10 per cent a year, which is more than twice as high as during the past ten years. In addition, even though unemployment might not be as big a concern as in other developing regions for the time being, if it were to grow at the speed it has grown during the past ten years, unemployment in 2015 would be above 10 per cent. Working poverty and unemployment would then make it impossible to considerably reduce US$2 a day poverty.

Figure 1.7.   Output per person employed in agriculture in South-East Asia (selected economies, index 1993=100, 1980-2001)

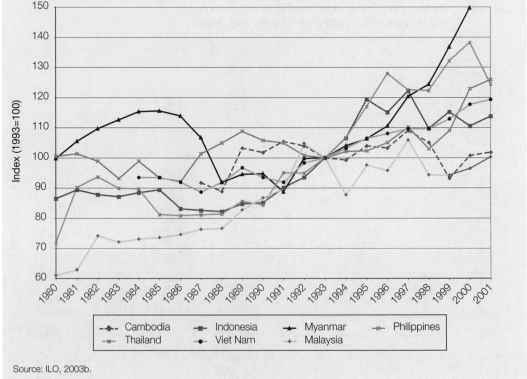

Source: ILO, 2003b.

**Figure 1.8.   US$1 and US$2 a day working poverty trends in South-East Asia
(1990-2015, percentage)**

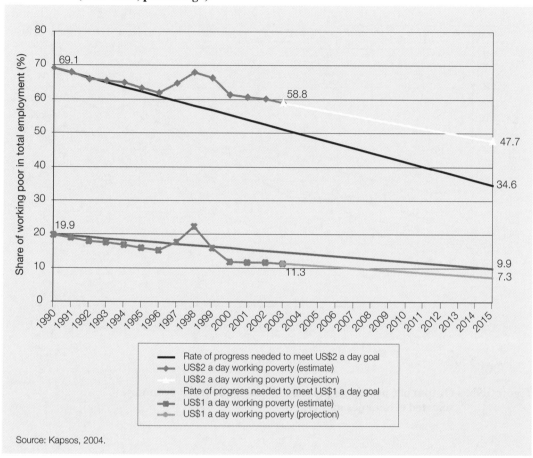

Source: Kapsos, 2004.

South Asia

Unemployment and employment-to-population ratios have not changed considerably over the past ten years despite solid GDP growth rates of over 5 per cent in South Asia.[13] Unemployment rates are just below 5 per cent and employment-to-population ratios are 57 per cent, which is the same level as in 1993. This indicates that there has been employment creation, but just enough to absorb the growing labour force (which is still growing at the fast rate of 2.3 per cent a year). The employment-to-population ratio is low: only the Middle East and North Africa region has a lower ratio.

The South Asia region has seen improvements in terms of productivity growth since 1993. Productivity grew by 3.3 per cent annually and the level of productivity in 2003 was 37.9 per cent higher than in 1993 (table 1.3). These trends indicate that besides East Asia no other region in the world has been as successful in terms of increasing productivity as South Asia. Figures 1.9a and 1.9b

---

[13] The South Asia region comprises Afghanistan, Bangladesh, Bhutan, India, Maldives, Nepal, Pakistan, and Sri Lanka.

Figure 1.9a. Growth in output per person employed in South Asia (total economy, selected economies, index 1993=100, 1980 to latest year)

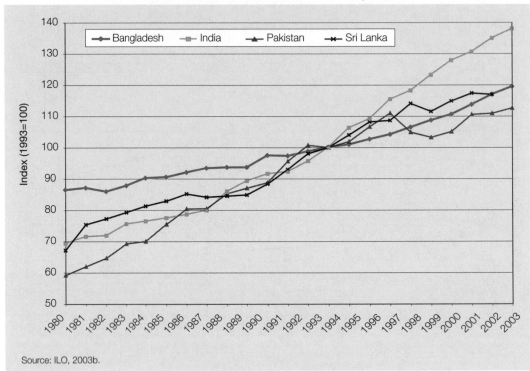

Source: ILO, 2003b.

Figure 1.9b. Output per person employed in South Asia (total economy, selected economies and years)

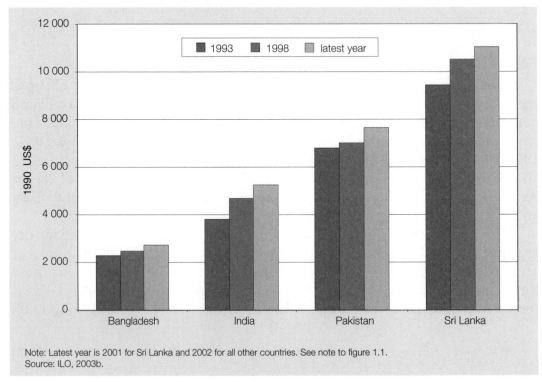

Note: Latest year is 2001 for Sri Lanka and 2002 for all other countries. See note to figure 1.1.
Source: ILO, 2003b.

show the development as well as the levels for a selection of economies in the region. These levels vary considerably between economies. Whereas Pakistan, Bangladesh and Sri Lanka have managed to improve productivity only slightly since 1993, India has managed to increase the output produced per person employed by almost 40 per cent within the same period (for more details on India, see box 1.6). Pakistan and Sri Lanka both started off well at the beginning of the 1990s, but with the onset of the Asian crisis in 1997, Pakistan entered into a period of productivity decline for two years and has not yet recovered. Sri Lanka witnessed a decline in productivity in 1998 and productivity in the country has more or less stagnated since then.

The improvements in agricultural productivity have, on average, been smaller than in overall productivity, an adverse development in a region where agriculture is the main provider of jobs (table 1.6). India, one of the best performers in the 1980s in terms of increases in agricultural productivity, has seen an increase of only 12 per cent since 1990. In the same period Sri Lanka has witnessed an increase of 40 per cent. Pakistan and Sri Lanka have the highest levels of output per person in agriculture, producing more than twice as much per person as India. Once again, motivation or willingness to work are not explanations, for the differences, but rather they are likely to be the result of differences in skills and access to technology.

The stability in labour market indicators together with increases in productivity were the main reasons why the region has seen considerable declines in

---

Box 1.6. Productivity, employment and poverty reduction in India

The Indian experience can be taken as a good example of the fact that growth in productivity usually goes hand in hand with growth in employment as well as poverty reduction. In the specific case of India, this is true for all three sectors, but employment creation varied tremendously. The service sector has seen impressive improvements in productivity and in employment. In contrast, the agricultural sector has witnessed the smallest improvement in terms of productivity but greater employment growth than the industrial sector. Meanwhile the industrial sector had the highest improvement in productivity but, as is often the case in this sector, at the cost of very little improvement in employment. In addition, wages in manufacturing saw a decline over the past 20 years (as can be seen in figure 4 of this box. (Wages in the sector are still high enough to enable people who work in this sector to live above the US$1 a day poverty threshold.) Overall, the shares of agricultural and industrial employment in total employment have been decreasing, whereas the share of service sector employment has risen. But even if this trend continues in the near future, with over 200 million people working in the agricultural sector, India will remain a largely agrarian economy for some time. As can be seen from figure 4 above, this very typical pattern in terms of sectoral shift went hand in hand with growth in GDP per capita.

Source: ILO, 2003b, and calculations based on the same source; Amjad, 2004; Islam, 2004.

1. Total and sectoral employment (index 1990=100, 1990-1995)

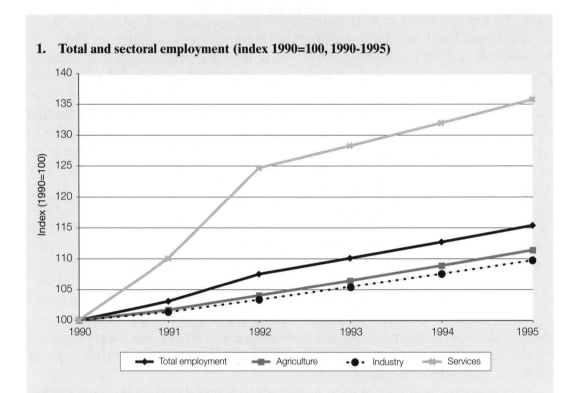

2. Output per person employed (total and by sector, index 1990=100, 1990-2002)

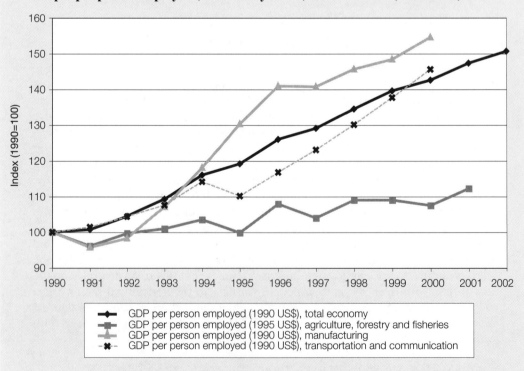

3. Employment by sector (total numbers, 1990-1995)

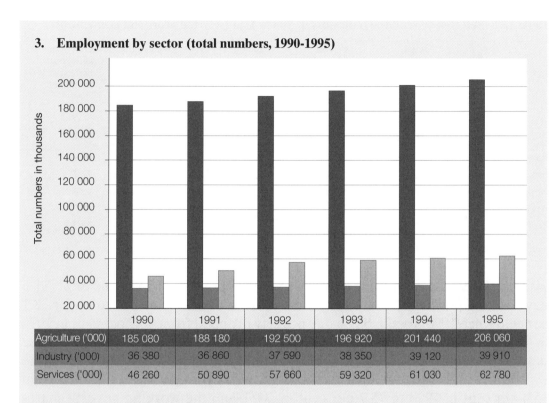

	1990	1991	1992	1993	1994	1995
Agriculture ('000)	185 080	188 180	192 500	196 920	201 440	206 060
Industry ('000)	36 380	36 860	37 590	38 350	39 120	39 910
Services ('000)	46 260	50 890	57 660	59 320	61 030	62 780

4. GDP per capita at PPP, 1980-2001 and real manufacturing wage index (1990=100), 1980-1999

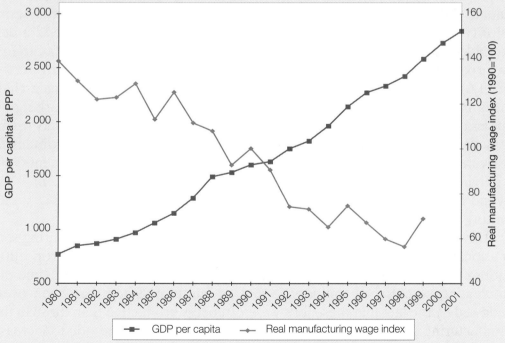

Note: Sectoral productivity data have different groupings from sectoral employment data. Agriculture is the same for both; manufacturing and industry are roughly comparable; and communication and transportation can be used as an indicator of the service sector.

Source: ILO, 2003b.

Table 1.6.   Selected agricultural indicators in South Asia (selected years and economies)

	Output per person employed 1980	Output per person employed 1993	Output per person employed latest year available*	Employment share of agriculture in total employment latest year available*	GDP share of agriculture earliest year available**
	1995 US$	1995 US$*	1995 US$	(%)	(%)
Bangladesh	286	318	397	62.1	22.7
India	528	686	762	66.7	22.7
Nepal	388	516	606	78.5	40.8
Pakistan	1 019	1 524	1 674	48.4	23.2
Sri Lanka	1 114	1 328	1 594	41.6	22.7

Source: *ILO, 2003b;   **World Bank, 2003.

extreme US$1 a day working poverty and total poverty. [14] In terms of US$1 a day working poverty, the rate has dropped from over 53 per cent to under 38.1 per cent since 1990. Total US$1 a day poverty dropped from 40.9 per cent in 1990 to 28.4 per cent in 2003 and is likely to further decrease in 2004. Despite these positive economic developments, these are still the second highest shares in the world (after sub-Saharan Africa). The US$2 a day poverty share declined from 85.4 per cent in 1990 to 75.7 per cent in 2003, and the working poverty shares declined from 93.1 to 87.5 per cent during the same period. This indicates that the productivity growth rates and the solid GDP growth rates of 5.5 per cent annually did help to create jobs and to lift people out of extreme poverty, but the majority of jobs were not decent enough to lift people above the US$2 a day threshold (figure 1.10). This situation will continue if trends in wages fail to follow productivity trends, as has been the case in India's manufacturing sector (box 1.6). The decent work deficit in this region remains one of the main challenges and can be tackled only with the right combination of labour market policies and macroeconomic policies. Even if the goal to halve the US$1 a day working poverty share in total employment by 2015 is reachable and contributes to the overall likelihood of this region reaching the Millennium Development Goal of halving extreme poverty by 2015, growth rates of over 10 per cent – far beyond historical rates – would be needed to halve the share of US$2 a day working poverty in total employment by 2015.

Development strategies have to keep in mind that the manufacturing sector's contribution to job creation has historically been lower than the proportion of jobs created in the service and the agricultural sectors. At the same time the job-creating potential of the service and agricultural sectors has been overshadowed by the fact that these jobs were often less productive than those in the manufacturing sector. Therefore the focus has to be on the one side to increase

---

[14] There have been differences in the poverty reduction process. The impacts of labour market conditions as well as economic conditions on poverty reduction depend on the institutional settings and other non-economic factors. For an analysis of some of the differences between some of the economies in the region see Amjad, 2004 and Islam, 2004.

**Figure 1.10.   US$1 and US$2 a day working poverty trends in South Asia
(1990-2015, percentage)**

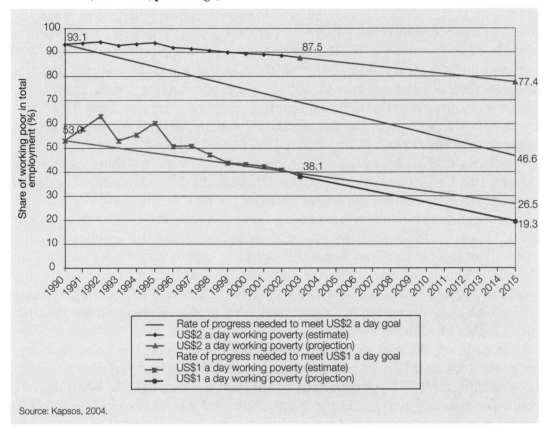

Source: Kapsos, 2004.

employment creation in manufacturing, and on the other side to make sure that the jobs created in services and agriculture do not further contribute to the poverty trap of low productivity and low wage jobs.

Middle East and North Africa

The region of the Middle East and North Africa (MENA) [15] is unique in the economic diversity of the economies covered. The GDP figures among the region's oil-producing countries are close to three times higher than the average for non-oil-producing countries. The regional aggregates of labour market indicators, therefore, are likely to mask the highly diverse socio-economic situations of the economies themselves, and these should thus be used with care.

There are, however, some notable features that characterize the region as a whole. First of all, MENA has a growing young population, with 37 per cent of the population below the age of 15 years in 2000, and 58 per cent below the age

---

[15] The Middle East and North Africa region comprises the subregions of the Middle East (Bahrain, Djibouti, Islamic Republic of Iran, Iraq, Israel, Jordan, Kuwait, Lebanon, Oman, Qatar, Saudi Arabia, Somalia, Syrian Arab Republic, United Arab Emirates, West Bank and Gaza Strip, Yemen), and North Africa (Algeria, Egypt, Libyan Arab Jamahiriya, Morocco, Sudan, Tunisia).

of 25 years. This raises the important question of whether the relatively high economic growth in the region will bring with it enough decent and productive employment creation to absorb the growing youth cohort when, on average, the working age population increases by 3 per cent a year. Youth unemployment is already a major challenge for the region; the youth unemployment rate, at 25.6 per cent in 2003 (ILO, 2004c), is the highest in the world. In addition, there is concern that population growth will outpace economic growth, despite the region's resource wealth, threatening future economic development. The fertility rate (births per woman) in the region is declining, but it is still higher than in other developing regions (Cordseman, 1998).

MENA differs from other developing regions in its low share of working poverty (the US$1 a day working poverty share in total employment was only 2.9 per cent in 2003, whereas about one-third of the people who have a job do not earn enough to lift themselves and their families above the US$2 a day poverty line). However, the inequality in the distribution of wealth implies that the majority of people have not benefited from the vast oil wealth generated over decades by many of the MENA economies. The distribution of poverty and working poverty in this region follows closely the division of the oil-producing states and non-oil-producing states, with the non-producing states showing much higher incidences.

In addition, the high unemployment rates in the region are a real challenge for policy-makers. MENA's unemployment rate – the highest regional rate – has hovered around the 12 per cent mark for at least the past decade. What the rate reflects is a steady increase in the number of total unemployed since 1996 (an average of 500,000 additional unemployed per year, generated mostly in the Middle East subregion) and an increase in employment, but not enough to absorb all of those seeking work. Figures 1.11a and 1.11b confirm that between 1993 and 2003, nominal unemployment (1993=100) grew faster than employment in the Middle East but not in North Africa. It should be noted, however, that most of the increase in employment was that of females, which can be viewed as a sign of some improvement in its own right, given the past restrictions on female work. The employment-to-population ratio for men actually stayed relatively constant (69.6 in 1993 and 68.6 in 2003), whereas this ratio for women increased from 20.4 to 23.5. This indicates improvement, certainly, but the female employment-to-population ratios in this region still remain the lowest in the world by far. Additionally, the quality of jobs created for women is often inferior to that of men (ILO, 2004b).

Compared to other regions — especially the Asian regions — productivity gains have been rather low with an average annual growth rate of 0.1 per cent and an increase of 0.9 per cent over the past ten years. The picture of the levels of productivity for the region (figure 1.12b) also mimics the natural resource distribution within the region; oil-producing countries such as Saudi Arabia and the United Arab Emirates have much higher labour productivity – on a par with some industrialized economies — than non-oil-producing countries such as

**Figure 1.11a.   Employment and unemployment in the Middle East
(index 1993=100, 1993 to latest year)**

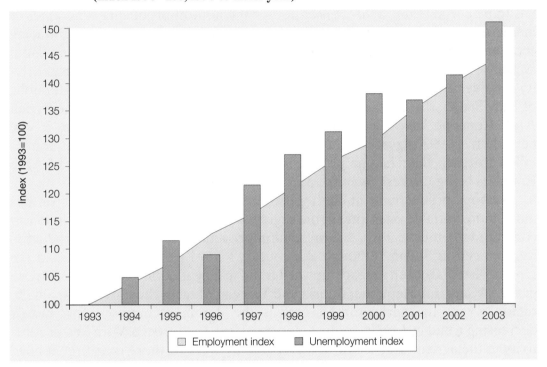

**Figure 1.11b.   Employment and unemployment in North Africa
(index 1993=100, 1993 to latest year)**

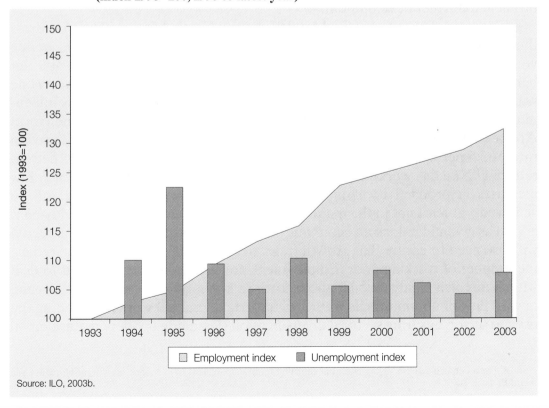

Source: ILO, 2003b.

Egypt, Morocco and Yemen. In terms of trends, there is no clear distinction between oil-producing and non-oil-producing economies. Having noted this, it has to be borne in mind that it is easier for the non-oil-producing economies to increase from their rather low productivity levels than it is for the oil-producing economies with their high levels. In three economies – Algeria, Jordan and Saudi Arabia – labour productivity in 2002 was lower than in 1993. Labour productivity however increased steadily during this period in Egypt, the Islamic Republic of Iran, Sudan, the United Arab Emirates and Yemen. Morocco and the Syrian Arab Republic have seen very little variation in labour productivity in the period after 1993 (figures 1.12a and 1.12b). A slight majority of the economies failed to reach their labour productivity level of 1980, with the United Arab Emirates being furthest away from its 1980 level.

Labour productivity in the agriculture, forestry and fisheries sector was much more variable over time in the region, but in general it remained quite low compared to other regions. A significant improvement in agricultural productivity occurred in Sudan, although the country's level remains the lowest in the region. There has been a steady upward trend in Egypt, a mostly increasing trend in the Syrian Arab Republic, Tunisia and Yemen (which is the only country in the region where the agricultural sector is the dominant employer), a mostly decreasing trend in Jordan, and a volatile pattern in Morocco. With low productivity in the agricultural sector in this region as a whole, there is an urgent need for employment policies that address rural labour market deficiencies. Otherwise the outflow of the population from rural into urban areas could become an obstacle to further development.

The main challenge for the Middle East and North Africa will be to address the unemployment situation, particularly the high unemployment among youths, as well as to make sure that the share of people working but still not being able to lift themselves and their families above the US$2 a day poverty line will decrease faster than during the 1990s and the early part of the new millennium (figure 1.13). To halve unemployment by 2015, the Middle East and North Africa would need GDP growth rates much higher than the historical growth rate of 3.5 per cent. At the same time higher growth rates would also help to reduce US$2 a day working poverty considerably. But given the persistently low increases in productivity it is unlikely that the growth rate needed will be achieved – at least not in the majority of economies. Decreasing unemployment is vital as it would unlock an economic potential not used so far,[16] but the region will also need to ensure that growth translates into higher wages so as to reduce the number of working poor. Employment policies should be designed to deal with issues of: a highly mobile labour force (a net outward flow of nationals and inward flow of non-nationals willing to undertake manual work); expanding the private sector; ensuring sectoral diversification (lessening the dependence on oil

---

[16] For a detailed analysis of the potential contribution of employment to economic growth in the region, see World Bank, 2004c.

Figure 1.12a.   Growth in output per person employed in the Middle East and North Africa (total economy, selected economies, index 1993=100, 1980 to latest year)

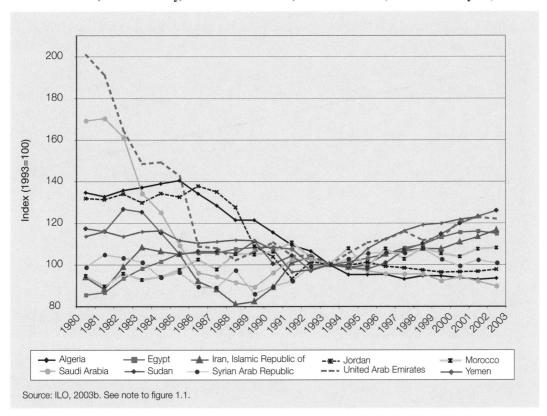

Source: ILO, 2003b. See note to figure 1.1.

Figure 1.12b.   Output per person employed in the Middle East and North Africa (total economy, selected economies, index 1993=100, 1980 to latest year)

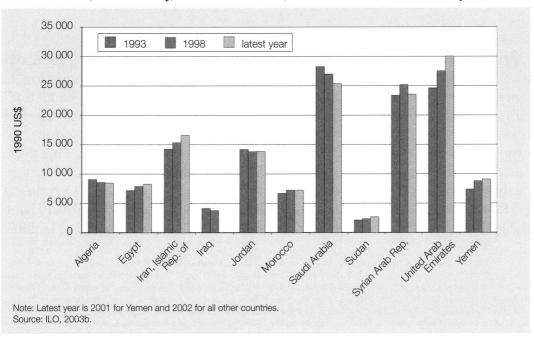

Note: Latest year is 2001 for Yemen and 2002 for all other countries.
Source: ILO, 2003b.

**Figure 1.13.   US$1 and US$2 a day working poverty trends in the Middle East
and North Africa (1990-2015, percentage)**

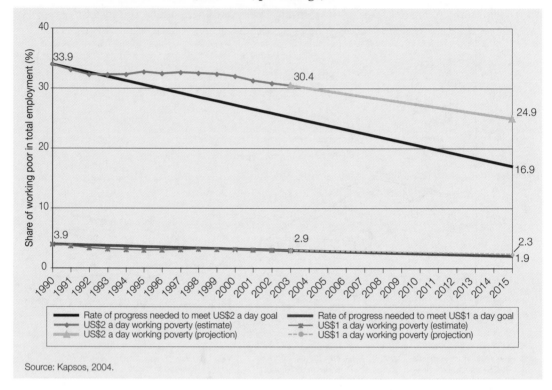

Source: Kapsos, 2004.

exports); improving educational standards and ensuring equal opportunity for education; increasing the economic activity of women; and bridging the gap in the supply and demand for youth employment (box 1.7).

Sub-Saharan Africa

Developments in sub-Saharan Africa [17] underline the fact that low productivity, low GDP growth rates, increases in total unemployment, stagnation in employment-to-population ratios and working poverty go hand in hand. Sub-Saharan Africa has the highest incidence of working poverty of all developing regions. Around 55 per cent of all people employed are not earning enough to lift themselves and their families above the US$1 a day poverty line. This share had decreased slightly during the late 1980s, but since 1990 it stayed continuously at a level as high as 55.8 per cent (table 1.1 and figure 1.15). In terms of US$2 a day working poverty the same stagnation took place since 1990, leaving the working poor share in total employment at just below 90 per cent in 2003.

---

[17] The Sub-Saharan Africa region comprises the subregions of **Central Africa** (Angola, Cameroon, Central African Republic, Chad, Congo, Democratic Republic of Congo, Equatorial Guinea, Gabon, Sao Tome and Principe), **eastern Africa** (Burundi, Comoros, Eritrea, Ethiopia, Kenya, Madagascar, Malawi, Mauritius, Mozambique, Réunion, Rwanda, Seychelles, Uganda, United Republic of Tanzania, Zambia, Zanzibar, Zimbabwe), **southern Africa** (Botswana, Lesotho, Namibia, South Africa, Swaziland), and **western Africa** (Benin, Burkina Faso, Cape Verde, Côte d'Ivoire, Gambia, Ghana, Guinea, Guinea-Bissau, Liberia, Mali, Mauritania, Niger, Nigeria, Senegal, Sierra Leone, St. Helena, Togo).

Box 1.7. The Arab brain drain

With unemployment soaring to worrying levels and the inability of Arab States to absorb their growing number of highly educated professionals, Arab citizens – particularly Arab youths – are increasingly migrating to try their luck in other areas of the world.

There are economic and political reasons why young graduates leave their native State, amongst which are:

- Avoidance of joblessness or the obligation to accept jobs far from their specialization
- Insufficient scientific and technological infrastructure
- Low income prospects for the highly skilled
- Political and social instability
- Avoidance of stringent administrative bureaucracies and other institutional constraints

A report of the Arab League found that more than 450,000 Arab university graduates were settled in European countries and the United States in 2001, resulting in a loss of human and economic potential to the Middle East and North Africa region and an overall negative impact on development. UNDP estimates that between 1998 and 2000, more than 15,000 Arab doctors emigrated abroad.

Source: UNDP, 2003.

The stagnation in both US$1 a day and US$2 a day total poverty follows these trends (table 1.2).

Sub-Saharan Africa's unemployment rate has seen no improvement in recent years and remained at 10.9 per cent in 2003 (table 1.3). The same is true for the region's employment-to-population ratio, which stands at around 66 per cent. This is quite high compared to other developing regions, but at the same time this indicator does not give a clear picture as to the quality of jobs and the conditions under which people work.

Sub-Saharan Africa is the only region that had seen decreases in labour productivity levels between 1993 and 2003 (table 1.3). This went hand in hand with slow GDP growth rates of under 3 per cent, a value that for an extremely poor region is not enough to push development forward. Out of the eight countries for which comparable data are available, GDP per person employed is only higher than in 1980 in one country, Ghana. Since 1983, productivity in Ghana grew solidly, which helped the economy double its GDP per capita over the period. Over the past ten years Ethiopia, South Africa and the United Republic of Tanzania also saw increases in productivity levels, but in the other economies for which data are available, productivity decreased over the period (figures 1.14a and 1.14b).

As agriculture plays a major role in most countries in the region, a look at the development in agricultural productivity is worthwhile (table 1.7). Ghana saw the largest reduction in agricultural productivity between 1980 and 2001.

**Figure 1.14a. Growth in output per person employed in sub-Saharan Africa
(total economy, selected economies, index 1993=100, 1980 to latest year)**

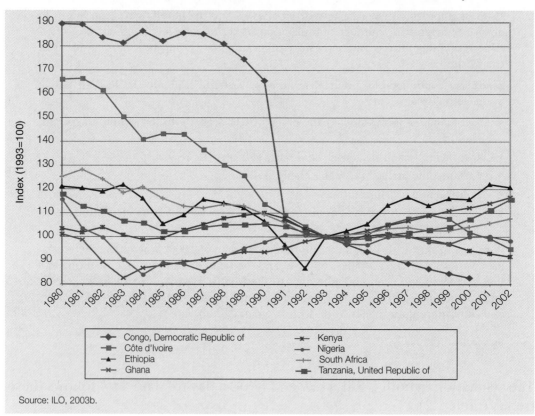

Source: ILO, 2003b.

**Figure 1.14b. Output per person employed in sub-Saharan Africa
(total economy, selected economies and years)**

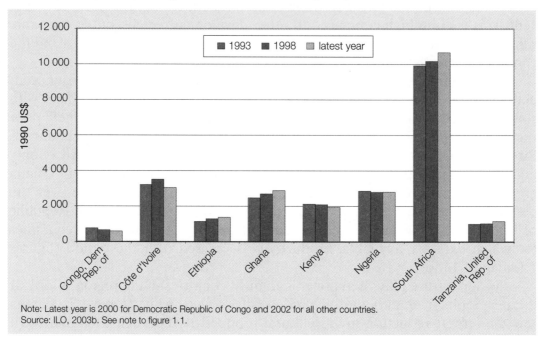

Note: Latest year is 2000 for Democratic Republic of Congo and 2002 for all other countries.
Source: ILO, 2003b. See note to figure 1.1.

Table 1.7. Selected agricultural indicators in sub-Saharan Africa (selected years)

	Output per person employed in agriculture	Output per person employed in agriculture	Output per person employed in agriculture	Difference in output per person employed in agriculture	Change in employment in agriculture between year closest to 1980 and closest to 2001
	1980 1995 US$	1990 1995 US$	2001 1995 US$	1980-2001	(in thousands)
Benin	941	1 161	1 819	878	220
Burundi	399	415	357	–42	n.a.
Cameroon	109	115	178	69	569
Chad	383	336	485	102	276
Congo, Democratic Republic of	150	155	127	–23	2 171
Côte d'Ivoire	1 355	1 142	1 348	–7	–508
Ghana	3 151	2 448	2 654	–497	279.03
Guinea	n.a.	222	262	40	375
Kenya	357	365	290	–67	79.9
Madagascar	534	532	515	–19	1 024
Malawi	216	167	261	45	n.a.
Mali	422	405	416	–6	829
Mozambique	n.a.	1 293	1 447	154	n.a.
Niger	199	169	177	–22	n.a.
Nigeria	480	672	940	460	–153
Rwanda	217	170	207	–10	879
Senegal	387	431	444	57	455
South Africa	2 432	2 790	3 256	824	–1 146
Tanzania, United Republic of	151	165	205	54	n.a.
Zambia	1 659	1 631	1 699	40	381
Zimbabwe	783	712	754	–29	n.a.

n.a.: no data available.
Source: ILO, 2003b.

But taking into account the country's growth rate in total productivity (figure 1.14a), Ghana was obviously able to create productivity growth in other sectors. Considerable increases in productivity in agriculture took place in Chad, Mozambique, Nigeria, Uganda and most impressively in Benin and South Africa. In Benin, Chad, Mozambique and Uganda, productivity growth went hand in hand with employment growth in the sector. South Africa and Nigeria have reached a phase in their development process in which the impact of agriculture on employment and GDP has begun to decrease while other sectors are becoming more important.

Prospects for sub-Saharan Africa look rather challenging if current trends persist (figure 1.15). If productivity growth continues at the very low rate of the

**Figure 1.15.   US$1 and US$2 a day working poverty trends in sub-Saharan Africa
(1990-2015, percentage)**

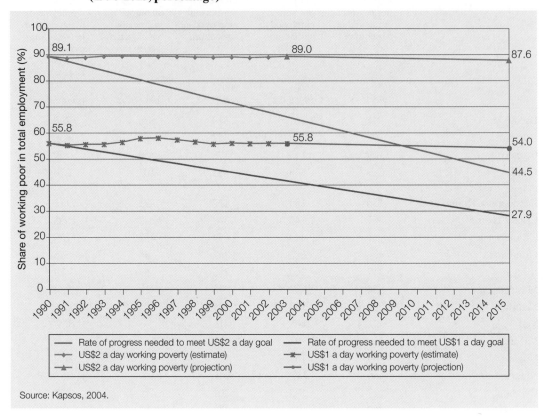

Source: Kapsos, 2004.

past 20 years, the high share of working poor and total poverty is likely to persist
given the region's high unemployment rates, insufficient capacity for job creation, rapidly expanding labour force and huge overall decent work deficit. To
halve unemployment as well as working poverty by 2015, sub-Saharan Africa
would need GDP growth rates much higher than in the past (table 1.4; ILO,
2003a, 2004a). This points to the need for politicians to focus on decent employment and improvements in labour productivity (for one example, see box 1.8
and also box 1.9) together with the employment content of growth. Even if the
region might not reach the Millennium Development Goal of halving poverty by
2015 – an extremely difficult challenge given that the region had the highest
share of extreme poverty in the world – any improvements in this regard would
lay the groundwork for a brighter future. The region now requires the concerted
efforts of governments together with the international community. While governments in the region should work on improvements in education, infrastructure and developing favourable investment conditions, the international community has to make sure that the region can participate more in trade and
thereby benefit from the positive effects of globalization.

Box 1.8.   Enhancing female productivity in agriculture as a simple means to raise overall productivity

In recent years, research has found mixed results in answer to the question of whether differences in yields between male and female farmers in sub-Saharan Africa exist, but the majority of studies found that yields of women are smaller than those of men. This result is often misused as an indication of lower labour productivity of women. In fact, IFAD's 1999 *Assessment of rural poverty in West and Central Africa* argues that lower yields should not be interpreted as indicating lower productivity among women farmers. The sex differences in yields are mainly the result of the following:

- The intra-household allocation of resources, such as of the quality and quantity of land;

- Women's greater difficulties in accessing financial resources, which limit their purchase of inputs, such as fertilizer and tools, and their ability to pay hired labour;

- Women's shortage of labour owing to their multiple responsibilities and their poor control over family labour.

In Burkina Faso, applied research on men and women who grew the same crop on individual plots provided more detailed findings, including the following. Most of the inputs, such as labour and fertilizer, went to the men's plots. However, female labour was more productive in growing vegetables. Overall the study estimated that the total household output could be increased by 10-20 per cent if some of the inputs from the plots controlled by men went to the plots controlled by women. In addition, the IFAD poverty assessment points to evidence that shows that, when they are available, resources such as organic fertilizer and credit are better managed by women than by men. Finally, if women were to get more support in managing their multiple responsibilities, agricultural productivity in sub-Saharan Africa could increase considerably.

Source: IFAD, 1999; IFAD/FAO/Government of Japan, 1998.

Box 1.9.   The Extraordinary Summit on Employment and Poverty Alleviation in Africa

On the initiative of President Compaoré of Burkina Faso, the Heads of State of the African Union (AU) held an Extraordinary Summit on Employment and Poverty Alleviation in Ouagadougou, Burkina Faso on 8-9 September 2004. The Summit was held in collaboration with the Regional Economic Communities, the ILO, the development partners and other involved parties.

The goals of the Extraordinary Summit were to:

- consolidate the New Partnership for Africa's Development (NEPAD), aimed at ensuring sustainable human development in Africa;

- re-emphasize the dedication of the Heads of State in making employment central in the fight against poverty, in the context of globalization and technological, economic, political and social change;

(continued overleaf)

- elaborate a Plan of Action with specific programmes for the creation of productive employment;
- establish an efficient and appropriate feedback mechanism for the follow-up to the conclusions and decisions taken at the Summit.

The Plan of Action worked on at the time of finalizing this report provides the means of translating broad principles into action by targeting priority sectors (such as agriculture and infrastructure projects) that favour job creation. The Plan places a special emphasis on the fight against HIV/AIDS and similar diseases and on the role of women and youth in these development strategies.

In his opening speech, the Director-General of the International Labour Organization (ILO), Juan Somavia, pointed out that "the women, men and youth and, unfortunately, even children of this continent are working hard every day. There is no poverty of effort in Africa. There is poverty of opportunity". He emphasized Africa's right to expect support and global fairness and said that "good national governance will not succeed unless we have good global governance". This can only be achieved through greater policy coherence on growth, investment and employment creation from the international community.

"We need a global approach", he said, adding, "No institution has all the answers, but we all have the mandates that oblige us to find solutions. By joining forces, we can forge a better path to a fair globalization."

The Summit was preceded by a Social Partners' Forum, entitled "Decent work, a driving force for Africa's development". It brought together 80 representatives of employer and worker organizations as well as 20 observers from non-governmental organizations (NGOs) and representatives of international institutions to discuss the following key points:

- The creation of employment as one of the best methods for combating poverty;
- The necessity to make decent work a worldwide goal;
- The need for a high and sustainable rate of economic growth as the first step in the fight against poverty;
- The protection of fundamental workers' rights and social dialogue as irreplaceable tools for development.

Source: ILO press release, 8 September 2004 (ILO/04/39); available at http://www.ilo.org/public/english/bureau/inf/pr/2004/39.htm and http://www.ilo.org/public/english/bureau/inf/event/ouagadougou/

Transition economies

The entry into the European Union (EU) of ten new member countries on 1 May 2004 has brought a fair amount of hope as well as uncertainty to the growth and employment prospects for the transition economies[18] as a whole. There is an expectation that membership in the EU will quicken the

[18] The transition region comprises the subregions of **Central and Eastern Europe** (Albania, Bosnia and Herzegovina, Bulgaria, Croatia, Czech Republic, Hungary, Poland, Romania, Slovakia, Slovenia, The former Yugoslav Republic of Macedonia, Serbia and Montenegro), **Baltic States** (Estonia, Latvia, Lithuania), and **Commonwealth of Independent States** (Armenia, Azerbaijan, Belarus, Georgia, Kazakhstan, Kyrgyzstan, Republic of Moldova, Russian Federation, Tajikistan, Turkmenistan, Ukraine). The ILO recognises that the transition process is not a permanent state. As a result, the next Trends Report will feature reclassified regional groupings to take into consideration the changed status of many of these economies.

pace of foreign investment in the region, open new markets and ultimately lead to what many hope will be akin to another "Irish miracle". At the same time there are fears that the opening of labour markets will encourage large-scale emigration to the richer EU economies, as the unemployed and underemployed seek job opportunities outside of the transition region. Which of these scenarios will arise remains to be seen and is very much dependent on the ability of the transition economies to create decent and productive employment opportunities within their own borders.

The current employment situation in the transition economies is characterized by high unemployment, which has been increasing since the economic transition process of the early 1990s. Employment declined significantly in the years immediately following the transition, as markets were privatized and production processes became more efficient. Since that time, the economic situation in the region has seen improvements. Output growth and labour productivity has increased, and despite large increases in US$1 a day working poverty in the beginning of the transition period, the region is nearly on track to halve the number of US$1 a day working poor by 2015. Recently, unemployment rates have stabilized, and the 9.2 per cent rate in 2003 is slightly less than the rate in 2002 (9.4 per cent, table 1.3). The transition region is also one of the few regions where women fare no worse than men in terms of unemployment (ILO, 2004b). Besides unemployment, underemployment is a major concern, most notably in the Commonwealth of Independent States, where the lack of decent employment opportunities in the formal market and administrative legislation impedes small business ownership, and forces many people to find work in the informal economy.

How did the region do in terms of labour productivity? Figures 1.16a and 1.16b show labour productivity growth in a selection of the transition economies where internationally comparable data are currently available. In the majority of these economies an upward trend in productivity is seen since 1990, particularly among the current EU member countries. Hungary, Poland, Slovakia and Slovenia all exhibited substantial growth in productivity since 1990, increasing on average between 3.1 to 4.9 per cent per year. In addition, figure 1.16b shows that these countries are among those with the highest levels of productivity for the region, meaning that the strong growth is not the result of a low starting point. Other countries in this region, such as Bulgaria, Czech Republic, Estonia, Kazakhstan, Romania and the Russian Federation have had a more erratic labour productivity growth pattern. In particular, labour productivity in the Russian Federation is currently below what it was before the collapse of the USSR, while Bulgaria has shown marked improvements since 1998.

Despite the strong gains in productivity growth for a number of the transition economies, the gains in employment remain disappointing. The size of the labour force and the share of the population employed both declined in the region between 1993 and 2003. Add to that the region's high unemployment rate, and it becomes obvious that much of these historical gains in productivity were at the expense of employment.

Figure 1.16a.   Growth in output per person employed in the transition economies (total economy, selected economies, index 1990=100, 1990 to latest year)

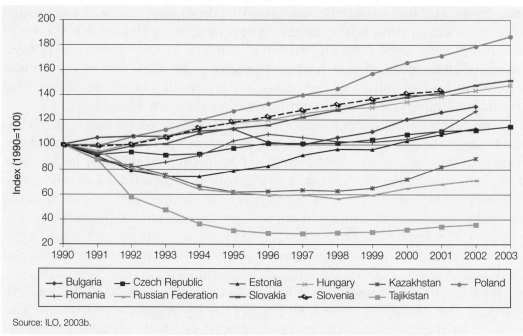

Source: ILO, 2003b.

Figure 1.16b.   Output per person employed in the transition economies (total economy, selected economies and years)

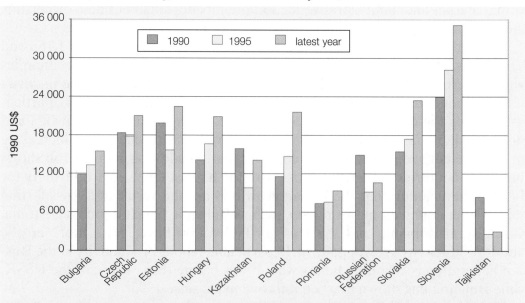

Note: To better reflect the transition period, figures 1.16a and 1.16b use different base years and a different selection of years than the other regions in this chapter. Latest year is 2003 for Czech Republic, Hungary, Poland, and Slovakia, and 2002 for all other countries. Figure 1.16a shows the trend in labour productivity growth; it does not say anything about the levels. Levels are shown in figure 1.16b. Therefore an economy can have higher growth rates over time but still have lower levels of labour productivity than other economies in the figure. To make the development comparable, figure 1.16a uses an index in which 1990 is the base year. This, in effect puts all economies on a comparable labour productivity scale, whereby all economies have equal values in 1990. The highest line in years following 1993 thereby shows the economy with the fastest growth in labour productivity since 1990.

Source: ILO, 2003b.

Some countries, however, have started to turn this scenario around. For example, since 1998 both employment and productivity have been increasing in Hungary as the result of economic reforms. By establishing itself as part of the European production network through foreign direct investment, Hungary has been successful in obtaining high growth rates since the middle of the 1990s, which has also translated into higher employment creation during this period (see box on Hungary in Chapter 2 of this Report).

In general, the employment prospects for the region will very much depend, among other things, on economic developments in the richer EU countries and the ability of the new member countries to successfully integrate into the EU production chains.

Industrialized economies

The rate of unemployment in the industrialized region [19] in 2003 was 6.8 per cent, with rates lower in the industrialized economies outside of Europe than those in Europe. Unemployment rates in the industrialized economies in Europe were 7.9 per cent, compared with 5.9 per cent outside of Europe (ILO, 2004a). Thus, despite the ongoing economic recovery in terms of GDP growth, labour markets have been slow to recover (see also box 1.10 on outsourcing and its contribution to unemployment). [20]

Over the past decade, employment in the industrialized economies outside of Europe expanded at a more rapid rate than the European industrialized economies. Total employment increased by 8.8 per cent in industrialized Europe (from 177 to 193 million), compared to 10.8 per cent in the industrialized economies outside of Europe (from 211 to 234 million). However, if the focus is on the percentage of people who have jobs (which is a better measure of employment), then labour markets in industrialized Europe show more improvements. Since 1993, employment as a share of the population in industrialized Europe increased from 50.3 per cent in 1993 to 51.2 per cent in 2003, compared to the industrialized economies outside of Europe where it increased from 60.6 per cent to 60.9 per cent (ILO, 2004a). Also, since 1998, industrialized Europe's employment growth, at 4.3 per cent, has exceeded that of the industrialized economies outside of Europe, at 2.7 per cent – indicating that some of the reforms in labour and product markets in Europe have begun to pay off.

---

[19] The industrialized region comprises the subregions of **European industrialized economies** (Austria, Belgium, Denmark, Finland, France, Germany, Greece, Iceland, Ireland, Italy, Luxembourg, Netherlands, Norway, Portugal, Spain, Sweden, Switzerland, Turkey, United Kingdom), and **industrialized economies outside of Europe** (Australia, Canada, Japan, New Zealand, United States). The Employment Strategy Department is currently revising regional groupings based on the realignment of economies within Europe. Regional groupings in subsequent Trends Reports will reflect these changes.

[20] The continued rise in oil prices (over 40 per cent in the past year) will likely have a dampening effect on growth and the recovery in labour markets. According to the International Energy Agency, the EU economies would likely be hardest hit (as they do not have their own oil reserves) and could face an impact of a half a percentage point of GDP growth in 2004. The impact in Japan is estimated to be a 0.4 percentage point decline, while in the US the rise in oil prices it is expected to take 0.3 percentage points off GDP growth for the year (International Energy Agency, 2004). Although industrialized economies have become more productive in their use of oil resources for manufacturing production, globalization has increased the importance of transportation – ships, trains, and aeroplanes – in getting goods and people to and from market, which has translated into a continued reliance on oil among rich and poor countries alike.

Box 1.10. Outsourcing in the industrialized economies

"Offshoring", i.e. the production of goods or purchasing of services from an overseas provider, has been increasing in many industrialized economies, causing concerns among workers that it is leading to widespread unemployment as jobs are being moved from industrialized to developing economies. Yet, data show that there is no net transfer of jobs from one part of the world to the other. Rather than jobs moving abroad, increases in productivity growth have eliminated many jobs that previously existed. This is particularly the case in the manufacturing sector. For example, during the past decade, steel production in the United States has increased from 75 to 102 million tons, but the number of workers in this industry has decreased from 289,000 to 74,000 employees.

Although outsourcing does account for some of the job losses in industrialized economies, statistically it is a small fraction of the employment turnover that occurs in industrialized economies on a yearly basis.

- The United States Department of Labor estimates that in the first three months of 2004, less than 2 per cent of mass lay-offs in the United States were the result of outsourcing. During that period, 4,633 of 239,361 employees were laid off because of their jobs moving to a foreign country.

- According to estimates by the Centre for Economic Policy Research, outsourcing to Eastern Europe led to an average loss of 8,000 jobs per year in Germany and 2,000 jobs per year in Austria during the period 1990 to 2001.

Statistics are, of course, only one side of the story and there is the likelihood that firms in industrialized economies will increase their offshoring activities in the future. It is therefore difficult to determine exactly how outsourcing will ultimately affect labour markets in industrialized economies. The challenges ahead require industrialized economies to ensure that the net effect of outsourcing is not simply to displace workers, but rather that the benefits that outsourcing can bring are properly weighted against the costs, and that these costs are minimized through active involvement of all the major actors.

One such example is that of HSBC bank in the United Kingdom, which reached an outsourcing agreement with UNIFI, the financial union. Following the bank's recent decision to outsource 4,000 jobs, the bank reached an agreement with the union to minimise the number of jobs lost and to find innovative solutions for re-deploying workers within the company.

Sources: International Institute for Management Development, 2004; US Bureau of Labor Statistics, 2004; Marin, 2004.

In the region as a whole, the gains in employment growth accompanied growth in labour productivity. This suggests that the growth in productivity – discussed in the next paragraph – was not at the expense of employment in the region, but rather it went along with growth in employment for the economy as a whole.

Figures 1.17a and 1.17b show labour productivity growth and levels in selected economies in the industrialized region. The industrialized region as a

**Figure 1.17a.   Growth in output per person employed in the industrialized economies
(total economy, selected economies, index 1993=100, 1980 to latest year)**

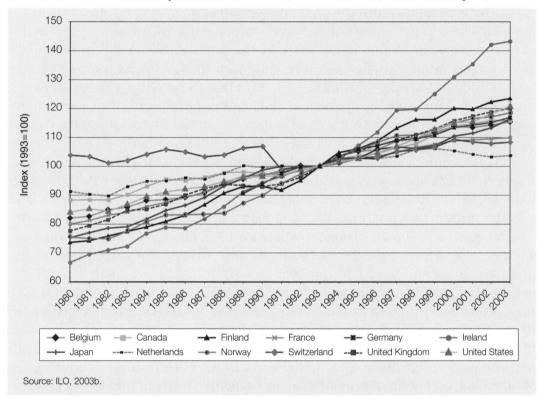

Source: ILO, 2003b.

**Figure 1.17b.   Output per person employed in the industrialized economies
(total economy, selected economies and years)**

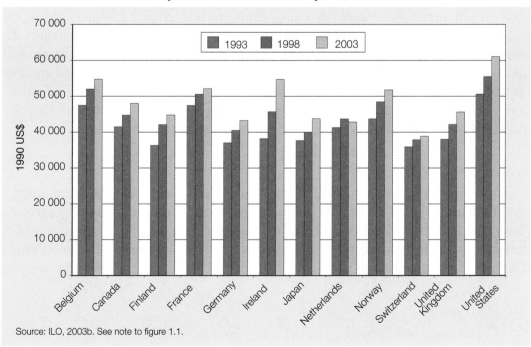

Source: ILO, 2003b. See note to figure 1.1.

whole has seen an average increase of 1.4 per cent annually in productivity – levels in 2003 were on average 15 per cent higher than in 1993. Since 1993, labour productivity in industrialized Europe has grown at an average annual rate of 1.3 per cent, while in the industrialized economies outside of Europe it grew by 1.4 per cent per year. In the first 5 years of the period (1993-1997), productivity growth rates in industrialized Europe outpaced those of industrialized economies outside of Europe – raising speculations that the productivity gap between the United States and Europe would close in the near future. This trend, however, reversed in the latter part of the decade as United States labour productivity growth rates accelerated at a faster rate than those of Europe.

At the country level, productivity growth is particularly strong in Ireland, where there has been average annual growth of 3.7 per cent since 1993. Productivity growth in Ireland has been spurred by high foreign direct investment and a highly productive pharmaceutical industry. Denmark, Finland, Greece and Sweden have also shown strong growth since 1993, all above 2 per cent on average per year. Meanwhile, the Netherlands and Switzerland lagged behind the other countries and have had minimal growth in labour productivity over the decade (less than 1 per cent annually; see figure 1.17a). According to the OECD, slow productivity growth in the Netherlands and Switzerland can be attributed to strong regulations in product markets. Enhancing competition in product markets may be one means of improving the relatively poor productivity growth performance, especially in non-traded services for both of these economies. In Switzerland, competitive pressures seem particularly low in the network industries, health, agriculture, business services, public procurement and distribution (OECD, 2003, 2004).[21]

It is expected that the expansion of the EU by ten new member countries in 2004 will increase the competitiveness of the industrialized Europe region, by reducing the costs of doing business and providing access to more markets. In turn, lower transaction costs within the region will improve efficiencies and increase productivity. In addition, productivity must be raised through quality improvements of the workforce (including more liberal immigration of workers), and through advances in technology and knowledge accumulation, thereby facilitating innovation and expansion into new markets.

1.3. Concluding remarks

The empirical analysis in this chapter provides evidence that productivity growth can and must go hand in hand with employment creation and poverty reduction, at least in the long run. But it also shows that this does not occur automatically and in the same way for all regions. It gives evidence that economies require a certain degree of productivity growth in order to improve labour mar-

---

[21] OECD Economic surveys, Netherlands 2004 and Switzerland 2003.

ket conditions and that labour markets need time to recover after major transitions or crises that have a negative impact on productivity growth.

Whereas productivity growth in East Asia and South Asia has been translated into stable labour market conditions during recent years (after some downturn at the beginning of the last century in East Asia), South-East Asia's labour markets are still recovering from the Asian financial crisis. But the region's solid productivity performance is likely to reduce unemployment and this in turn will help to further reduce poverty. Latin America and the Caribbean have only recently witnessed a recovery in labour markets as a result of almost no productivity increases for over a decade and slight improvements in the past two years. Meanwhile the labour market situation in the Middle East and North Africa and in sub-Saharan Africa, specifically vis-à-vis high unemployment rates, has seen no improvement, along with declining or low growth in productivity. In the transition region, there have been improvements in productivity and employment, particularly among the new EU Member States. Other economies in this region are still bearing the heavy costs of the transition process and are not yet on the path of productivity growth, GDP growth and employment creation. Finally, some economies in industrialized Europe are experiencing GDP growth rates of less than 2 per cent and productivity growth rates of just above 1 per cent. These rates are not translating into adequate employment creation and therefore more needs to be done on the labour demand side to stimulate employment opportunities in the region.

Poverty reduction and working poverty reduction are often but not always the mirror image of productivity gains. In regions with high productivity growth, poverty has decreased; in regions with low or no productivity growth, poverty and working poverty remained more persistent. As can be seen from figure 1.18, the goal of halving the share of US$1 a day working poverty amongst the employed in the world by 2015 can be reached if GDP growth rates continue on their recent growth path. But even though it is likely that half of today's working poor will be able to work themselves and their families out of extreme poverty by 2015, 40 per cent of the working people in the world will not earn enough to lift themselves and their family members above the US$2 a day poverty line. This indicates a severe lack of decent employment opportunities in the developing world. This lack will likely become a constraint for further development as poor people cannot contribute to overall demand, nor can they invest in the education, well-being or health of their children to make sure that they can escape the poverty trap.

There can be no doubt that this regional analysis hides important examples of individual economies where these general rules might not be applicable. But it can be taken as a first step towards the further analysis of the linkages between productivity, employment and poverty reduction discussed in this Report.

**Figure 1.18.   US$1 and US$2 a day working poverty trends in the world
(1990-2015, percentage)**

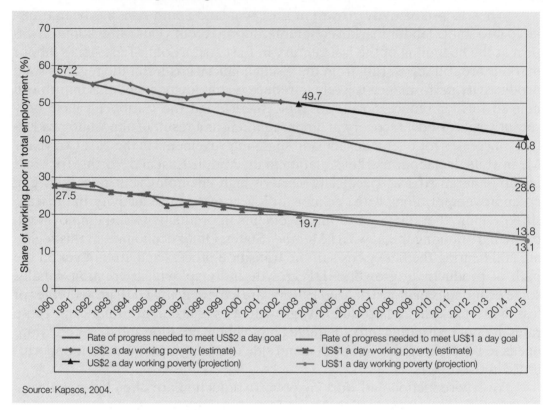

Source: Kapsos, 2004.

References

Amjad, R. 2004. *Solving Pakistan's poverty puzzle: Who should we believe? What should we do?*, paper presented at the 19th Annual Meeting of the Pakistan Society of Development Economists (Islamabad), Jan.

Asian Development Bank (ADB). 2004. *Asian Development Outlook 2004* (Manila) (http://www.adb.org/Documents/Books/ADO/2004/ado2004.pdf).

—. 2003. *Asian Development Outlook 2003* (Manila) (http://www.adb.org/Documents/Books/ADO/2003/ado2003.pdf).

—. 2004. 2002. *Asian Development Outlook 2002* (Manila) (http://www.adb.org/Documents/Books/ADO/2002/ado2002.pdf).

Cordseman, A. 1998. *Demographics and the coming youth explosion in the Gulf* (Washington, DC, Center for Strategic and International Studies) Jan. (http://www.csis.org/mideast/reports/demograp.pdf).

ECLAC. 2004. *Foreign Investment in Latin America and the Caribbean, 2003* (New York, NY).

FAO. 2004. AQUASTAT country profiles, Haiti (http://www.wca-infonet.org/servlet/CDSServlet?status=ND01ODMuMTQzOTQmNz1lbiY2MT13ZWItc2l0ZXMmNjU9aW5mbw~~).

IFAD. 1999. *Assessment of rural poverty in West and Central Africa* (Rome, West and Central Africa Division).

IFAD/FAO/Government of Japan. 1998. *Agricultural implements used by women farmers in Africa* (Rome).

ILO. *World Employment Report* (all years) (Geneva).

—. 2004a. *Global Employment Trends* (Geneva), Jan. (http://kilm.ilo.org/get2004/download/trends.pdf).

—. 2004b. *Global Employment Trends for Women 2004* (Geneva) (http://kilm.ilo.org/get2004/download/trendsw.pdf).

—. 2004c. *Global Employment Trends for Youth 2004* (Geneva) (http://mirror/public/english/employment/strat/download/getyen.pdf).

—. 2004d. *Panorama Laboral 2003* (Lima) (http://www.cinterfor.org.uy/public/spanish/region/ampro/cinterfor/newsroom/hechos/pl2003.htm).

—. 2003a. *Global Employment Trends* (Geneva), Jan.

—. 2003b. *Key Indicators of the Labour Market, 3rd edition* (Geneva).

—. 2003c. *Economically active population 1950-2010, ILO database on estimates and projections of the economically active population (5th edition) for all countries and territories with a population of over 100,000 at mid-year 2000* (Geneva, LABORSTA, LABPROJ) (http://laborsta.ilo.org).

IMF. 2004. *"Harnessing cyclical gains for development: Economic prospects" Global development finance 2004*, (Washington, DC).

—. 2003. *World Economic Outlook* (Washington, DC), Sep.

International Energy Agency (IEA). 2004. *Analysis of the impact of high oil prices on the global economy* (Paris), manuscript.

International Institute for Management Development (IMD). 2004. *World Competitiveness Yearbook 2004* (Lausanne).

Islam, R. 2004. *The nexus of economic growth, employment and poverty reduction: An empirical analysis*. Issues in Employment and Poverty Discussion Paper series (Geneva, ILO).

Kapsos, S. 2004. "Estimating growth requirements for reducing working poverty: Can the world halve working poverty by 2015?" (Geneva, ILO). Background paper prepared for the *World Employment Report 2004-05*, Employment Strategy Paper No. 2004/14.

Marin, D. 2004. "A nation of poets and thinkers - less so with Eastern enlargement? Austria and Germany" (London, Centre for Economic Policy Research (CEPR), Discussion Paper 4358) (http://www.cepr.org/pubs/dps/DP4358.asp).

OECD. 2004. *Economic survey Netherlands* (Paris).

—. 2003. *Economic survey Switzerland* (Paris).

Republic of Korea, Ministry of Labor. 2004. *Social pact for job creation* (http://www.molab.go.kr:8787/English/news/sub_Content1.jsp).

UNDP. 2003. *Arab Human Development Report 2003* (New York).

US, Bureau of Labor Statistics. 2004. *Mass Layoff Statistics* (http://www.bls.gov).

US Library of Congress. 2004. (Washington, DC) (http://countrystudies.us/haiti/48.htm).

World Bank. 2004a. *World Development Indicators (WDI)* (Washington, DC).

—. 2004b. http://www.worldbank.org/wbi/reducingpoverty/case-Indonesia-PovertyReduction.html

—. 2004c. *Unlocking the employment potential in the Middle East and North Africa: Toward a new social contract* (Washington, DC).

—. 2003. *World Development Indicators (WDI)* (Washington, DC).

World Commission on the Social Dimension of Globalization. 2004. *A fair globalization: Creating opportunities for all* (Geneva, ILO).

Xie, A.; Lam, S. 2004. Global Economic Forum, the latest views of Morgan Stanley Economists (http://www.morganstanley.com/GEFdata/digests/20040324-wed.html#anchor2).

2. Does productivity help or harm employment growth?

2.1. Introduction

One of the core elements of the International Labour Organization's Global Employment Agenda addresses the twin issues of promoting higher productivity and creating employment opportunities in order for countries to improve standards of living for their citizenry and obtain long-term sustainable growth. [1] Thus, the ILO is not just concerned with the creation of employment, but that of productive employment, making the distinction between the creation of low-quality jobs and the creation of decent-quality jobs.

In their national agendas, both developed and developing countries focus on improving worker productivity as a means to achieving these goals. At the same time, however, there is often fear among workers that increases in productivity are synonymous with the substitution of capital-intensive production techniques for labour, leading to mass destruction of jobs. How then can these two issues be reconciled?

There is no escaping the fact that productivity gains can lead to job losses as technological progress improves the efficiency of the production process, allowing firms to produce more output with fewer workers. At the same time productivity gains lead to employment creation as well, since technology also creates new products and new processes, which lead to the expansion of markets and additional job opportunities. This *creative destruction* of employment means that less productive firms will leave the market, and new more productive ones will take their place, perhaps in different industries, different sectors and even different locations. Thus, analysing what is gained as opposed to what is lost as the result of increasing productivity becomes critically important and the basis for developing responsible employment policies.

In this regard, the growth effects of employment shifts between sectors are as significant as the growth within sectors. [2] In all regions of the world a shift in employment has been taking place – away from agriculture towards non-agricultural sectors. On balance, the increase in sectoral employment has been most dramatic in the service sector, which accounts for over two-thirds of employment in developed economies and between 10 and 80 per cent (and rising) in developing economies. Although jobs in the service sector fall on both sides of

---

[1] Core element 2 of the ILO's Global Employment Agenda calls for "Promoting technological change for higher productivity and job creation and improved standards of living" (ILO, 2003c).

[2] See, for example, Baily et al., 1992; Pieper, 2001; Piacentini and Pini, 2000.

the "decent work" spectrum, productivity and employment growth have been increasing rapidly in some of the service industries, leading to a win-win situation for the economy as a whole.

In order to harness the development potential of structural changes, however, developing economies, in particular, must focus on a two-pronged strategy of improving the productivity of workers in dynamic *niche* industries and, at the same time, focusing on those sectors of the economy where the majority of labour is concentrated. This focus would give them the tools to move from low- to high-productivity activities. Raising productivity in burgeoning industries, such as those in information and communication technology (ICT) is important for economic growth, but neglecting segments of the economy with greater concentrations of labour can lead to widening inequality. Along these lines, the informal economy, which can constitute a large number of hidden employed persons in the service sector, should not be neglected.

This chapter addresses the specific issue of employment trade-offs in productivity growth. It provides a framework for the analysis by focusing on the time dimension of productivity growth in dynamically changing economies. Its hypothesis is that there will be trade-offs between productivity growth and employment, due to structural and frictional changes – which lead to the displacement of workers at the sectoral level. But, over the longer run – and at the aggregate level – markets have historically compensated for these changes, as higher rates of productivity growth have been accompanied by higher rates of employment growth. Thus, during the medium run it is essential to develop pro-growth progressive policies at the micro- and macro-levels – to ensure growth in the long term – while at the same time providing adjustment strategies (in the form of financial assistance and retraining) for displaced workers.

Section 2.2 provides an overview and conceptualization of the productivity–employment relationship and sets the conditions for a trade-off by focusing on specific time horizons (i.e. short, medium and long run). In section 2.3, this trade-off is examined in a developing-country context of labour surplus and the role of the informal economy is assessed. Section 2.4 shifts to a sectoral analysis in highlighting employment–productivity dynamics. Section 2.5 gauges the contribution of the service sector to aggregate employment productivity growth. Finally, section 2.6 draws the chapter's conclusions.

2.2.   How does productivity growth affect employment?

This question has concerned economists and the general public for centuries. There is no denying that rapid and sustained productivity growth has lifted advanced industrialized nations to their present-day standards of living and, by any historical standards, has allowed them to eradicate mass poverty. However, the very technological innovations and capital-intensive investments that are the mainsprings of this productivity growth are constantly feared as instigators of mass job destruction – a description for which they have often, and rightly, been held responsible. Economic growth continues to go hand in hand with structural change, which often entails a fair amount of "creative destruction"[3] as old jobs are lost in declining industries and new jobs are created in the expanding sectors of the economy. It is a point of history that economies adapt to such changes, but there are particular costs for workers that cannot and should not be ignored. And the minimization of these costs in order to ease the transition of workers should be the focus of policy.

Workers once feared they would be replaced by machines, as they now feel threatened by computer technology. In the 1800s, at the dawn of the Industrial Revolution, a group of English workers (known as the Luddites) launched a campaign to destroy the machinery that was putting their jobs at risk and undermining their way of life. Although these protests were ineffective in slowing the pace of industrialization, they brought to light a number of issues concerning the plight of workers. The demonstrations against the Industrial Revolution were not only concerned with the rise of mechanization but also with the deterioration in workers' rights – decreasing minimum wages, the banning of trade unions and an overall decline in their working conditions. Politically, the Luddite protestors of 1812 were successful in sparking public debate on the negative as well as the positive dimension of the Industrial Revolution. Similarly, today's "anti-globalization" protestors have successfully called for open debate on the "winners and losers" dimension of technological progress and productivity growth.[4]

In our global society, with the asymmetries that characterize globalization, we cannot ignore the dual side of productivity gains or gloss over the fact that productivity gains often lead to job loss. Since 1995, 3 million jobs *per year* have been lost in the manufacturing sector worldwide – due in large part to productivity increases.[5] In order to increase the acceptance of change among workers, there must be a fair distribution of these gains so that society as a whole is better off – not just a privileged few.

This Report acknowledges that the world cannot and should not stop the forces of technological change leading to productivity growth. What society can achieve is to ensure that the worker has a smoother transition and protection in the form of security, opportunities, basic workers' rights and representation, the four main dimensions of decent work.

The link between employment and productivity

Employment, productivity and aggregate output are linked to each other, as follows:

$$Output = Employment \times Productivity.$$

This equation means, for example, that any given level of output can be achieved either with high productivity and low employment (in which case the employment intensity of economic growth is said to be low) or, conversely, with low productivity and high employment (a high-employment intensity).

---

[3] Joseph Schumpeter coined the phrase "creative destruction" in his seminal work, *Capitalism, Socialism and Democracy* to denote a "process of industrial mutation that incessantly revolutionizes the economic structure from within, incessantly destroying the old one, incessantly creating a new one".

[4] For a more elaborate discussion on the dimensions of globalization, see World Commission on the Social Dimension of Globalization, 2004.

[5] Alliance Bernstein, 2003.

Thus, the question "As enterprises become more productive, do they need fewer workers and thus shed them?" has no straightforward answer. Four general points can be made, however. First, there is a range of sources of productivity increase that may have no direct or indirect effect on reducing the level of employment. Increases in product quality, greater capacity utilization, the more efficient use of materials and the better organization, training and treatment of labour are changes that can increase productivity without causing declines in employment levels. Second, a productivity increase that leads to expanded market share and therefore employment creation at the enterprise or country level can prompt an employment decrease in competing enterprises or countries. This is the *displacement effect* and would need to be factored into any analysis of net employment effects. Countries are constantly concerned with the loss of industry competitiveness and market share because of their effects on employment and output.

Third, productivity increase based on mechanization and robotization can reduce the demand for labour. At the enterprise level, the net employment effect will be determined by market demand. More specifically, it will depend on *whether the reduced demand for labour in per unit output is offset by an increase in labour demand due to output expansion*. Finally, a decrease in labour demand due to productivity increase may be offset by the increased demand for labour in the same or other sectors, as a result of the creation of new products or the expansion of markets. In developed countries, for example, the decline in rural employment due to tractorization and other advances was offset by increased demand for workers in urban manufacturing and services.

Thus, although the immediate impact of productivity gains can lead to labour displacement in one sector, over the longer term the market can compensate with gains in another sector, depending on the evolution of product demand and output expansion. However, this may take time as labour markets adapt to structural changes. Consequently, many of the misgivings about the relationship between employment and productivity are based on generalizations concerning trade-offs that occur often but not always in the short run between these two variables in a given sector.[6] A more robust evaluation of the relation between employment and productivity growth must be sensitive not only to the timeframe considered, but also to the ways in which markets, actors and institutions respond to the growth of productivity. Such "compensatory mechanisms" and their interrelation are vital to an understanding of how productivity growth at one location in an economy affects employment and output growth at the aggregate level.

A highly stylized view of these compensatory mechanisms is described in table 2.1.[7] A subsequent discussion in this chapter will dwell in greater detail on how reality often stands at some distance from a theoretical or mechanistic view.

---

[6] The distinction between short, medium and long run varies considerably by industry, but usually constitutes a period of time when certain factor inputs (such as size of the plant) are fixed. Most economists agree on the definition of 3-5 years for the short run, 5-20 years for the medium-long term and 20+ for the very long term.

[7] For a more elaborate discussion of compensatory mechanisms, see Pianta, 2000; Spezia and Vivarelli, 2002; and Vivarelli, 1995.

Table 2.1. Theoretical benefits of productivity growth: Compensatory mechanisms of an economy

Declining product prices	Productivity increases could allow products to be produced at lower cost which, in turn, could result in lower prices. Lower prices could then increase demand for the product, (as well as result in higher real incomes for consumers). However this virtuous scenario assumes that product prices respond to productivity gains and that consumers respond to such price changes through an increase in demand. Suppose, for example, that the demand response is weak compared to the decline in prices, too weak to compensate for the labour-saving effect of productivity increases. Employment would then decline.
Increased wages	The producer could pass along some of the increased profits from productivity gains in the form of higher wages. This, in turn, could boost purchasing power and increased demand for goods and services, not only in the sectors in which the productivity gains have occurred, but in different sectors of the economy where employment growth would as a consequence be stimulated. These benefits, however, assume that producers do not appropriate all of the gains of productivity growth in the form of higher profits.
Increased investment	Not all the gains of higher productivity are likely to be distributed as lower product prices or higher wages. Some gains will be in the form of higher profits which could be reinvested and create more employment opportunities. In a globalizing world, however, the question arises of where the profits have been made, and where the proceeds are reinvested.
Increased employment overall	Even with job displacement in some industries, higher productivity resulting in higher real incomes could lead to shifts in product demand and result in employment creation. Shifts in product demand, however, might not be confined to the domestic market.
New products	Productivity improvements result from product innovations as well as process innovations. The former leads to the creation of new and improved products, expanding output and creating employment opportunities. The latter, however, lead to improvements in the efficiency of production, which can be labour-displacing.

Employment and productivity over the business cycle

For the most part, both employment and productivity growth are pro-cyclical, increasing during boom times and decreasing during recessionary periods. However, due to costs incurred when adjusting their workforce, firms may not react immediately to business cycles, causing employment, including lay-offs and rehiring, to operate with a lag. In an attempt to smooth these costs, changes in employment do not fluctuate as greatly as output.

This lag causes productivity growth to respond in a somewhat inverse manner to employment: productivity may decline more than employment at the onset of a recession, whereas productivity may rise more than hiring in an upturn. One reason for this is that during economic recoveries employers are often hesitant to rehire workers until they are sure the recovery can be sustained; and they will squeeze as much work out of the current workforce as possible. In this case productivity will increase, while employment is stagnating or even declining. One example is the stagnation in the United States labour market during the recent economic recovery. Although the recession was short-lived (from March to November 2001), employment growth remained weak through the first half of 2004 because employers, unsure about the future, refrained from hiring permanent employees. Using a number of cost-cutting strategies, US companies were able to increase output, with the same number or fewer workers, causing productivity to increase considerably over this period.

A market selection process can also occur during recessions, forcing the more unproductive firms out of the market and leaving only the most efficient firms – those that are able to produce more with the same or fewer resources. In an attempt to increase their competitive positions and consolidate their share in the market, firms trim and re-organize their staff. Firm restructuring of this kind can boost aggregate productivity growth, even though output and employment are declining, creating a counter-cyclical relationship. For example, a study in the United Kingdom presents evidence showing that productivity growth for dying firms was less than that of firms that remained (and those that entered) during the recession of the early 1980s, lending support to the idea that the process of restructuring can increase aggregate productivity growth.[8]

Another, more debatable issue is how business cycles are influenced by structural as well as cyclical factors taking place in the economy, such as stock market crashes or political shocks. Cyclical changes involve temporary shocks in the economy, which can affect demand. These factors can lead to temporary loss of jobs until the economy starts to recover, at which point workers are reinstated in their previous positions. Structural factors, on the other hand, involve more permanent changes in the economy, such as technological changes and changes in the structure of consumer demand. When workers lose jobs as a result of structural change, their jobs are permanently removed and they must seek work in other industries or sectors.

Whether employment gains or losses are cyclical or structural in nature can often be difficult to discern: employment fluctuations that might initially seem to be short run in nature (lasting 3-5 years), could actually be part of a longer term adjustment in the economy. A recent study by the Federal Reserve Bank of New York suggests that both structural and cyclical changes contributed to stagnant employment growth during the most recent recession in the United States (see box 2.1).[9] The bias towards job losses in the manufacturing sector since 2001 gives this idea strong appeal. As shown in figure 2.1, employment in the manufacturing sector declined by 17.1 per cent between the first quarter of 2000 and the first quarter of 2004, a loss of close to 3 million manufacturing jobs. In contrast, in the service sector, employment increased during the same period by 2.2 per cent, a gain of 2.3 million service jobs. This scenario in manufacturing is indicative of the general falling trend in manufacturing employment worldwide.

---

[8] Disney et al., 2003.

[9] Groshen and Potter, 2003.

Box 2.1. Jobless growth in the United States

Much attention has been given to the "joblessness" of the economic recovery in the United States following the country's recent recession. While the impact of the recession on GDP growth was brief and relatively mild,[1] its effect on employment has indeed been far more serious and pronounced. Since the onset of the US recession in March 2001, real GDP has recovered and grown by over 7 per cent from its pre-recession level. Employment growth, on the other hand, has only recently begun to recover. An analysis of the causes reveals that the lack of employment growth during the period was of both a cyclical and structural nature.

In the context of the current situation in the United States, it is clear that several cyclical factors are affecting the country's labour market. Most notably, the recent recession was marked by substantial declines in business inventories and investment, a severe correction in the stock market, and a collapse in venture capital and other forms of business and entrepreneurial financing. The initial recovery period in 2001-2002 showed rapid labour productivity gains, despite sluggish growth in output. This was mainly the result of a decline in employment growth (see graph below). Even as output increased after 2002, employment growth continued to be sluggish until early 2004, implying that firms worked off inventories and increased production with existing workers rather than hiring new employees.

Structural changes are also playing an important role in the ongoing employment stagnation in the United States. A recent study by the Federal Reserve Bank of New York[2] notes that an increasing number of lay-offs in the previous two recessions have been permanent, indicating that structural changes such as permanent declines in demand, increasing international outsourcing of employment, technological change and production reorganization are taking place in many industries. As the permanent lay-offs characteristic of periods of increasing structural change force the unemployed to find new jobs (often requiring new skills), longer average job search times and slower employment growth result. Workers in the country's manufacturing sector have been hit the hardest. These workers, whose jobs have been permanently eliminated, need assistance in the form of unemployment benefits, but also access to education and training programmes, so that they can acquire the education and skills needed to move into those industries experiencing job growth.

Employment vs. GDP growth in the United States, 1994-2004 (index, 1994 = 100)

Legend: GDP constant · Total employment (Household Survey) · Productivity · Employment-population ratio

[1] The National Bureau of Economic Research estimates that the recession lasted 8 months, from March to November 2001. While the recession's impact on GDP is clear in quarterly data, the downturn does not register in annual GDP figures. [2] Groshen and Potter, 2003.

Graph sources: US Department of Labor, Bureau of Labor Statistics, 2004a; US Department of Commerce, Bureau of Economic Analysis, 2004 and UN Population Division, 2001.

Figure 2.1.   Employment in services and manufacturing (in thousands), United States, 2000-2004

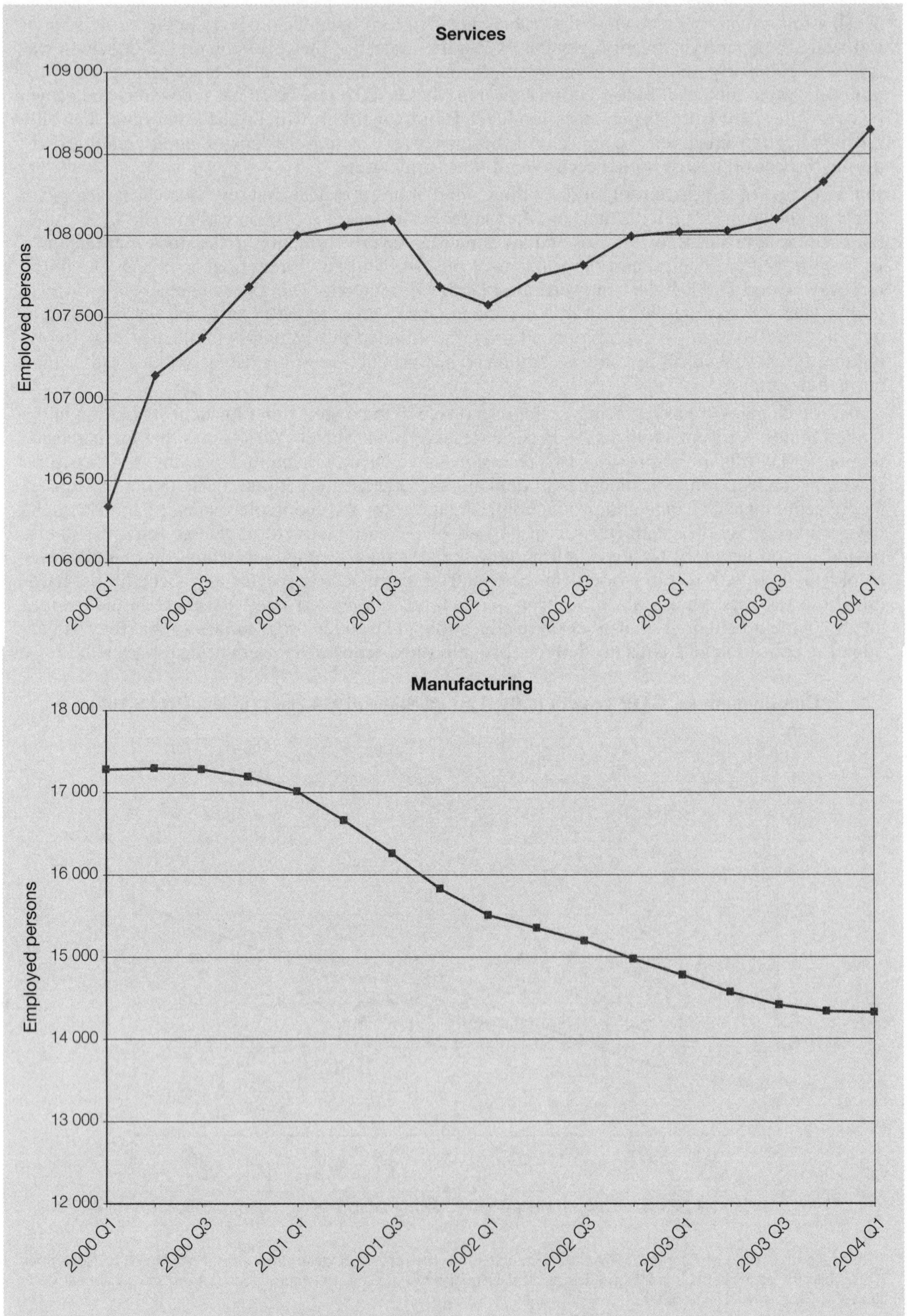

Source: US Department of Labor, Bureau of Labor Statistics, 2004b.

A longer-term perspective: Adjusting to structural and frictional changes

An analysis of the trade-offs between employment and productivity growth would be limited unless it looked beyond the short run to a longer-term horizon, in which firms have adequate time to adjust to the demand requirements of the economy. In the short run, labour market disturbances tend to be governed by the business cycle. Over the medium and longer term, labour market institutions, technological change and aggregate demand policies play a greater role in determining the demand and supply of labour. Trade-offs between employment and productivity growth are quite common during business cycles and to some extent even during the medium term, as labour continues to adjust to structural changes in the economy. But over time, most countries show a positive relationship between productivity and employment growth. The reason for this is determined by a number of factors, but one primary reason is that output in an economy is not fixed. An exclusive focus on the supply-side dimension of employment ignores the fact that changes in demand occur over time, increasing output growth and creating jobs to meet a growing demand. This is the case because technological progress ultimately leads to the expansion and creation of new markets. For example, there is now demand for products that were non-existent 15 years ago – and labour markets inevitably adapt to these changes. Thus, while not elaborated in this chapter, the demand-side aspects – including macroeconomic policies and conditions, the overall environment for innovation and investment (and the relation between the two) – would be necessary for a fuller understanding of the link between labour productivity growth and long-run sustainable growth.

The income levels of consumers are a prime determinant of the structure of product market demand. When income per capita increases, people change their tastes and develop new demands directed towards luxury goods and services. Particularly important in this respect is Engel's law, stating that with an increase in income people spend comparatively less on primary products, creating demand for manufacturing and service goods. The shift in consumption towards service goods has been particularly pronounced in developed economies.[10]

Demand patterns heavily influence structural change and employment dynamics, since labour shed in one sector can be absorbed in other sectors. The process is of course not instantaneous and frictions in the market (e.g. skill matching, wages, differences in labour and product market regulation) mean that labour requires time to adjust. This is one reason why it is not surprising in a climate of rapid structural change that a maximum level of employment may be difficult to attain. It is also a strong argument for the role that labour market institutions must play in improving the efficiency of labour markets and providing security for workers.

The employment impact of outsourcing

Outsourcing (the contracting out of business functions previously performed in-house) has heightened concerns among workers about job security. More

---

[10] Schettkat and Russo, 2001.

particularly, the increasing trend of *offshoring* (the contracting out to foreign as opposed to domestic affiliates) has prompted many to suggest that the phenomenon is leading to a reallocation of jobs from developed to developing economies. Newspapers in some industrialized economies carry headlines warning workers of *"Jobs Lost Abroad"* and cite alarming statistics on job flight to foreign destinations.[11] One study noted that, in the ICT-using sector, "3.3 million jobs in America will move offshore by 2015".[12]

Whether these warnings are justified depends on many factors, but two events that have fundamentally changed the way labour markets function will help put the debate into a better perspective.[13] First, technological change in the form of information and communication technology has increased the number of jobs that can be moved to offshore locations—meaning that the outsourcing phenomenon is no longer limited to the manufacturing sector but also includes the outsourcing of highly skilled jobs in the service sector. Second, the opening up of labour markets in China and India has brought a vast number of low-wage semi-skilled workers into the global production system.

The implication of these two events is a heightened sense of competitive pressure on employees as labour markets become increasingly more integrated on a global scale. This has increased anxiety among workers, particularly those who cannot easily relocate in order to find employment (older workers and single parents with children, for example). At the same time, the globalization of production has helped to drive down wages in certain sectors of developed economies, as they face increased competition from labour in lower-wage economies.

It is certainly true that many multinational firms have shifted production facilities to developing economies to take advantage of lower labour costs – yet it would be an overstatement to assert that a large share of developed economy jobs have gone overseas. Recent statistics based on job losses due to outsourcing in some of the developed economies illustrate the previous point:

- In the United States, by far the largest outsourcer of the industrialized economies, estimates of job losses due to outsourcing represent only a small fraction of jobs lost in a given period. For example in the first three months of 2004 less than 2 per cent of mass lay-offs in the United States were due to outsourcing (this includes domestic outsourcing).[14]

- In Europe the outsourcing phenomenon is not yet as widespread as in the United States. Germany is by far the largest outsourcer in Europe, perhaps due to its proximity to Eastern Europe. Outsourcing in Germany resulted in a loss of roughly 8,000 jobs per year from 1990 to 2001, mainly to Eastern Europe. This figure represents only 0.2 per cent of Germany's labour force, which comprises 40 million people. It is also a small fraction of total jobs lost on a yearly basis.

---

[11] See, for example, an article in *The New York Times* dated 15 February 2004.

[12] See Forrester Research, 2002.

[13] For a more detailed discussion, see Polaski, 2004.

[14] See box 1.10 in Chapter 1 of this Report for further discussion.

- Additionally, outsourcing is a two-way street: economies might lose jobs due to *outsourcing*, but they also gain jobs as the result of *insourcing*. Another study based on the United States shows that its economy *insources* far more business than it *outsources*: in 2003, it outsourced approximately US$77 billion worth of "business, professional and technical services" to foreigners and insourced over US$130 billion. [15]

But statistics can only give a partial picture, and if one downplays the current statistics and focuses instead on the increasing trend in jobs being outsourced then a different depiction of the phenomenon emerges. For example, half of the major companies in the United States currently engage in some form of outsourcing and more expect to do so in the coming years. [16] Additionally the expansion of outsourcing across occupational groups, including highly skilled jobs in the service sectors suggest that all phases of the production process can be "globalized". As one study notes:

> Even if many of the outsourced jobs are low-skilled call centre positions, reports of software programmers and ... analysts being outsourced creates in millions of workers the fear that a college education and a professional job are no longer enough. [17]

There is also a growing concern that the quality of jobs being created in the developed economies has been declining over recent years – due mainly to outsourcing. The concern is that growth in employment is being driven by jobs with less decent working conditions (in terms of pay and job security) than those that have been lost. The evidence regarding this is mixed. A study by the OECD shows that over the past ten years part-time employment has accounted for half of total employment in the OECD economies. [18] In addition, there has been strong growth in temporary employment. The trend in part-time and temporary employment has been particularly strong among women and youth – and accounts for their growing numbers as employed. The determination of whether this trend represents a decline in working conditions depends on whether part-time and temporary work represents a "choice" or "an option of last resort".

The OECD study also adds that "there is little to support the notion that increased employment is the result of a proliferation of low-paying jobs". Since 1993 in the European Union as a whole and in the United States, employment has grown more in industries and occupations with above-average wages, than those with below-average. The study finds, however, that although earnings inequality has remained low and relatively stable in many of the EU economies and in Japan, in fact it has widened in the United Kingdom and in the United States.

Exactly how outsourcing will ultimately impact on growth and employment in developed and developing economies remains to be seen. Sentiment is strong

---

[15] See Parry, 2004. Business, professional and technical services refer to computer programming, telecommunications, legal services, banking, engineering, management consulting, call centres, data entry, and other private services.

[16] Sperling, 2004.

[17] Ibid.

[18] OECD, 2003.

among those in the business community that in spite of today's low figures on outsourcing, the future may bring a massive transformation in how goods and services are produced.[19] The challenge for economies will be how to integrate themselves into the global production process in order to create decent employment opportunities for those seeking work. For developing economies it undoubtedly will require increasing the absorptive capacity of their labour force and institutions – the ability to utilize technology transferred from the developed economies. For developed economies it requires a stronger focus on innovation and expansion into new markets.

The benefits from outsourcing can be derived through a number of channels – global linkages in the supply chain have created opportunities for increased income in the developing economies, which has increased demand for more skill-intensive products in developed economies. The challenge for both the developed and developing economies, however, is to adapt to the rapid changes in technology, which are speeding productivity gains and the rate of job creation and destruction, and to provide social safety nets for workers who are displaced during the process.

As mentioned earlier, it is certainly true that globalization has been the cause of the loss of competitive advantage in certain labour-intensive industries in the industrialized economies, leading to a loss of jobs.[20] But there has been no net transfer of jobs to developing economies – and studies have shown that the decline in industrial employment across economies is due more to gains in the efficiency of production than to the loss of jobs to developing economies – a trend that has been occurring worldwide.[21] Innovations in the production process have increased efficiencies in traditional industrial sectors, not only in developed economies but also in the developing economies, as increasingly more output can be produced with less workers. According to one study, "between 1995 and 2002 roughly 22 million jobs were lost globally, a decline of 11 per cent. Yet over the same period, global industrial production increased by more than 30 per cent – a remarkable gain in productivity".[22]

In addition to social protection for workers, international labour standards are necessary in order to ensure that low-cost labour is not synonymous with the exploitation of labour – and that decent work prevails. Some developing economies that have entered into the global supply chain have done so through the "low road" option to development. These economies compete based on low-cost, low-skilled labour – a growth strategy that is not sustainable, because it often does not lead to productive work. For example, although the quantity of work has been increasing in the manufacturing sector in Mexico with the rise of the *maquiladoras* (maquila factories), the quality of employment has not improved, leading to a "decent-work deficit" (see box 2.2).

---

[19] McKinsey and Company, 2004.

[20] See, for example, Kucera and Milberg, 2003.

[21] See, for example, Ghose, 2003.

[22] Alliance Bernstein, 2003.

Box 2.2. Decent work and *maquiladoras* in Mexico

Mexico's recent labour market experiences highlight the distinction between the quantitative and qualitative elements of job creation as noted in the ILO's Global Employment Agenda. In purely quantitative terms the Mexican labour market has, for the most part, been able to absorb its increasing supply of labour. Yet, despite economic restructuring and policy reforms, the Mexican labour market continues to be hampered by a decent work deficit. Although participation rates are comparable to other Latin American countries and unemployment is low, most Mexicans are employed in poorly paid jobs (in both the formal and the informal economy), characterized by stagnant or declining wages, little job security, inadequate social protection and a lack of training.

One illustration of Mexico's labour market is the growth of the maquila economy. During the 1990s, the maquila's size in Mexico's manufacturing sector expanded tremendously in terms of output and employment. Output expanded nearly 40 per cent annually between 1990 and 1999. By 2000, the sector was exporting US$80 billion worth of goods, a figure larger than that of Brazil's total exports (Palma, 2003). Employment nearly tripled from 446,436 in 1990 to nearly 1.3 million in 2000.

Yet, despite its enormous increases in production, the maquila economy continues to have few linkages with the rest of the Mexican economy. Maquila (which means literally *in-bond plants*) factories were initially developed to allow American companies to take advantage of Mexico's low-cost labour in order to assemble products for re-export to the US market. This was done through a provision that allowed American firms to be taxed only on the value-added component of the imported assembled goods, thus removing any incentive to establish linkages with Mexican industries. For example, under this programme, United States car manufacturers could send unassembled car parts to maquila factories in Mexico for assembly. The assembled car would then be exported back to the United States for sale there and abroad. The US company would only be taxed on the value-added to the car parts during assembly, which was minimal. The strong dependence on imported inputs means that the maquila still adds very little value to the goods being produced. Thus, gross output per employee has increased, but productivity (measured as value added per employee) has not. As a result, wages have remained stagnant (see accompanying graph in this box).

The maquila sector's principal benefit to the Mexican economy is as an employer of mostly unskilled and relatively cheap labour. Recently, however, competitive pressure from other low-labour-cost countries and the slowdown in economic growth in the United States has led to a decline in maquila employment of more than 15 per cent between 2001 and 2003, because large numbers of factories have relocated to China. Preliminary evidence shows that between June 2001 and June 2002, 545 maquila factories left Mexico, equivalent to one in every seven (Palma, 2003).

The future for the maquila economy is tied to its ability to remain internationally competitive without relying on "low-road" development practices. With this aim, second- and third-generation maquila factories have moved away from simple assemblage to manufacturing and knowledge-intensive product design. The shift in work structure has lead to an increase in the skill intensity of maquila labour, as some plants are using more skilled workers and providing more training for current employees (Carillo, 2003). This "high road" competitive strategy has the potential to defray low-cost competition and develop greater linkages with the domestic economy.

(continued overleaf)

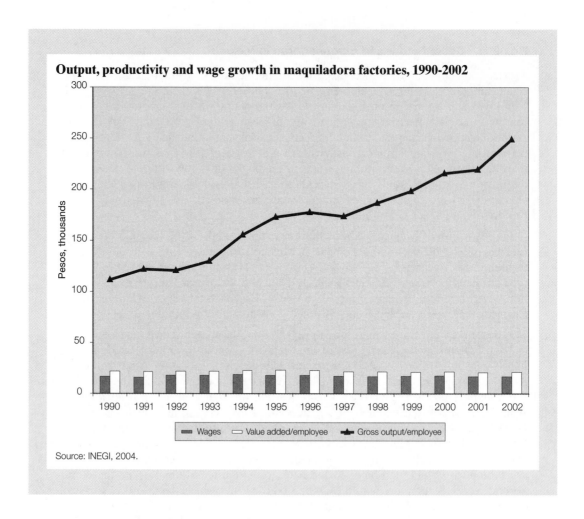

Output, productivity and wage growth in maquiladora factories, 1990-2002

Source: INEGI, 2004.

Empirical evidence on employment and productivity growth

Figure 2.2 provides a snapshot of the long-run interaction between employment and productivity growth from 1980 to 2000.[23] Although a weak negative relationship between productivity and employment growth can be distinguished, the global picture is quite diverse. More than two-thirds of the countries are in the northeast quadrant, exhibiting both productivity and employment growth. Within this group there is no positive or negative relationship between the two variables.

A closer look at figure 2.2 suggests a distinctive concentration of specific "country clubs". For example, the four countries in the northwest quadrant (Bulgaria, Czech Republic, Poland and Hungary) and the country in the southwest quadrant (Romania) are all transition economies that experienced a sharp fall in employment during the 1990s, after the collapse of the Soviet Union. The deep transitional crisis and subsequent large structural changes in these economies greatly affected the labour markets of this region. Firms closed, many people

---

[23] These data are taken from the Groningen Growth and Development Centre (GGDC), Total Economy Database (2004) for a cross-section of 66 countries, in which all parts of the world are included. See also ILO, 2003b, Chapter 18.

Figure 2.2. Relation between average annual growth rates of employed persons and labour productivity, selected economies, 1980-2000

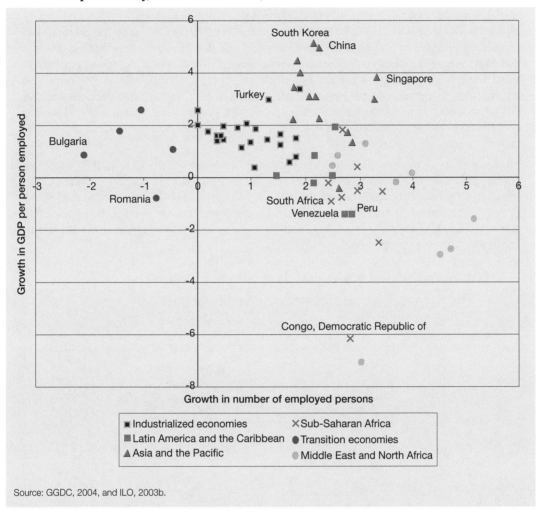

Source: GGDC, 2004, and ILO, 2003b.

lost their jobs, and only the most productive businesses survived. On the whole, the growth rates of output and productivity turned negative or at best remained modestly positive. Hence the loss of jobs during the previous decade was not the result of productivity growth but of stagnating productivity levels during the communist era (see case study on Hungary, box 2.3).

The southeast quadrant of figure 2.2 shows a fair number of economies with positive or even very high growth rates of employment but negative productivity growth. These countries are mainly located in sub-Saharan Africa, Latin America (Brazil, Venezuela and Peru) and the Middle East and North Africa. The high employment growth in these economies is primarily explained by high population growth and growing informal economy activity. Some resource-rich economies such as South Africa and Venezuela also belong to this group because, in spite of their resource abundance, these countries fail to create enough productive jobs to raise average income levels. Because of factors such as political

Box 2.3. Case study: Labour productivity and employment in Hungary

The Hungarian economy provides an interesting example of employment–productivity trade-offs incurred as the result of intense structural transformation due to the change from a centrally planned to a market-oriented economy. As in all centrally planned economies, full employment was achieved and maintained through huge amounts of hidden unemployment. From the beginning of the transition in 1992 until 1997, nearly 2 million jobs were lost. Though output decreased, it was not in proportion to the employment declines, causing labour productivity to increase considerably. Economic growth improved after 1997, leading to a period of employment creation which was also accompanied by continued productivity growth.

Hungary's experience can roughly be divided into two phases: from 1992 to 1997 and from 1998 to 2002 (see the following graph). During the first period, employment declined at the expense of labour productivity gains, owing mainly to the effects of downsizing public enterprises and the need to make them efficient. Unemployment continued to rise during the economic downturn of the early 1990s and even the recovery that followed was unable to create employment opportunities.

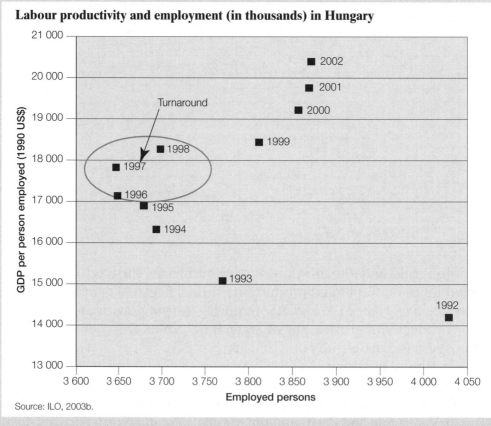

Labour productivity and employment (in thousands) in Hungary

Source: ILO, 2003b.

The government introduced a controversial austerity programme in 1995, aimed at speeding up the privatization process and reducing government debt in order to bring interest rates and inflation under control. The reforms encouraged foreign direct investment and stimulated exports, one of the main engines of growth, which increased considerably after 1997 with the devaluation of the Hungarian forint. Although initially employment continued to decline, a closer look at the sectoral composition of employment during this period reveals an increase in employment in construction, financial services, retail trade, catering, and the transport and communication industries.

By establishing itself as part of the European production network through foreign direct investment, Hungary has been successful in obtaining high growth rates since the mid-1990s, which has also translated into employment creation. At the same time, businesses have adopted more efficient practices, leading to gains in productivity growth.

Although Hungary has achieved impressive labour productivity over the decade, the employment rate is still relatively low. In 1992, employment as a share of the working-age population was 50 per cent. Additionally, rising domestic labour costs mean that Hungary is losing its competitive edge in low-skilled industries. Some multinationals in low value-added industries are already relocating further east to Ukraine, some to Asia (mainly China). To maintain its growth, Hungary needs to improve the skills of its labour force and upgrade its knowledge base through increased investment in research and development (R&D), to be more competitive in higher skilled industries.

Source: Román, 2003.

instability and inequities in the economy many of the jobs created are also in the less productive informal economy.

The upper northeast quadrant is dominated by the high-growth economies of the Asian and Pacific rim (e.g. China, the Republic of Korea, Singapore). Their high growth in productivity and employment can be explained by an export-led growth strategy using an abundant and increasingly skilled workforce that was able to take advantage of its relatively low labour cost to increase its competitiveness and expand into new markets.

In the lower part of the northeast quadrant is a heavy concentration of industrialized economies, showing no discernable pattern between employment and productivity growth. Productivity levels in this region are the highest in the world, which accounts for slower growth than that of the East Asian "catch-up" economies. At the same time, considerable diversity is present in this region, as it comprises economies both within and outside Europe. In essence, nothing has done more to keep the notion of a trade-off between employment and productivity alive than the comparative evolution of these two key variables in the European Union and the United States. This phenomenon, known as "the Atlantic Divide", is discussed in more detail below.[24]

Employment/productivity trade-offs in Europe and the United States:
The Atlantic Divide

Table 2.2 separates the growth of aggregate output into the contribution of employment growth and labour productivity growth in Europe and the United States. From 1970 to 1990, the rate of annual output growth was similar in Europe (2.8 per cent) and the United States (3.2 per cent). However, whereas

---

[24] The European-US employment and productivity differential has generated a large literature. A particularly perceptive analysis is given by Gordon (1997). Various issues of the *World Economic Outlook* by the International Monetary Fund (1995, 1999) have also addressed this topic.

Table 2.2.   Employment and productivity in the United States and Europe, 1970-2000 (percentage)

Economic region	1970-1990	1990-2000
United States		
Employment	2.1	1.3
Productivity	1.1	1.9
Output	3.2	3.2
Europe (EU 11)		
Employment	0.4	0.6[1]
Productivity	2.4	1.5[1]
Output	2.8	2.1[1]

Note: Annual growth rates (in per cent).

[1] 1991-2000. For Europe, the growth rates are from 1991 to 2000 rather than from 1990 to 2000 in order to eliminate the only substantial (but artificial) one-time upward shift in the employment series: the inclusion of some 10 million East Germans in the employment statistics.

Source: OECD, various years.

Europeans relied almost exclusively on productivity growth to increase their output, American output growth in the same period was much more labour-intensive, with employment growth contributing two-thirds of output growth. Europe achieved much higher productivity growth than the United States in 1970-1990, which can mainly be attributed to the process of "catching-up". During the catching-up process countries tend to have really high growth rates, then once they catch-up (i.e. their levels converge to the leaders), growth will slow. Part of the strong growth in Europe's productivity during this period was undoubtedly due to its efforts to attain productivity levels similar to those in the United States. During this period, however, Europe was much less successful in providing its slowly growing labour force with jobs (as evidenced by the 0.4 per cent growth rate over the period) than the United States was at integrating a much more rapidly expanding labour force into the labour market. This suggests a trade-off between employment and productivity growth in the two regions.[25]

The numbers for the 1990s, in which the relative productivity performance of the European Union and the United States underwent a fundamental change triggers doubts about the idea of an employment–productivity trade-off. Particularly in the second half of that decade, the United States experienced a marked acceleration of productivity growth, which is widely attributed to the growth of the "new economy" through information and communication technologies. For the first time in the post-war era, the United States outperformed Europe in terms of productivity growth. This "productivity miracle" in no way put an end to the "employment miracle" of the preceding decades. Employment growth slowed somewhat, but this was clearly due to slower labour force growth, as evidenced by

[25] One issue not dealt with here is that a comparison of labour productivity growth and changes in *unemployment* will easily do away with the trade-off hypothesis on the Atlantic Divide. Whereas productivity growth slowed down, and labour input growth slightly accelerated, unemployment rates in many European countries – notably Germany – have continued to rise (Landmann, 2004, figure 2).

the almost continuous fall of the unemployment rate throughout the decade: from 5.6 per cent in 1990 to slightly more than 4 per cent in 2000. Not surprisingly, European productivity growth decreased (as levels converged to those in the United States). The productivity slowdown had no noticeable effect on employment growth and was translated almost entirely into slower output growth.

Productivity growth and better jobs

Another issue in the relationship between productivity and employment concerns the quality of jobs being created. Productivity growth might be related to the creation of more jobs, but if these jobs are of lower quality, for example, with lower skill levels, then a quality trade-off with potential impact on slower income growth may be the result.

Labour quality can be measured in various ways. One way is to measure the labour skills in terms of literacy and educational attainment of the labour force. Measures of labour force quality conclude that the quality of jobs has substantially increased over time, although the direct impact on productivity is hard to show.[26] Another direct measure of labour quality concerns the payment to labour.

Unfortunately, comprehensive measures of real wages (covering the total economy, all occupations and including all components of labour compensation) can only be obtained for a limited number of countries, mostly for the OECD region. Figure 2.3 shows the relationship between the growth in labour productivity and real labour compensation per hour from 1985 to 2000. A clear positive relationship between the two variables can be seen, strongly suggesting that in the long run, higher productivity is accompanied by higher labour compensation.

2.3. Productivity and employment in developing economies

The preceding discussion argues from the standpoint of both theory and evidence the conditions under which employment and productivity growth go together. Often, when economists talk about workers moving into other sectors after job loss, they assume that certain mechanisms are in place to ensure that a beneficial outcome occurs. Unfortunately this is not always the case. For example, the worker who loses her job in the garment industry might be able to find a job of equal or better conditions in the service sector, provided, of course, that sufficient demand exists, that she possesses the adequate skills or can quickly obtain them, that she has access to labour market information, that there is no discrimination in the labour market, and that there are no barriers to mobility. In short, the various "compensatory mechanisms" discussed earlier in section 2.2 and table 2.1 often remain at the level of theory, rather than reality. A case study was done by Karaömerlioglu and Ansal (2000) based on the experiences of Turkey to understand how these "mechanisms" might work in a developing country with some agricultural and industrial research capacity. The results of the study are summarized below in table 2.3.

---

[26] See, for example, Van Ark et al., 2004.

Figure 2.3.   Relation between growth in labour productivity and real labour compensation, 1985-2000 (in 1990 US dollars)

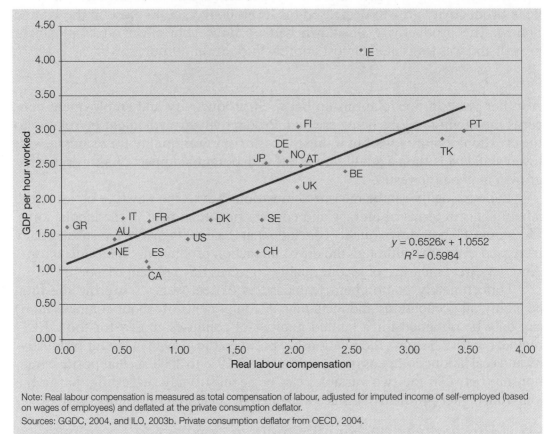

Note: Real labour compensation is measured as total compensation of labour, adjusted for imputed income of self-employed (based on wages of employees) and deflated at the private consumption deflator.
Sources: GGDC, 2004, and ILO, 2003b. Private consumption deflator from OECD, 2004.

In general, national socio-economic factors affect employment creation. The macroeconomic conditions, industrial structure and firm characteristics all determine how productivity gains will impact on employment creation. For most developing countries, reality is often marked by substantial unemployment, underemployment, and poverty – and stalled "structural transformation" out of low-paying activities to higher value-added ones. The reasons are manifold: indeed, to address them is to review the voluminous history of development economics, which is well beyond the scope of the present chapter. The central question, however, is whether the analysis in section 2.2 applies equally well to developing countries, characterized by labour surplus and a variety of institutional shortcomings. Given that in the short term, when output is fixed, a focus on productivity growth could be at the expense of job creation, the question is: Does the productivity–employment trade-off apply equally to developing countries with underutilized or unused labour?

The answer must clearly be in the affirmative for at least four reasons.

1.   The first is the general point that no country can afford to neglect improving the productivity of its workforce since productivity drives wage increases and

Table 2.3. Productivity growth and "compensation mechanisms" in developing countries

Does productivity growth lead to:	Scenario in developing economies	Evidence from the Turkey case study
Declining product prices?	Although productivity gains may lead to lower product prices, this may not result in increased demand from consumers and businesses. Firstly, because user and buyer industries do not always exist in a developing economy, which limits the scope for increased demand from industries in the supply chain. Secondly, the slow growth rates in many developing economies suggest that consumer demand may respond weakly to price changes. In this case no additional employment gains will result.	Productivity gains often led to an increase rather than a decline in prices of the product – because of the new features and higher quality of production. When demand did increase as in the case of manufacturing, where demand increased by 211 per cent from 1981 to 1995, the employment gains were minimal.
Increased wages?	Initially any increases in wages will be much lower than the productivity gains, and may also be biased towards those with specific skills. Based on these limitations there may not be sufficient increased demand to stimulate additional job creation.	There were productivity gains in manufacturing during 1980-89, but this did not lead to sectoral wage increases – in fact, real wages in manufacturing declined during this period.
Employment creation from increased investment?	The gains from productivity are not always reinvested back into the business. Profits may instead be consumed or reinvested in other ventures, often outside of the local economy. Additionally, when reinvestment in the firm does occur it can often be in the form of capital-intensive/labour-saving technologies in a drive to increase competitiveness.	Investments were generally in the form of capital intensive/labour-saving technology, which did not result in employment gains.
Employment creation from new products?	Since most of the new technology in developing economies is imported, they do not benefit from employment gains that generally are associated with new product innovation – developing economies are technology imitators, not technology creators at initial stages. Additionally, most of the technology comes to developing economies once it has matured in developed economies so they experience the mainly negative employment effects that are associated with process innovation.	The majority of new technology was imported and only negative employment effects were experienced. Often industries had license agreements with multinationals restricting independent new product development. In few cases where there was new product innovation no significant employment impact occurred.

Source: Karaömerlioglu and Ansal, 2000.

thus brings about an improvement in the standard of living of a country. Moreover, as the rate of economic growth increases, the "lion's share" of this higher rate of growth is typically accounted for by productivity improvement. [27] The employment-displacing effects of productivity growth can in

---

[27] Due to diminishing returns of capital and labour.

some instances not be avoided: indeed, they ought not to be as they are part of the structural transformation to becoming a wealthier country.

2. The second reason is that no enterprise that operates on global markets, regardless of where it is located, can afford to forego productivity increases, irrespective of their employment consequences. With the exposure to competition that comes with the greater integration of global markets, a company's autonomy to pick and choose its production technologies declines.

3. Strong empirical support is behind the third reason, and that is that productivity and employment growth can go together. The development of the East Asian "miracle economies" with their export-oriented development strategy is, of course, instructive in this regard. Three observations are of particular note here. It will be recalled from figure 2.3 that a positive relation generally exists between productivity and wage growth. A closer look reveals that the relationship is not one-to-one. In fact, over the past decades, labour's share in national income has been declining in many countries. Having wages grow, but grow with a lag, or grow at less than the rate of productivity growth, has in fact been a hallmark of the export-oriented East Asian miracle economies. Limiting wage growth was a means of ensuring the external competitiveness of export industries which, in turn, allowed for expanded market share and thus continued employment and wage growth. Box 2.4 describes the experience of the Republic of Korea in this regard. As a strategy for employment-absorbing output growth, but one that also allows for rising wages and also profits for reinvestment, it proved effective. The second observation is, quite simply, that structural transformation does not happen overnight. The Asian model was characterized by the substantial intervention of the State and well-functioning institutions in the promotion of key industries and, indeed, key firms within those industries. Rapid growth nevertheless coexisted with underemployment and poverty, much as it does at present in China and India. Indeed, even an advanced economy such as Japan combines a highly productive export-oriented manufacturing sector with a relatively low productive and domestic-oriented service sector. The third observation is that early industrialization in the successful Asian economies was based on their factor endowment, the abundance of low-cost labour. While low-cost, labour-intensive production might appear to be the antithesis of a productivity-led growth strategy, such a conclusion would be erroneous. Why? Because even relatively unskilled industrial employment in the early stages of the export-oriented strategy *was more productive than its pre-industrial alternative*. The message here is that a productivity strategy need not be one that ignores the factor that developing countries have in abundance – labour. And, as mentioned in box 2.2, a low-wage, low-skilled development strategy is *unsustainable* in the long run: it can only be viewed as the starting point for the *transition to higher value-added activities* (by establishing linkages with other sectors of the economy

and upgrading the skills of the workforce) which, again, describes the trajectory associated with the Asian miracle economies.

4.   The fourth reason is even more compelling. The magnitude of underemployment and poverty in the developing world is a reflection, not of the absence of economic activity of the poor, but of the unproductive nature of that activity. It stands to reason that a focus on improving the productivity of the working poor (those who work but still earn less than US$1 a day) is a direct route to poverty reduction. Evidence of this last-mentioned claim is shown in table 2.4. Chapter 3 of this Report further elaborates the linkage between productivity and poverty reduction.

Table 2.4 presents an empirical exercise undertaken for this chapter in order to investigate the link between productivity and poverty reduction.[28] This exercise examines the relationship between productivity and poverty from 1970 to 1998 and also addresses the link between inequality and poverty reduction. The results show that both productivity growth and levels are strongly, negatively associated with changes in poverty rates. In the case of US$2 a day poverty, productivity appears to have a relatively stronger impact on reducing poverty, whereas in the case of US$1 a day poverty, the impact of productivity is slightly less. The income inequality coefficient has the expected sign, but is not statistically significant in any of the cases.

All else being equal, over a period of 28 years, a US$1000 per worker increase in labour productivity will reduce the US$1 a day poverty rate by 1.5 percentage points. In terms of US$2 a day poverty, the same increase in worker productivity levels is associated with a 2.6 percentage point reduction in the poverty rate.

The results are similar when one examines the impact of *productivity growth* on poverty over the same period. The estimates predict that, all else being equal, for every 1 per cent increase in the rate of productivity growth, the US$1 a day poverty rate will be reduced by 1.75 per cent. Slightly more robust results are obtained when using the US$2 a day poverty rate; a growth in worker productivity is associated with a 2.8 per cent reduction in the poverty rate.

In general, the main reason why productivity growth impacts poverty is because productivity is the main determinant of income growth. Gains in productivity mean that there is more real income in the economy that can be distributed to workers in the form of increased wages. This analysis shows that in developing economies it is not only employment that is necessary for poverty reduction, but also *productive employment* – employment that leads to increased wages, allowing workers to rise above the poverty level.

It is also important to note that there is a two-way relationship or *virtuous* circle between productivity growth and poverty reduction.[29] Productivity growth raises incomes and reduces poverty. But the reduction in poverty can in turn loop back to improved productivity performance as those that move from poor

---

[28] For a detailed methodology, see appendix 2.1 and Sharpe, 2004.

[29] For a discussion of this relationship, see Sharpe et al., 2002.

Box 2.4.   The wage–productivity gap in the Republic of Korea and the role
          of social dialogue

The Republic of Korea has a history of strong trade union activism dating back to the late 1940s. In particular, its experience in dealing with unions is interesting because of the relationship that unions had with the Government, which in the past exerted considerable wage leadership, and tied growth in wages to growth in productivity.

The active involvement of the State

The Republic of Korea was concerned with minimizing capital–labour conflict to secure industrial peace, and motivating workers to improve productivity. The Government initiated a procedure for announcing wage guidelines in the late 1970s which strongly influenced decision-making by firms. The major purpose of the guidelines was to prevent wages increasing faster than productivity. Although there was no mechanism for enforcement, state control of the allocation of cheap credit and scarce foreign exchange forced compliance from many of the larger firms. Labour costs decreased rapidly due to the Government's direct intervention (which could not have happened in a competitive market). The liberalization of political institutions, which started in 1987 and subsequently led to an explosion in wages, strongly suggests that wage repression was indeed part of the labour market scene prior to this date.

The importance of having a high rate of output growth

As an export economy, the Republic of Korea had to be competitive in international markets, especially in terms of its unit labour costs. Additionally, with such a competitive advantage, the Republic of Korea had a very high rate of output growth, which allowed it to absorb excess labour from other sectors of the economy (such as agriculture). The rate of wage growth was based on labour productivity and the Government was in favour of distributing the profits to workers in terms of wage increases. The State also encouraged firms to provide more social benefits to employees. The rate of real wage increase was 5.7 per cent a year from 1981 to 1986. This rate grew significantly from 1989 to 1992 (as a result of liberalization) and continued to increase through 1996. The productivity gains and increased demand in manufacturing goods lead to substantially higher wages for manufacturing workers and increased employment creation in this sector.

The wage–productivity gap in Korean manufacturing

The "wage–productivity gap" (defined as the difference in the percentage growth rate of annual real wage and real value added per worker in manufacturing sector) is shown in the graph opposite. For most of the two decades covered, wages increased slightly below the productivity growth rate and never produced wage inflation, except during the industrialization phase of late 1970s, when the Republic of Korea pushed ahead with an ambitious programme of heavy industrialization, and at the same time there was a serious tightening of the labour market due to massive migration to the Middle East. In 1974 there were 395 Korean workers in the Middle East; by 1981 this number had expanded to 162,000.[1]

Another element in Korean wage history is the sharp fall in the share of wages in each of the two periods following the oil shocks. In order for the economy to rebound after the two oil shocks, there was a sharp fall in wages, which lead to a reduction in unit labour costs. Here again state paternalism was important, since it ordered labour inspectors to ensure that wage increases were accompanied by productivity increases.[2]

After 1997

After the economic crisis and the subsequent programme imposed by the International Monetary Fund, relations with the Government and the social partners were strained, which lead to the signing of the Social Pact (1998). This three-way dialogue at the national level facilitated the adoption of a set of economic and social measures to cope with the crisis, as well as maintaining social stability in a situation of severe economic downturn. However, once the crisis was over, this tripartite dialogue was abandoned, which lead to new industrial conflicts. Due to the economic buoyancy after 1999, unemployment decreased, but the mistrust between Government and social partners remained. As seen in the graph opposite, after the economic crisis of 1997 real wages decreased considerably and have not kept pace with productivity growth.

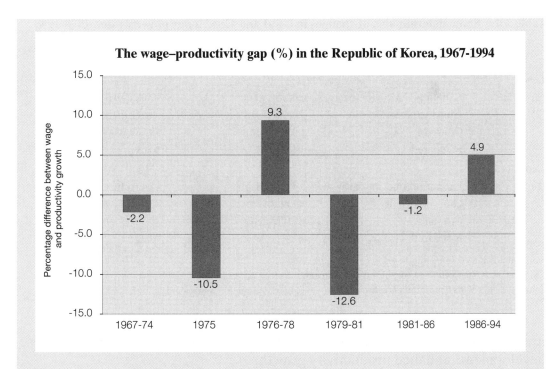

The wage–productivity gap (%) in the Republic of Korea, 1967-1994

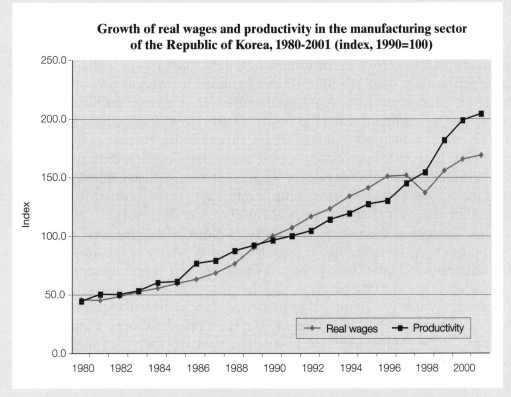

Growth of real wages and productivity in the manufacturing sector of the Republic of Korea, 1980-2001 (index, 1990=100)

[1] Migration News, http://migration.ucdavis.edu/mn.   [2] In 1974 and 1975, the LCSPNC (Law concerning the special measures for safeguarding national security), which was enacted in 1972, expanded the scope of compulsory arbitration to all industries.

Sources: ILO, 2003b; Mazumdar, 2004.

Table 2.4.   Some determinants of changes in US\$1 and US\$2 a day poverty rates, 1970-1998

	Variable name	Change in US\$1 a day poverty rate	Change in US\$2 a day poverty rate
Levels			
(1)	Labour productivity levels	–0.0015(0.000)**	–0.0026(0.000)**
(2)	Gini coefficient	0.0676(0.318)	–0.0623(0.376)
	Constant	24.857(0.044)*	58.389(0.000)**
	R-squared	0.41	0.61
Growth rates			
(1)	Labour productivity growth	–1.754(0.686)*	–3.471(1.043)**
(2)	Gini coefficient	3.299(2.166)	2.763(3.294)
	Constant	–4.910(2.284)*	–8.191(3.474)*
	R-squared	0.26	0.32

Note: Standard errors in parentheses.
* Significant at 5 per cent.   ** Significant at 1 per cent.
Source: See appendix 2.1 for details regarding data sources and estimation methodology.

to non-poor status enjoy better health and acquire more education. Both these developments enhance productivity growth.

The results of this analysis provide support for the view that productivity growth is essential for poverty reduction and should be a priority for developing countries. Consequently, the challenge developing countries face is to promote higher productivity growth for long-run sustainable growth while at the same time offering short- and medium-term solutions for providing an abundance of labour with decent employment opportunities. In principle, public policy could play a role by compensating the losers of the growth process, through such avenues as income support and retraining programmes. But in many developing economies there are significant barriers to the development of such programmes, including high cost and ineffective government structures. In these circumstances, most especially, providing employment opportunities for the poor is essential in order for them to "work themselves out of poverty".

The foregoing discussion is consistent both with observed practices in developing countries and, indeed, with ILO policy advice in the area of employment-intensive infrastructure projects. These are self-targeting, poverty reduction projects that are characterized by their more intensive use of labour than equipment. While it cannot be argued that labour-based methodologies are always appropriate, they could be so in certain circumstances. For example, in less competitive contexts, such as in economic activities that are more sheltered from market competition, where capital is excessively expensive relative to the returns on the project, and, of course, where income-generating activities are needed for the poor. Box 2.5 elaborates the concept of employment-intensive methodologies.

Are employment-intensive infrastructure projects a prescription for favouring "employment" over "productivity"? Here, too, such a conclusion would be mis-

Box 2.5.   The macro-impact of labour-intensive employment programmes

The critical importance of infrastructure in catalysing development is well known. Opening up and linking isolated rural areas, roads and improved transport may play a critical role in facilitating the growth of poverty-reducing non-farm activities. From the point of view of poverty reduction, there are at least two more reasons for providing particular attention to investment in the infrastructure and construction sector. The first relates to the large size of this sector in a typical developing economy and the second to options available in terms of choice of production technology.

The macroeconomic case for using labour-based – instead of equipment-intensive – technology in the infrastructure and construction sectors has been made in many developing countries on a number of grounds. Labour-based programmes provide lower unit costs, increased employment generation, higher contribution to GDP, higher multiplier effects, higher levels of household income and consumption, reduced foreign exchange requirements and, hence, reduced import dependency. These conclusions apply to countries characterized by surplus labour, low wages and weak local industrial capacity (in tools and equipment production). The labour-based approach should be considered as a strategy for the short and medium term. When a country achieves a certain level of development and the surplus labour becomes exhausted, such an approach should no longer be required.

Although more comprehensive and longer term analysis of the impact on poverty of employment-based investments is required, macroeconomic comparative analyses of labour versus equipment-based investments clearly show that for a given investment, the labour-based approach yields better results on household income and consumption (which increases by at least twice as much). Programme benefits include:

- Stimulating employment in low-income groups by providing at least three times more employment for unskilled labour.

- Spending about 50 per cent more on local resources and at least twice as much on local wages.

- Generating about twice as much indirect employment – mainly through the increased use of local resources and hence strengthened inter-sectoral linkages.

- Saving foreign exchange, improving the current account.

Concrete investment–employment–poverty linkages thus achieve much higher multiplier effects for the economy, and in particular for the poor and low-income groups, than policies that do not explicitly address these linkages.

Labour-based approaches are not limited to rural projects and could also be applied in urban situations where they would contribute simultaneously to an improvement in the living conditions of the urban poor and improvements to the urban environment. Upgrading urban slums (clearing and paving of roads, improving drainage), and management of solid wastes are examples of such activities.

Source: ILO, 2004, p. 5.

leading. First, participants in employment-intensive infrastructure projects are *employed at a higher level of productivity than their alternative economic activities could provide.* The self-selecting nature of their participation in such projects can be taken as a proxy for this. Second, as noted in box 2.5, the multiplier effects of such projects have a more direct and positive spillover effect on the communities in which poor people live. As a result, employment-intensive infrastructure projects can overcome difficulties in the transmission from sectors where productivity is growing to sectors where poor people live and work. Moreover, the effects are quantifiable, as figure 2.4 shows in a comparison of economic outcomes of employment versus equipment-based production methods in Uganda. The labour-based method yields three times the impact on employment creation and twice as much effect on generating GDP in the economy. Through direct and indirect channels the employment created using labour-intensive methods is estimated to be 107,657 compared to only 36,418 using the equipment-based approach. The reason for the higher GDP impact in the labour-based methodology is that a higher proportion of income and consumption remains in the local economy.

Even in developing economies characterized by underutilized (or unutilized) labour, the statement that countries should focus on employment at any cost, irrespective of productivity, is misguided. Were a country to do so it would be a prescription for widening inequality between it and wealthier countries, where the main source of economic growth and growth in standards of living is through productivity increases. Rather, policy focus needs to be on both employment and productivity growth. That said, two principles are of relevance. First, as

Figure 2.4   Comparison between equipment and labour-based investment project, Uganda, 1996

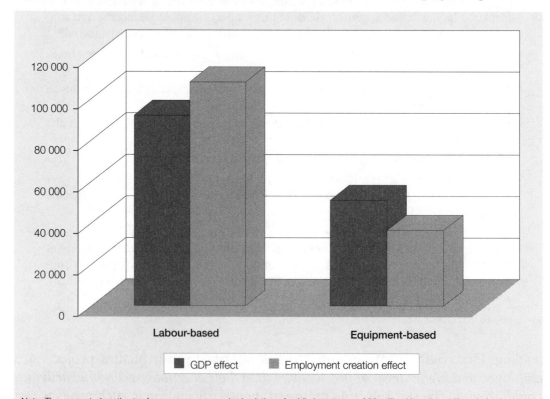

Note: These are study estimates from a macroeconomic simulation of public investment of 30 million Ugandan shillings in feeder roads rehabilitation and maintenance. GDP figures are in millions of Ugandan shillings.
Source: Taylor and Bekabye, 1999.

the successful economies in Asia have shown, industrialization begins by capitalizing on the abundant factor – low-cost, unskilled labour. It makes economic and social sense to build an economy on the factors in which a country has comparative advantage. Experience has shown, however, that such a strategy is transitional, and that the route to greater wealth and higher incomes is by increasing the productivity of the labour force.

The second principle is that both the labour intensity of early industrialization and the employment bias in employment-intensive infrastructure projects cannot be taken as evidence of opting for employment growth over productivity growth. Such a conclusion neglects the lower productivity associated with alternative economic activities. As the sectors in which productivity is growing most rapidly are unlikely to be those in which productivity growth would have the greatest impact on poverty reduction, it makes sense to focus attention on employment and productivity growth on the sectors and areas where they can have the greatest impact on poverty. This idea is now followed up in more depth by looking at the informal economy, where most underemployment is concentrated. The issue here is: Are productivity improvements in the informal economy feasible and do they constitute a meaningful contribution to structural transformation?

The role of the informal economy in structural change

As noted above, structural transformation is both time-intensive and occurs in an unequally distributed fashion in developing countries. The time-lag for structural change to impact on growth, in combination with the effects of demographic transition, has resulted in an explosive growth of urban sprawl in cities such as Mexico City, Jakarta, Calcutta, and Lagos. As a result, these economies are confronted with large labour surpluses of underemployed people who find their way into informal employment, largely in the service sector. Developing economies have only been partly able to absorb these surpluses by creating new employment opportunities.

This section deals with the specific role of the informal economy in the process of structural change. The crucial question is: Can the informal economy positively contribute to the dynamics of structural change? This section presents the conditions under which this might be the case.

The expansion of the informal economy[30]

With respect to the productivity–employment trade-off, the informal economy is typically biased towards employment growth at the expense of productivity growth. Consequently, the informal economy is characterized by substantial economic activity and substantial underemployment. The informal economy is also heavily biased towards unskilled labour. Despite these drawbacks, it has

---

[30] This section is based on the ILO's work on skills development in the informal economy. See http://www.ilo.org/public/english/employment/skills/informal/who.htm

also become increasingly recognized that the small-scale enterprises character-istic of the informal economy have substantial growth potential. These informal small-scale enterprises provide many jobs and are an important source of income, as they are easy to start up and rely primarily on unskilled labour. Fur-thermore, they are a source of capital formation for small entrepreneurs. Facili-tating small-scale entrepreneurship by reducing entrance costs for informal economy workers can be considered a labour-biased development strategy to offset the distortionary tendencies (underemployment) of capital-biased tech-nological change.[31]

Only recently have labour statisticians began to capture the informal econ-omy in quantitative terms. Still, there are some problems in defining informal economy employment, and statistics often lack comparability.[32] Nevertheless, some preliminary results and estimates have been published by the ILO, includ-ing a percentage share of employment in the urban informal economy in total urban employment, as shown in table 2.5.

Self-employed workers comprise the majority of employment in the infor-mal economy. In many developing countries, the number of self-employed in non-agricultural activities has been increasing as workers are attracted by the possibility of greater opportunities in urban areas. As a consequence, a substan-tial proportion of urban informal activities are located in the service sector, a topic that will be discussed later in this chapter.

During the 1990s, own-account and family workers[33] represented nearly two-thirds of the total non-agricultural labour force in Africa, half in South Asia, a third in the Middle East, and a quarter in East Asia and Latin America. A dramatic increase in self-employment has also marked the transition process of the former centrally planned economies of Europe. In the 1990s, own-account workers made up a quarter of total employment in Poland, one-fifth in Romania and one-tenth in the Czech Republic, Hungary and Slovenia.

In Latin America the urban informal economy was the primary job gener-ator during the 1990s; informal economy employment increased by 3.9 per cent a year, while formal economy employment grew by 2.1 per cent. On average 60 per cent of new jobs were created by micro-enterprises, own-account workers and domestic services. Urban informal employment in Africa was estimated to absorb about 60 per cent of the urban labour force and generate more than

---

[31] For further discussion, see Little, Mazumdar and Page, 1987 and Vandenberg, 2004.

[32] The Resolution concerning statistics of employment in the informal economy, adopted by the Fifteenth Inter-national Conference of Labour Statisticians, defines the informal economy as "a group of production units, which form part of the household sector as household enterprises or, equivalently, as unincorporated enterprises owned by house-holds ...." Within the household sector, the informal economy comprises (i) "informal own-account enterprise" that is owned and operated by own-account workers, either alone or in partnership with members of the same or other house-holds, which may employ contributing family workers and employees on an occasional basis, but do not employ em-ployees on a continuing basis; and (ii) "enterprises of informal employers" that are owned and operated by employers, alone or in partnership with members of the same or other households, which employ one or more employees on a con-tinuous basis.

[33] Self-employed workers can be separated into employers, own-account workers and unpaid family workers.

**Table 2.5.	Percentage of total employed in the urban informal economy, selected countries, selected years**

Country	Year	Total	Male	Female
Benin	1999**	46.0	50.0	41.0
Ethiopia	1999*	49.2	37.1	64.0
South Africa	1999**	21.3	16.1	28.4
Tanzania	1995**	67.0	59.7	85.3
Brazil	1997**	27.3	27.4	27.1
Mexico	2000**	19.4	17.8	22.2
Peru	1999*	53.8	48.9	60.6
India	2000**	51.3	53.7	40.6
Nepal	1999**	64.8	64.1	60.7
Pakistan	2000**	63.8	64.1	60.7
Philippines	1995**	17.3	15.8	19.4
Georgia	1999**	14.2	20.7	7.4
Lithuania	2000**	41.3	49.6	26.5
Russian Federation	1999*	4.5	4.4	4.7
Turkey	2000*	10.2	10.4	9.4
Ukraine	1997**	4.9	4.5	5.3

* According to the ILO's harmonized definition.   ** According to the national definition.

Source: KILM 7a and 7b – Employment in the Informal Economy. ILO, 2003b.

93 per cent of all new jobs in the region in the 1990s. In Asia, it was estimated that the informal economy absorbed between 40 and 50 per cent of the urban labour force, before the 1997 financial crisis, displaying large differences across countries in the region. In the newly industrializing Asian economies, the informal economy accounted for less than 10 per cent of labour absorption, while in countries such as Bangladesh, Nepal and Pakistan it grew by over 60 per cent.

Large share of women in informal employment

There is also a gender-specific dimension to informal employment as represented by the large share of women who hold informal jobs. Women comprise between 60 and 80 per cent of total informal employment and tend to be concentrated in a narrow range of activities in lower-skill, lower-pay tasks (food processing, garment sewing and domestic services). Moreover, in addition to constraints faced by workers and producers in the informal economy with regard to access to assets, markets, services and regulatory frameworks, women face additional gender-specific barriers, which include restrictions to entering into contracts, insecure land and property rights and the constraints of household and childcare responsibilities. The recent widespread strategy of firms in the formal economy of advanced and developing countries to subcontract production to family enterprises has helped to link women's home-based labour to the formal production system under informal, flexible employment arrangements.

A potential positive contribution for creating better jobs?

The expansion of employment in the informal economy in many developing countries is directly linked to imbalances in the process of structural change. Thus, the challenging task ahead is to transform this large pool of human potential into a more productive one. Increasing the productivity of the informal economy workers will mean higher incomes and subsequently improved working conditions and living standards.

In this regard, it is worthwhile to distinguish between informal activities that are complementary (those that play a role in the vertical chain of formal production) and those that are substitutes for, and thus competing with, formal activities. Examples of the latter are food stalls, street vending, the production of low-quality apparel and shoes or simple mechanical work. These activities are sometimes perceived as a threat to their formal economy counterparts. On the other hand, activities that are considered to be complementary to formal production processes play a different role in the economy. Take, for example, informal transport services, the production of intermediary goods or informal types of education and learning, which are not available in the formal sector and are required to smooth the vertical chain. Lowering entrance costs for these small-scale enterprises, either in the formal or the informal economy, may create beneficial spillover effects for the formal economy.

For small businesses to develop they must gain access to important facilities such as capital loans, market information, simple technology and sufficient protection of property rights. Once this occurs the urban informal economy may even achieve a modest surplus that can be used to develop business linkages with the formal economy. Ultimately, this upgrading will lead to a decline in inequality, and will help to create a sizeable middle class that can stimulate social and political stability and enhance aggregate domestic demand.

Clearly a large informal economy is not a sign of favourable economic development. On the contrary, it points to the existence of a dual economy. But, given the existence of the informal economy and the problems of matching demand and supply of labour in the formal economy, the only option is to focus on the growth potential of the informal economy as an additional means of fighting poverty. The challenge then becomes one of providing assistance and improving the productive performance of these informal small-scale enterprises. Fundamental to this strategy is lowering the costs of formalizing business and building commercial and financial institutions to enhance economic integration of small-scale enterprises (see box 2.6).[34] For more on small-scale enterprises, see Chapter 5 of this Report.

Section 2.4 now discusses the policy strategies conducive to breaking or reducing the trade-off between productivity growth and employment in order to realize long-run growth potential.

---

[34] For additional literature, see de Soto, 2000.

> **Box 2.6.   Formalizing the informal economy: The role of the National Productivity Institute in South Africa**
>
> The burden of turning informal business activities into formal ones lies in the cost of becoming formalized, a process that can be frustrating because of excessive rules and regulations. Formalization often requires the entrepreneur to accept and apply regulations concerning, among other things, the organization of the production process, the hiring and firing of labour, minimum wages, business administration, insurance and responsibility. Implementation of these laws can be costly and at times prohibitive.
>
> The administrative abilities of the entrepreneur are also often unequal to the legal requirements necessary for registering (as a cook, a hairdresser, or a carpenter, for example) in the formal economy. In addition, in many countries, a reliable, extensive network is at least as important as personal or entrepreneurial capabilities in gaining access to the formal sector (de Soto, 2000).
>
> Responding to this need, the National Productivity Institute (NPI) in South Africa developed a programme to help build productive capacity by working with informal businesses – particularly small, medium and micro-enterprises (SMMEs) – and helping them to become formal businesses. The main aim of the NPI is to build the country's productive capacity, by taking into consideration the interests of its three social partners: government, labour and business.
>
> In order to meet the productivity needs of the SMMEs, the NPI instituted the Productive Behaviour and Competencies Programme (PBCP). Its purpose is to provide education and training to small-business owners in order to reduce waste, improve efficiency and utilization of resources, and improve product and service quality. The programme targets key areas of the economy that would most benefit from productivity gains: manufacturing, tourism and hospitality, agriculture, and services.
>
> One outstanding example of the programme's work is with *The Sweet and Chocolate Factory* in Atteridgeville (Pretoria district), which started as a community project supplying sweets and chocolates to schools and the local community. The PBCP programme aided the factory's managers in a more efficient reallocation of resources, by helping them to keep records and identify and correct production-related errors. These small changes, by reducing wastage and allowing managers to keep a closer track of production, have almost quadrupled the factory's daily output.
>
> Source: National Productivity Institute, 2003.

2.4.   Focusing on sectors where employment is concentrated

Increasing productivity and employment for long-run sustainable growth requires a twin strategy of investing in dynamically growing sectors while at the same building capacity in sectors where the majority of labour is employed. A strategy of investing only in dynamic sectors in attempts to "leapfrog" may not be enough to reduce poverty, mainly because the fastest growing sectors may often not be where the majority of the poor are employed and may require skills and training that the poor do not possess. The growing ICT sector in India (as described later, in box 2.8) is a case in point. Currently India's ICT sector employs about 800,000 people, a figure that is expected to increase to 2 million by 2008.[35] But job growth in the rest of India's economy has not been sufficient to provide adequate employment opportunities for the over 400 million people who make up the labour force, two-thirds of whom are located in the rural sector and lack the education and skills to compete for these ICT jobs. The challenge then is to *broaden the dynamic sectors of the economy, such as ICT, while deepening their linkages with other sectors in the economy – sectors where the majority of labour is employed.* At the same time, it is paramount to ensure that workers can be provided with skills and training for labour absorption in these growing areas of the economy, a strategy that requires increasing the productivity of workers in labour abundant industries.

This strategy will have the largest impact on workers' lives not only in the short and medium run, but also in the long term. In the short and medium term it will provide workers with decent employment opportunities, defined by security, opportunities, basic workers' rights and representation; in the long term, workers will be equipped with the necessary skills and training to compete for job opportunities in a dynamic economy.

A dynamic economy is exemplified by a great deal of "job churning", meaning that jobs are created and destroyed on a continuous basis. This process takes place both within (intra) and between (inter) sectors. Understanding employment dynamics at the sectoral level is helpful to appreciate how trade-offs between employment and productivity growth at the sectoral level may or may not exist at the aggregate level.

Table 2.6 illustrates the trend in sectoral employment growth by world region from 1950 to 1990. In all regions a considerable shift has been taking place away from agriculture towards the non-agricultural sectors of the economy, i.e. industry and services. On balance the service sector attracted the largest share of the increasing pool of labour, whereas the employment trends in industry diverged quite substantially between the advanced regions on the one hand, and developing regions on the other.

The shift in employment towards services is a "stylized fact" of post-war economic development. Table 2.7 shows that as an economy becomes more developed (i.e. moves towards high income) the contribution of its service sector to GDP increases. Nevertheless, compared to productivity growth rates in industry, the service sector trailed industry in most countries. Labour apparently does not exclusively shift towards the productivity champions as most theories on structural change predict. In spite of lower productivity growth rates, the service industry was the largest contributor to net employment creation. How can this be explained?

The attraction of labour by services is a very diverse process. First, economic growth in general implies the increasing contribution of services as a response to an increased demand for trade, transport, communication and social services. This service–employment growth effect can be considered partly as a classic type

---

[35] *The Economist*, 2004.

Table 2.6. The sectoral distribution of employment, according to region, 1950-1990

	Total employment(thousands)				Percentage distribution		
	Agriculture	Industry	Services	Total	Agriculture	Industry	Services
World							
1950	809 864	179 203	217 457	1 206 524	67	15	18
1970	930 196	317 957	408 001	1 656 154	56	19	25
1990	1 225 709	500 702	779 448	2 505 859	49	20	31
Europe							
1950	100 360	81 015	72 072	253 447	40	32	28
1970	64 120	123 563	116 581	304 264	21	41	38
1990	42 496	126 345	179 878	348 719	12	36	52
North America							
1950	9 389	26 711	36 767	72 867	13	37	50
1970	4 518	31 731	61 922	98 171	5	32	63
1990	4 128	37 003	101 348	142 479	3	26	71
Oceania							
1950	1 737	1 678	1 975	5 390	32	31	37
1970	1 964	2 499	3 865	8 328	24	30	46
1990	2 563	2 857	7 419	12 839	20	22	58
East and South-East Asia, excluding China							
1950	95 191	15 007	24 729	134 927	71	11	18
1970	104 620	34 240	54 793	193 653	54	18	28
1990	135 283	62 191	108 063	305 537	44	20	35
Asia							
1950	578 785	51 688	79 082	709 555	82	7	11
1970	699 140	124 841	167 168	991 149	71	13	17
1990	964 963	263 750	331 787	1 560 500	62	17	21
Latin America and the Caribbean							
1950	32 573	11 559	16 015	60 147	54	19	27
1970	40 107	21 145	34 140	95 392	42	22	36
1990	44 515	41 364	89 326	175 205	25	24	51
Africa							
1950	87 020	6 553	11 547	105 120	83	6	11
1970	120 347	14 178	24 324	158 849	76	9	15
1990	167 043	29 384	69 391	265 818	63	11	26

Source: ILO, 2003a.

Table 2.7. Share of the service sector in economy, according to income level, 1980-2000

Income level	Services share (% of GDP)	
	1980	2002
Low-income countries (≤$735)	38	46
Lower middle-income countries ($736-$2935)	39	56
Upper middle-income countries ($2936-$9075)	48	60
High-income countries (≥$9076)	58	71[1]

Note: $ = US$.
[1] 2001 value.
Source: World Bank, WDI, 2004.

of economic development based on the integration of markets, the increase of scale-enhancing specialization and the division of labour. As a result, many service activities have become independent activities, outsourced from agriculture and, to an even larger extent, the industrial sector in which they were once embedded.

Secondly, employment growth in the service sector can be a residual – and result from a lack of productivity growth in the rest of the economy. In particular, demographic pressures in rural areas, which lack sufficient employment opportunities, have caused large flows of rural–urban migration. These migrants are mostly absorbed by the urban informal service sector. The service sector is much more able to absorb hidden unemployment than the industrial sector, because of the possibilities of small-scale production and less capital-intensive work.

Many service activities are labour-intensive and, as noted above, the possibilities of raising productivity may be limited. Debate is ongoing on just how limited these possibilities are. Although the service sector has the most employment and represents the lion's share of output in developed economies, it has historically been characterized as technologically *non-progressive*, with little opportunity for productivity growth and facing relative constraints on wages and prices of goods in the sector.[36] An even more dire view was that the expansion of the service economy was akin to an urban crisis, as in Baumol's much-cited 1967 article, "Macroeconomics of unbalanced growth: The anatomy of urban crisis".[37]

It should be noted that productivity levels in some service sectors are already fairly high, particularly in many modern business service sectors. The inherent problems of measurement in this industry have caused productivity in many of the service industries to be underestimated (see box 2.7). Evidence is mounting that other "more traditional" industries in the service sector (such as distribution, retail, and transport and communication) are profiting from technological and organizational innovations in the economy, and also exhibiting substantial increases in productivity growth. Contrary to Baumol's view, more recent studies[38] have shown that rapid changes in ICT have expanded the productivity and marketability of many service industries that serve as the primary employer for a large proportion of the labour force. Not only are some service industries the highest productivity performers in the economy but also the most progressive, as they are the strongest users of ICT and have greatly expanded their market size and tradability by e-commerce.

---

[36] Adam Smith, in *Wealth of Nations* in 1776, and Karl Marx, in *Das Kapital* in 1873, adopted the physiocratic concept of productive and unproductive labour; neither gave the service sector an explicit treatment as a distinct activity. In this framework, the service sector was implicitly viewed as immaterial and unproductive, because it could not reproduce the economic system or create wealth for nations by adding value to materials (as could agriculture and manufacturing).

[37] Baumol, 1967.

[38] Miles and Kastrinos, 1995; Triplett and Bosworth, 2003; Andersen and Corley, 2003.

Box 2.7. Productivity measurement in the service sector

One of the most interesting debates surrounding productivity measurement involves the apparent *productivity paradox*. The term derives from Robert Solow's celebrated 1987 phrase, "You can see the computer age everywhere but in the productivity statistics." This paradox arose because those industries using new technology the most seemed to have the lowest levels of measured productivity. Numerous reasons have been advanced for this apparent paradox, one explanation being that the attempts to measure productivity in these industries were (and for the most still are) based on flawed statistics. This has been particularly the case in the ICT-using industries in the service sector.

As productivity statistics are derived from output measures, any errors in output will automatically feed into productivity measures. Measurements of output in the service sector do not fit the standard definitions, which were derived based on concepts for the manufacturing sector. Three issues underlie the problems in measurement of output and productivity in the service sector: definition, aggregation and quality consideration.

Defining the service and its output

Often, service sector production is not as clearly definable in tangible terms as in, for example, a "goods"-producing sector such as manufacturing. The intangible nature of some service industries makes it difficult to quantify (and sometimes even identify) an industry's output. For example, what is the output of a bank? Is its primary service the provision of customer accounts, or loans, or an optimal portfolio? How the primary service is perceived will determine a different mix of outputs (and inputs) that will alter the productivity measurement.

Another difficulty in defining a service is the role of customer involvement. "Goods"-producing industries produce an output, which is then sold to the market. Even if no one purchases the product, the industry has still generated an output, which can be stored in inventory. But what happens in the case of a service where the role of the consumer is implicit in determining output? A teacher, for example, is teaching – to an empty classroom. Here there is no output because there is no consumer involvement. But place just one student in the classroom and an output is produced. It is the same teaching, the same service, but without a consumer involved in the process, no output is generated.

Aggregation

Another issue in defining a service is the heterogeneity of units within types of services. Service transactions are generally not as homogeneous as manufactured goods because of the personalized aspects of the service sector (e.g. banking and finance) and consumer services (e.g. medical care, cleaning, and computer services). This is especially a problem when aggregating the number of transactions undertaken. The concept of aggregation of heterogeneous services is referred to as "bundled services". The difficulty in their measurement lies in first identifying and then finding some way of aggregating these diverse units. To return to the example of the banking industry, a bank account may provide services such as online banking, the use of ATM and bankcards, or safekeeping of funds. All these services must be aggregated to take account of their heterogeneous nature.

(continued overleaf)

Quality considerations

Finally, conventional measures of output and productivity do not capture the effect of quality changes in a good or service, unless this effect shows up in the price measure. And conventional measures of price movements (consumer price indices, producer price indices) do not consider changes in the quality of a good or service. A classic example here is the personal computer, whose prices have decreased steadily but whose quality continues to increase over the years.

This has lead to the concept of *hedonic* pricing, which takes quality into consideration. This statistical technique derives the relationship between a product's price and its characteristics. It is used to adjust the price index so that it removes the effects of variation in quality over time. Not applying hedonic prices will underestimate the output measure based on the volume of goods and services produced if there has been an increase in their quality. This is of particular importance in the increased quality of the healthcare industry and the computer industry, for example, both of which have been underestimated.

Hedonic pricing is more widely used in the United States to deflate output in industries (such as health services and telecommunications) where rapid technological changes have occurred. Thus, when estimating productivity for these industries, a more realistic picture is derived of changes in output, which is reflected in higher productivity figures. The effect is also to raise the average rate of productivity growth for the country. Such measures are not generally taken into account in many countries, which may be one of the reasons their economies seem to lag behind the United States in terms of productivity growth. For example, the British Office for National Statistics (ONS) recalculated productivity growth in the computer industry using hedonic pricing and found that growth rates had tripled.

Source: Andersen and Corley, 2003.

A word of caution should be noted here, because this does not apply to all service industries. Employment in this sector comprises the dual sides of the decent work spectrum: both high-skilled, high wage jobs and low-skilled, low wage components. The interesting question of how the sector has contributed to productivity growth for the economy as a whole is explored in section 2.5.

2.5. The impact of service sector growth on productivity growth

The service sector is important for a policy focus because it represents an overwhelming majority of output and labour in most developed economies. Additionally, in the developing economies the growth of services is expanding rapidly in terms of output, employment and in some cases productivity. Thus, both employment and productivity gains can be achieved in this rapidly expanding sector, warranting further investigation into the impact of the service sector expansion on the total economy.

As mentioned above, employment in this sector lies at both ends of the decent work spectrum. In some economies, the growth in services is attributed to a lack of employment in agriculture and industry, which pushes labour into less productive urban service sector jobs, such as those in petty trade and personal services.

In other economies, labour is pulled by high productivity service sectors. The impressive growth in India's service sector is one example (see box 2.8). In sum, increasing service sector employment can either indicate a successful transition of the economy towards higher productivity levels, or reflect high numbers of hidden unemployed people in low-productivity services.

To delve deeper into this issue, the contribution of service sector productivity and employment to growth in the economy as a whole is examined. This is done based on calculations of employment and productivity differences by sector. First, the difference between productivity growth in the service sector and the total economy is calculated, which tells us whether sectoral growth is contributing positively or negatively to growth in the economy as a whole. Next, employment is calculated similarly to determine whether those sectors that exhibited above-average productivity increases also saw increases in employment. This exercise is done for a sample of countries that had service productivity data available in the ILO's KILM database. The countries available represent both developed and developing economies.

Figures 2.5a and 2.5b give the results of calculations for two service industries (transport and communications, and wholesale and retail trade), as well as the manufacturing sector, for two periods: 1980-2001 (figure 2.5a) and 1995-2001 (figure 2.5b). Although the figures obtained do not cover all the sectors in the total economy, transport and the retail trade industries represent approximately 25 per cent of employment in the economies analysed.[39] Figures 2.5a and 2.5b demonstrate i) the contribution of the service sector to productivity growth for the economy as a whole, and ii) whether or not there are employment–productivity trade-offs.

Figure 2.5a shows that, in transport and communications, all 15 economies, with the exception of Indonesia and the Republic of Korea, have above-average productivity growth, meaning that productivity gains in this industry contributed positively to growth in the economy as a whole. Additionally, in over two-thirds of the economies that showed gains in productivity growth, this was accompanied by gains in employment. Thus, in these cases, employment was pulled into high-productivity activities in the service sector. An impressive employment performance in transportation and communication services can be seen in India. Contrary to its recently lagging industrial development, high employment and productivity growth in this industry indicate that India's service sector can be a vital source of employment creation. In stark contrast to India, employment in Indonesia is being pushed into low-productivity services as employment has failed to rebound from the impact of the Asian crisis in 1997 (for more on South-East Asia, see Chapter 1 of this Report).

---

[39] Additionally, these figures do not include the community and personal services industry, which was the main focus of Baumol's analysis. However, Triplett and Bosworth (2003) and the US Bureau of Labor Statistics calculate labour productivity for personal services in the United States, obtaining figures of 1.8 per cent and 1.7 per cent respectively for 1995-2000, which was higher than growth for the total economy during that period (1.2 per cent).

Box 2.8.   Growth in India's software industry

The service sector in India has recently been dominated by growth in the information and communication technology (ICT) sector. Numerous American and European companies are increasingly shifting their ICT services (back-office and call-centre operations, long-distance sales, insurance and medical data entry services) to India, either by opening their own businesses there or by outsourcing processes to Indian service providers. The ICT sector has become an oft-repeated success story and has placed the country on the global map of rapidly growing industry.

India's service sector is the most dynamic sector in the economy, primarily due to growth in the ICT sector, which accounts for 20 per cent of goods exported and over 3 per cent of the country's GDP.

The Indian software industry has grown by roughly 50 per cent in the past 6 years. Although this constitutes only a small fraction of total employment, the number of jobs in software and related industries jumped from just over 500,000 in 1999 to 700,000 in 2004.

India's success in the ICT business has been principally due to domestic capabilities and domestic entrepreneurs. Conventional explanations for the country's success in this industry highlight the comparative advantage argument. The software industry uses those resources (low-cost, high skilled human resources) in which India has international comparative advantage (and uses less physical infrastructure and financial capital where it has a comparative disadvantage). For example, the annual average wage for computer professionals is 10-20 per cent of that in the United States. This wage factor is one of the main reasons for this boom; India's wages are lower than their counterparts both in the United States and Europe. In addition, India has one of the largest reserves of English-speaking scientists and engineers in the world.

On the supply side, India is the largest producer of human capital for the software industry, producing over 100,000 ICT professionals in the late 1990s and over 65,000 engineers annually. In addition, over 200,000 Indian expatriates are working as ICT professionals in the United States as part of the H-1B visa programme. This undeniably helped India in establishing networks between American and Indian companies. As in all success stories, a little luck is always involved, which came in the opportune form of the ICT industry boom and the liberalization of the Indian economy in the early 1990s. Another plus is the difference in time zones, complementing India's working hours with those of the United States and allowing round-the-clock project work between the two countries.

Finally, the spread of the Indian diaspora in the United States, particularly in Silicon Valley, was instrumental in the development of this sector. First, it created networks that facilitated economic exchange and increased the transfer of knowledge between the two countries. Second, the "brain drain" has evolved into a vital mechanism for India's booming ICT sectors, with Indian workers being trained in software development in the United States.

Source: Arora et al., 2001.

In the wholesale and retail trade industry, a different scenario is found to that of the transportation and communication industry. Over half of the economies had productivity growth that trailed growth for the total economy. In some economies, such as Brazil and Mexico, employment growth accompanied negative labour productivity growth, resulting in a (reversed) employment–productivity trade-off. This can be explained by labour flowing in the direction of the low-productive urban service sector, as a result of increasing population pressure and lagging employment opportunities in (rural) agriculture and (urban) industry. In other words, labour is not pulled by high service sector productivity growth, rather it is being pushed by lagging dynamics in other sectors. The United States, Sweden and Taiwan, China, were the only economies having both above average gains in productivity and employment growth in this sector.

Performing a similar analysis for the manufacturing sector provides a useful benchmark for comparison across sectors. As expected, productivity growth in this sector has contributed positively to productivity growth for the economy in all of the countries in the sample. At the same time, the gains in productivity have accompanied trade-offs in employment in all economies, with the exception of India and Indonesia.

An interesting note is that productivity growth in the transport and communication industry is just as high as in the manufacturing sector, suggesting that growth in employment-intensive service industries can substitute for employment losses in the manufacturing sector – without fear of negative long-term effects on wages and sustainable growth.

How has the situation changed over time? Figure 2.5b presents the same analysis performed from 1995 to 2001 to see if these relationships have held over time.

In the transport and communication sector there was a substantial increase in productivity gains. Most economies still had productivity gains that were above average for the economy, while two-thirds of those economies also had above-average gains in employment. Japan, the Czech Republic and Indonesia were the only three economies with productivity gains less than the average for the total economy. During the 1990s, India also showed a slowdown in employment growth in this sector, possibly as the result of increasing gains in productivity. Across the board, however, employment gains remained above average for most of the sample economies.

In the wholesale and retail sector there was an increase in productivity growth from the previous period. Half of the economies have above-average productivity growth and, of those economies, about three-quarters also have above-average growth in employment. Mexico, which had negative productivity growth in the 1980-2000 period, is characterized by a significant increase in both productivity and employment growth. At the same time, the considerable increase in productivity in the United States (which can partly be explained by the 'Wal-Mart effect", i.e. the presence of big-box retailing which came onto the

Figure 2.5a. Difference between sectoral and total economy annual average growth in productivity and employment, 1980-2001

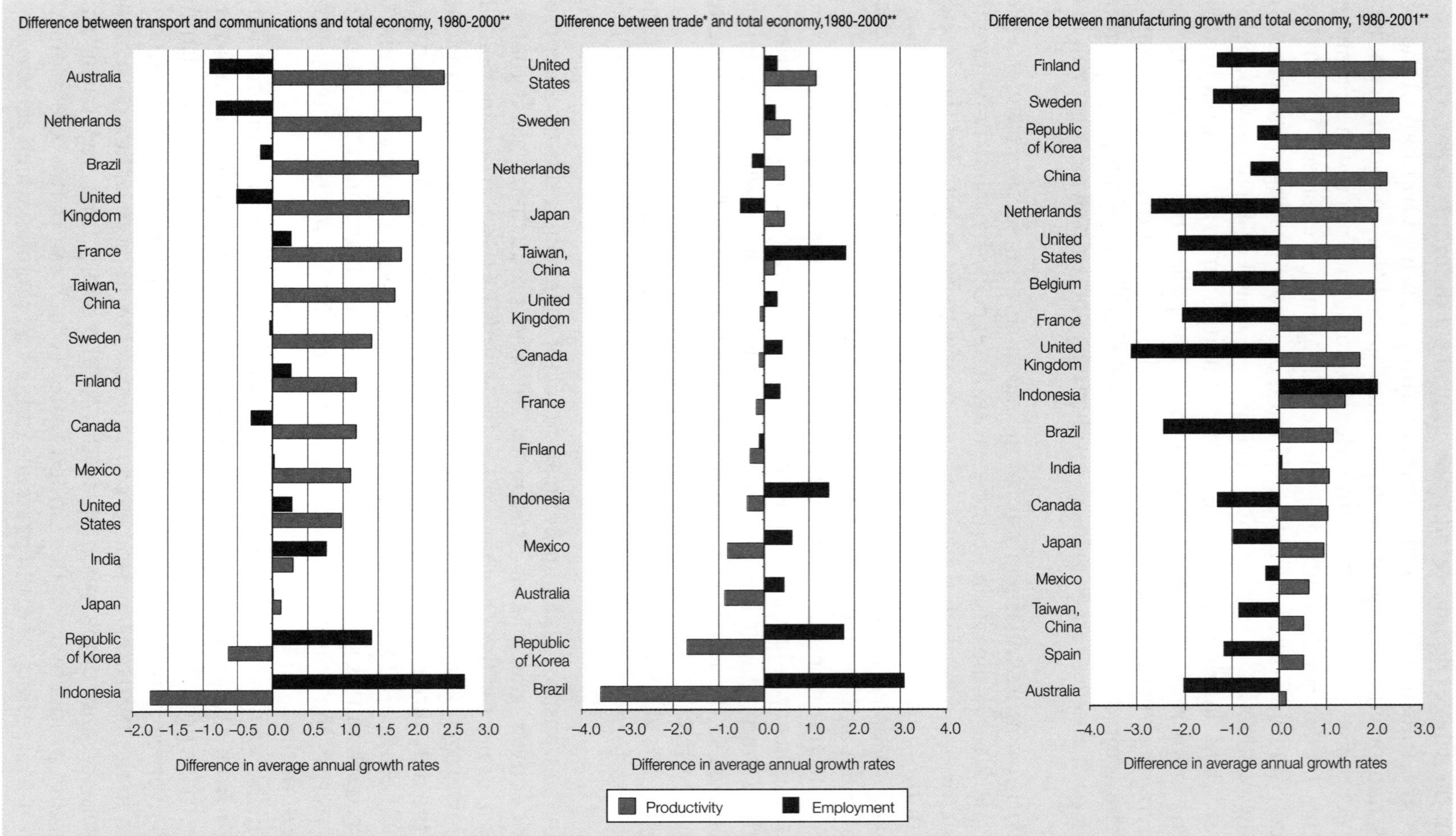

Difference between transport and communications and total economy, 1980-2000**

Difference between trade* and total economy, 1980-2000**

Difference between manufacturing growth and total economy, 1980-2001**

Productivity   Employment

* Denotes wholesale and retail trade.   ** Not all economies had data available for this period; see appendix 2.2 for details.

Source: Author's calculations based on ILO, 2003b data, and GGDC, 2004.

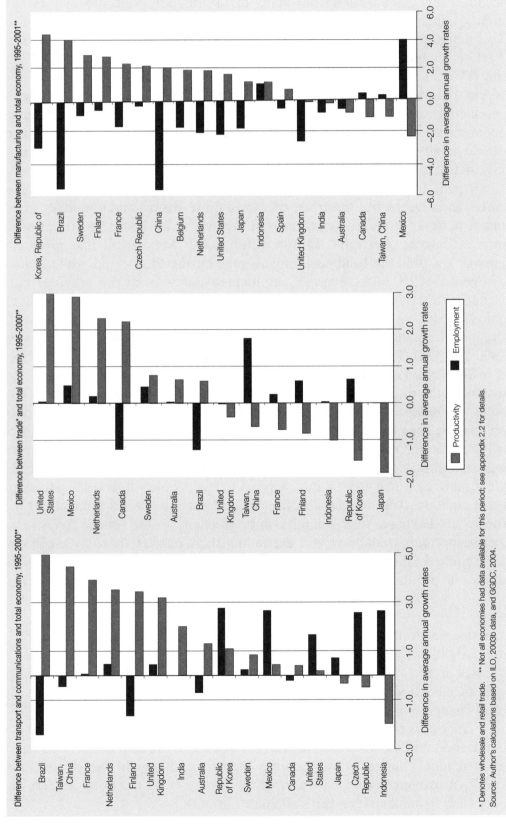

Figure 2.5b. Difference between sectoral and total economy annual average growth in productivity and employment, 1995-2001

* Denotes wholesale and retail trade. ** Not all economies had data available for this period; see appendix 2.2 for details.
Source: Author's calculations based on ILO, 2003b data, and GGDC, 2004.

scene in the 1990s pushing out many of the smaller, boutique-style establishments) appears to have had almost no impact on job creation in the trade sector. This is arguably a cyclical phenomenon and can be explained by the recession of 2001, which led to a decline in employment for the economy as a whole. During the 1990s a reverse pattern is also observed in Brazil. Employment shifts out of services towards industry, indicating that labour is released from the low-productive service sector as industrial activity picked up. However, in most economies with below-average productivity growth, there is higher than average employment growth, suggesting that employment is being pushed into low-productive jobs.

Again, in the manufacturing sector, productivity gains are well dispersed across the regions, but the trade-off is still quite strong, and a number of economies became productivity laggards in this sector. In descending order of magnitude, Canada, Australia, Taiwan (China) and Mexico all had productivity growth less than the total economy average during this period, while India saw a reversal of its above-average employment gains from the previous period. Canada, Taiwan (China) and Mexico showed higher than average employment gains. Mexico's astounding growth during this period can be linked to growth in the maquila sector, which doubled from 1,703 establishments to 3,590 between 1990 and 2000 (INEGI, 2002).

Thus, although labour has been pushed into low-productive services in some instances, the majority of cases show that *employment has been drawn to service employment that is highly productive.* Why has productivity and employment been on an increasing trend in this sector and become stronger over time? One reason is the rise in incomes in many countries. As income rises, earners spend more on leisure and service-related activities such as health, education and financial services, many of which are still mainly provided by people – thus leading to employment creation. Additionally, advances in ICT have deepened connections within the sector, having a strong impact on productivity in the service industries and increasing their tradability and expanding their market share by e-commerce. Consequently, the results show that service sector expansion can have a positive impact on productivity and employment growth for the economy as a whole.

2.6. Concluding remarks

This chapter addresses the existence of trade-offs between employment and productivity in both developed and developing economies, using a framework that focuses on the relationship over the short, medium and longer term, and pays specific attention to employment–productivity dynamics as the result of structural change.

Trade-offs between employment and productivity growth exist, most often, in the short and medium term as the result of short-run deviations and structural and frictional changes in the economy. Structural change in the form of shifts in employment across sectors is part of the "creative destruction" process and is necessary to achieve long-run sustainable growth.

In the longer term, in most economies, productivity and employment growth go hand in hand. This is particularly the case in the industrialized economies of Europe, North America, and many parts of Asia. This has not been the case in developing economies in either the African or Latin American regions where growth in employment and productivity has followed different trajectories, suggesting that a focus on productivity gains is a prescription for low employment growth.

The analysis in this chapter has shown that such a suggestion is not warranted. The presence of long-run trade-offs between productivity and employment in developing economies does not mean that this theory is not applicable to developing economies, but rather that there are inadequacies in the markets, conditions and institutions which block these economies from experiencing such gains. *No country can afford to neglect to focus on improving the productivity of its workforce. Productivity is the engine that drives wage increases and leads to improvements in the standard of living of a country.* At the same time a strategy focusing on maximizing employment does not have to mean a sacrifice in productivity – as the experience of employment-intensive investment programmes has shown.

A policy strategy for increasing productivity and employment over the long run should therefore entail a dual strategy of investing in dynamically growing sectors of the economy while also building capacity in sectors where the majority of labour is employed. Focusing on sectors where the majority of labour is employed is one way to bridge the gap between trade-offs in the interim and long-run growth in both. This has significance for both developed and developing economies alike. For developing economies, this entails investing in strategic growth sectors by acquiring and internalizing the knowledge developed elsewhere if they are to "catch up", while at the same time improving worker productivity in traditionally low-productivity sectors, such as in the informal economy. It also means establishing forward and backward linkages in the supply chain between fast-growing sectors and those in which labour is dominant. For developed economies, it entails being at the forefront of knowledge expansion and innovation in order to create new technology, which provides workers with opportunities to expand into new markets and, at the same time, maintaining the employability of those workers in declining markets.

History shows that economies adapt to structural change. However, in order to increase the acceptance of change there should be a smoother transition for workers and a distribution of productivity gains from the "winners" so that society as a whole is better off, rather than a small segment of the population. This strategy calls for additional measures such as compensation for dislocated workers during periods of loss, skills retraining and employability – for example, making training systems more demand-driven and facilitating self-employment and business start-ups through interest-free credit programmes for those who have difficulty relocating. In developing economies where such programmes cannot be made available, providing technical assistance to informal entrepreneurs, facilitating the legalities of becoming formal businesses and providing productive employment opportunities (through labour-intensive programmes) are essential in order for the poor to "work themselves out of poverty".

References

Alliance Bernstein. 2004. *US weekly economic update*, various issues.

—. 2003. *US weekly economic update*, various issues.

Andersen, B.; Corley, M. 2003. *The theoretical, conceptual, and empirical impact of the service economy: A critical review*, UNU WIDER Discussion Paper No. 22.

Arora, A.; Arunichalam, V.S.; Asunoi, Jai; Fernandes, Ronald. 2001. "The Indian software services industry", in *Research Policy*, No. 30, pp. 1267-1287.

Baily, M.N.; Hulten, C.R.; Campbell, D. 1992. "Productivity dynamics in manufacturing plants", *Brookings Papers on Economic Activity*, pp. 187-249.

Baumol, W.J. 1967. "Macroeconomics of unbalanced growth: The anatomy of urban crisis", in *The American Economic Review*, No. 3, pp. 415-426.

Borensztein, E.; De Gregorio, J.; Lee, J.W. 1998. "How does FDI affect economic growth?", in *Journal of International Economics*, Vol. 45, pp. 115-135.

Carillo, J. 2003. "Los retos de las maquiladoras ante la pérdida de competitividad", in *Comercio Exterior*, Vol. 53, No. 4, April.

De Soto, H. 2000. *The mystery of capital: Why capitalism triumphs in the West and fails everywhere else* (New York, Bantam Press).

Disney, R.; Haskel J.; Heden, Y. 2003. "Restructuring and productivity growth in UK manufacturing", in *The Economic Journal*, No. 113, pp. 666-694.

Groningen Growth and Development Centre (GGDC). 2004. *Total economy database*, available online at http://www.ggdc.net/homeggdc.html

Forrester Research. 2002. *3.3 million US services jobs to go offshore*, Forrester Research Brief, 11 November.

Ghose, A.K. 2003. *Jobs and incomes in a globalizing world* (Geneva, ILO).

Gordon, R.J. 1997. "Is there a trade-off between unemployment and productivity growth?", in D. Snower and G. de la Dehesa (eds.): *Unemployment policy* (Cambridge, Cambridge University Press), pp. 433-463.

Groshen, E.L.; Potter, S. 2003. "Has structural change contributed to a jobless recovery?" in *FRBNY Current Issues in Economics and Finance*, No. 8 (www.newyorkfed.org/rmaghome/curr_iss).

Hussmanns, R.; du Jeu, B. 2002. *ILO compendium of official statistics on employment in the informal sector* (Geneva, ILO), STAT Working Paper, pp. 16-28.

ILO. 2004. "Productive employment for poverty reduction and development", GB.289/ESP/2.

—. 2003a. *Economically active population 1950-2010: ILO database on estimates and projections of the economically active population (5th edition)* (Geneva, LABORSTA, LABPROJ) (http://laborsta.ilo.org).

—. 2003b. *Key Indicators of the Labour Market (KILM), 3rd Edition* (Geneva).

—. 2003c. *Global Employment Agenda* (Geneva) (http://www.ilo.org/public/english/employment/empframe/practice/index.htm).

—. 1999. *Key Indicators of the Labour Market 1999 (KILM)* (Geneva).

—. 1997. *World Labour Report 1997-98* (Geneva).

International Monetary Fund (IMF). 1995. *World Economic Outlook* (Washington, DC).

—. 1999. *World Economic Outlook* (Washington, DC).

Instituto Nacional de Estadística, Geografía e Informática (INEGI). 2004. *Industria maqui-ladora de exportación, indicadores anuales* (Mexico City) (http://dgcnesyp.inegi.gob.mx/bdine/j15/j1500601.htm).

Karaömerlioglu, D.; Ansal, H. 2000. "Innovation and employment in developing countries", in M. Vivarelli and M. Pianta (eds.): *The employment impact of innovation: Evidence and policy* (London, Routledge).

Kucera, D.; Milberg, W. 2003. "Deindustrialization and changes in the manufacturing trade: Factor content calculations for 1978-1995", *Review of World Economics*, No. 2, pp. 601-624.

Landesmann, M.; Stehrer, R. 2001. "The European unemployment problem: A structural approach", in P. Petit and L. Soete. (eds.): *Technology and the future of European unemployment* (Cheltenham, Edward Elgar).

Landmann, O. 2004. "Employment, productivity and output growth", background paper for the *World Employment Report 2004-05*, available on the CD-ROM version.

Little, I.; Mazumdar, D.; Page, J. 1987. *Small manufacturing enterprises: A comparative analysis of India and other economies* (New York, Oxford University Press).

Mazumdar, M. 2004. "Employment elasticity in manufacturing", background paper for the *World Employment Report 2004-05*, available on the CD-ROM version.

McKinsey and Company. 2004. *Offshoring roundtable – transcript* (http://www.mckinsey.com/ideas/offshoring/roundtable/).

Migration News (http://migration.ucdavis.edu/mn).

Miles, I.; Kastrinos, N. 1995. *Knowledge-intensive business services: Users, carriers and sources of innovation* (Luxembourg, Commission of the European Communities, Directorate General for Telecommunications, Information Market and Exploitation of Research, Innovation Programme), EIMS Publication No. 15.

National Productivity Institute. 2003. *Report on the productivity capacity building programme for SMMEs* (South Africa).

OECD. 2004. *Economic outlook* (Paris).

—.2003. *Economic outlook* (Paris).

—.1999. *OECD Economic surveys: Hungary* (Paris).

Palma, G. 2003. *Trade liberalization in Mexico: Its impact on growth, employment and wages* (Geneva, ILO), Employment Paper No. 55.

Parry, R. 2004. "Globalization: Threat or opportunity for the US economy?", in *FRBSF Economic Letter*, No.12, 21 May.

Piacentini, P.; Pini, P. 2000. "Growth and employment", in M. Vivarelli and M. Pianta (eds.): *The employment impact of innovation: Evidence and policy* (London, Routledge).

Pianta, M. 2000. "The employment impact of product and process innovations", in M. Vivarelli and M. Pianta (eds.): *The employment impact of innovation: Evidence and policy* (London, Routledge).

Pieper, U. 2001. *Sectoral regularities of productivity growth in developing countries – A Kaldorian interpretation*, Maastricht Economic Research Institute on Innovation and Technology.

Polaski, S. 2004. *Job anxiety is real – and it's global*, Policy Brief, Carnegie Endowment for International Peace, May.

Román, Z. 2003. "Labour productivity and employment in the Hungarian economy", background paper for the *World Employment Report 2004-05*, unpublished (Geneva, ILO, Employment Sector, Employment Trends Unit).

Sala-i-Martin, X. 2002 *The world distribution of income (estimated from individual country distributions)*, National Bureau of Economic Research, Working Paper No. 8933, May (www.nber.org/papers/w8933).

Schettkat, R.; Russo, G. 2001. "Structural dynamics and employment in highly industrialized economies", in P. Petit and L. Soete (eds.): *Technology and the future of European unemployment* (Cheltenham, Edward Elgar).

Sharpe, A.; St-Hilaire, F.; Banting, K. 2002. *The review of economic performance and social progress: Towards a social understanding of productivity* (Ottawa and Montreal, Institute for Research on Public Policy, Centre for the Study of Living Standards, distributed by McGill-Queens University Press) (www.csls.ca).

Sharpe, A. 2004. "Productivity growth and poverty reduction in developing countries", background paper for the *World Employment Report 2004-05*, available on the CD-ROM version.

Sherwood, M.K. 1994. "Difficulties in the measurement of services", in *Monthly Labour Review*, 11-19 March.

Sperling, G. 2004. *The effects of offshoring*, Progressive Politics, Vol. 3, No. 2, June (http://www.americanprogress.org/site/pp.asp?c=bijrj8ovf&b=105690).

Spezia, V.;Vivarelli, M. 2002. "Innovation and employment: A critical survey," in N. Greenan, Y. L'Horty and I. Mairesse (eds.): *Productivity, inequality and the digital economy* (London, MIT Press).

Spletzer, J.R.; Faberman, R. Jason; Arber, Sadeghi; Talan, David M.; Clayton, Richard L. 2004. "Business employment dynamics: New data on job gains and losses", in *Monthly Labour Review*, pp. 29-42, April.

The Economist. 2004. "The remote future", 19 February.

—. 1997. "One lump or two?", 23 October.

The New York Times. 2004. "Jobs lost abroad: Host of new causes for an old problem", 15 February.

Taylor, G.; Bekabye, M. 1999. *An opportunity for employment creation: Labour based technology roadworks – The macro-economic dimension* (Geneva, ILO), Employment-Intensive Investment Branch Working Paper.

Triplett, J.E.; Bosworth, B.P. 2003. "Productivity measurement issues in service industries: Baumol's disease has been cured", in *FRBNY Economic Policy Review*, September, pp. 23-33.

UN Population Division. 2001. *World population prospects: The 2000 revision* (New York).

US Department of Commerce, Bureau of Economic Analysis. 2004. *National income and product account* (http://www.bea.doc.gov/bea/dn/home/gdp.htm).

US Department of Labor, Bureau of Labor Statistics. 2004a. *Current population survey* (http://data.bls.gov/servlet/SurveyOutputServlet).

—. 2004b. *Current employment statistics* (http://data.bls.gov/servlet/SurveyOutputServlet).

Van Ark, B.; Frankema, E.; Duteweerd, H. 2004. "Productivity and employment growth: An empirical review of long and medium run evidence", background paper for the *World Employment Report 2004-05*, available on the CD-ROM version.

Vandenberg, P. 2004. "Productivity and SMEs: Conceptual and empirical issues related to employment impacts and poverty reduction", background paper for the *World Employment Report 2004-05*, available on the CD-ROM version.

Vivarelli, M. 1995. *The economics of technology and employment: Theory and empirical evidence* (Aldershot, Edward Elgar).

World Bank. 2004. *World Development Indicators 2004* (Washington, DC).

World Income Inequality Database (WIID). 2000. Version 1.0, 12 September, available online at http://www.wider.unu.edu/wiid/wiid.htm

World Commission on the Social Dimension of Globalization. 2004. *A fair globalization: Creating opportunities for all,* (Geneva, ILO).

Appendix 2.1

Methodology and sources for section 2.3 of Chapter 2

The results in table 2.4 of the chapter examine the relationship between productivity, poverty and income distribution. The first step in constructing the database needed to undertake multivariate analysis of the relationship between poverty, labour productivity and income inequality was to select match countries from the Penn World Table and World Income Inequality databases for which Sala-i-Martin (2002) provided poverty rate estimates. The countries for which Gini coefficient time-series were available were then retained for at least ten years. There were only 27 countries left after the selection: 12 in Latin America (Brazil, Chile, Colombia, Costa Rica, Dominican Republic, Ecuador, Jamaica, Mexico, Panama, Peru, El Salvador, Venezuela), 13 in Asia (Bangladesh, China, Hong Kong, Indonesia, India, the Republic of Korea, Sri Lanka, Malaysia, Pakistan, Philippines, Singapore, Thailand, Taiwan (China) and two in Africa (Ethiopia, Tanzania).

Initially, the intention was to undertake a cross-sectional analysis for the years 1970 and 1998 using levels of each of the three variables. But because of the incomplete Gini coefficient time-series, a cross-sectional analysis for the earliest year for which the Gini coefficient was available (and closest to 1970) and another one for the latest year (and closest to 1998) was done. Associating labour productivity levels to Gini coefficients was easy because labour productivity estimates are available for each year from 1970 to 1998. But this was not the case for poverty rates. Therefore, poverty rates had to be assigned to Gini coefficients on the basis of closeness to the years of availability. For example, if the earliest year of availability of a Gini coefficient was 1972, it was assigned the 1970 poverty rate. The Ordinary Least Square procedure and linear functional form were then used to estimate the coefficients.

To study the relationship between variations over time in each variable, the earliest and latest year available were used to calculate average annual growth rates for labour productivity and Gini coefficients and percentage change for the poverty rates. Therefore, the growth rates for some countries were for shorter periods than for others. Then the same statistical procedure was used as that for level comparisons. Some similar regressions were also run with World Bank data for both levels and growth rates, with results broadly supporting those discussed in section 2.3 of this chapter.

Appendix 2.2

Methodology and sources for section 2.5 of Chapter 2

The difference between industry and total economy annual growth rates in productivity and employment was estimated by:

1. Calculating the compounded annual average growth rate in employment and productivity in the particular industry and in the total economy for the same period.
2. Subtracting the growth rate of the total economy from the growth rate of industry to determine the sector's contribution to the total economy.

Thus, the sectoral contribution was obtained as follows:

$$L\hat{Y}_{iC-TC} = (L\hat{Y}_{iC} - L\hat{Y}_{TC}); \text{ and } \hat{E}_{iC-TC} = (\hat{E}_{iC} - \hat{E}_{TC}),$$

where $L\hat{Y}$ = growth in productivity, $\hat{E}$ = growth in employment, í = each sector (transport, trade, manufacturing), T = total economy, and C = particular country.

The above calculations were made for countries with sectoral data available during the period 1980-2001. For some economies data were not available for these specific years, in which case the closest year that data were available was used (see table A2.1).

Table A21.   Sectoral data available by country

Sector	Country	Latest year data available
Transport and communication	Australia	1998
	Brazil	1996
	Canada	1998
	Czech Republic	1998
	France	1998
	United Kingdom	1999
Trade	Australia	1999
	Brazil	1996
	Canada	1998
	France	1999
	Japan	1998
	United Kingdom	1999
Manufacturing	Australia	2000
	Brazil	1998
	China	1999
	Czech Republic	2000
	India	2000
	Spain	2000
	Sweden	2000

3. Why agriculture still matters

3.1. Introduction

In developing countries especially, the performance of the agricultural sector often depends on conditions outside policy-makers' reach. The weather, world prices (depending on how much the world demands of agricultural products and how much the rest of the world produces), external trade barriers and market access all play a role in determining agricultural outcomes. As a result, the agricultural sector is arguably more vulnerable and more dependent on a fair globalization[1] than any other sector. At the same time, most development economists and development agencies agree that neglecting the agricultural sector during the process of industrialization can constrain the development process. This view is supported both analytically and empirically. Economic development needs industrialization but, in many economies, industrialization also requires the development of the agricultural sector. This is certainly true for those developing economies in which agriculture is the main source of employment. The task of formulating sound policies is therefore to find the right balance in fostering the development process in all three sectors (agriculture, industry and services) at the same time.

Added to the importance of the development of the agricultural sector for the development of the economy as a whole is the sector's contribution to reducing poverty. Poverty is a multi-dimensional phenomenon, but with 75 per cent of the world's poor living in rural areas and given that the agricultural sector employs 40 per cent of developing countries' workers and contributes over 20 per cent of their GDP, there is convincing evidence as to why examining this sector is a good starting point for finding solutions to poverty. Moreover, agriculture has the greatest dominance of female employment in the poorest regions of the world. Therefore a focus on this sector can also contribute to greater gender equality in the world of work.

During the 1990s, researchers and policy-makers largely neglected the agricultural sector, while favouring modernization through the development of the manufacturing and service sectors. Declining official investment in agricultural development provides evidence for this trend.[2] Interestingly, this shift away from agriculture went hand in hand with a lower rate of poverty reduction. The main reasons why the sector's potential has been relatively ignored for a decade appear to be a steady decline in commodity prices, in tandem with the increased competition that developing economies face from large agricultural subsidies in the developed world and the related problems of market access. Conventional

---

[1] World Commission on the Social Dimension of Globalization, 2004.

[2] Dorward et al., 2001.

wisdom maintains that these factors make returns in agricultural investment unattractive compared with investment in more modern economic sectors. Yet the intensity with which developing countries have been fighting to persuade developed economies to reduce trade barriers is evidence that the high potential of this sector – particularly for poverty reduction – is once again attracting attention. This renewed awareness is also reflected by international agencies such as the World Bank (2003 and 2004), UNDP (2003) and the UN (2003).[3]

Indeed, agriculture is not only about decreasing commodity prices and subsidies. It is also about employment opportunities and chances for poor people to work themselves out of poverty. Beginning from this basic, human perspective, section 3.2 of this chapter analyses why growth in general matters for poverty reduction and why a focus on growth alone has its limits. Section 3.3 shows that poverty is predominantly a rural phenomenon (at least for the time being) and that the rural poor work mainly in agriculture and increasingly in non-farm activities such as agro-processing and input supply activities. If growth is important for poverty reduction and the poor are mainly in rural areas, it follows that growth in the agricultural sector should have a strong impact on poverty reduction. This argument is advanced in section 3.4. But if there are limitations to a growth focus in general, then agriculture will be similarly limited. By focusing on the two main components of growth, productivity and employment, these limitations can (to some extent) be overcome. Section 3.5 thus argues that productivity growth and employment growth must go hand in hand to maximize the impact on poverty reduction. Section 3.6 draws policy conclusions based on the results of the present analysis and section 3.7 offers some concluding remarks.

3.2. Growth matters for poverty reduction

One central finding established by many development institutions and researchers in the past two decades is that poverty is reduced primarily through economic growth – a finding that has elicited both well- and ill-informed policy prescriptions. Substantial primary research and international agency reports have been devoted to this topic.[4] Early ILO studies acknowledged the large role that economic growth plays in reducing poverty levels, but warned that other factors may intervene to reduce or reinforce the growth effects. While levels of per capita national income are good predictors of poverty in general, many countries have poverty levels that diverge from those predicted on this basis. Considerable scope thus remains for determining anti-poverty policy.[5] The divergence from the expected level of poverty reduction associated with national income attracts various explanations, ranging from the institutional to structural. Whether

---

[3] The UN Economic and Social Council recently called for a wide-ranging integrated approach to rural development. See ECOSOC: Draft Ministerial Declaration, E/2003/L.9. Besides this renewed interest in agriculture, the UN Food and Agriculture Organization (FAO), has for a long time been mandated to focus on the agricultural sector and provides – amongst others – fully detailed, comprehensive analyses of the agricultural sector (see http://www.fao.org).

[4] IFAD, 2001; World Bank, 2001; World Bank, 2002.

[5] Lipton, 1998.

Box 3.1 . The Millennium Development Goals

In September 2000, the United Nations' Member States unanimously adopted the Millennium Declaration. After consultations among international agencies including the World Bank, the International Monetary Fund, the Organisation for Economic Co-operation and Development, and the specialized agencies of the United Nations, the UN General Assembly recognized the Millennium Development Goals as part of the road map for implementing the Millennium Declaration.

The Goals, along with the specific targets set for each, commit the international community to an expanded plan of action aimed at encouraging sustainable and equitable development, one that promotes human development as the cornerstone for sustaining social and economic progress, and recognizes the importance of creating a global partnership for development. The goals and related targets, set out below, have been commonly accepted as a framework for measuring development progress.

Eradicate extreme poverty and hunger

Target 1: Halve, between 1990 and 2015, the proportion of people whose income is less than US$1 a day.

Target 2: Halve, between 1990 and 2015, the proportion of people who suffer from hunger.

Achieve universal primary education

Target 3: Ensure that, by 2015, children everywhere, boys and girls alike, will be able to complete a full course of primary schooling.

Promote gender equality and empower women

Target 4: Eliminate gender disparity in primary and secondary education, preferably by 2005, and at all levels of education no later than 2015.

Reduce child mortality

Target 5: Reduce by two-thirds, between 1990 and 2015, the under-five mortality rate.

Improve maternal health

Target 6: Reduce by three-quarters, between 1990 and 2015, the maternal mortality ratio.

Combat HIV/AIDS, malaria, and other diseases

Target 7: Have halted by 2015 and begun to reverse the spread of HIV/AIDS.

Target 8: Have halted by 2015 and begun to reverse the incidence of malaria and other major diseases.

Ensure environmental sustainability

Target 9: Integrate the principles of sustainable development into country policies and programmes and reverse the losses of environmental resources.

Target 10: Halve by 2015 the proportion of people without sustainable access to safe drinking water and basic sanitation.

Target 11: Have achieved by 2020 a significant improvement in the lives of at least 100 million slum dwellers.

Develop a global partnership for development

Target 12: Develop further an open, rule-based, predictable, non-discriminatory trading and financial system. Includes: a commitment to good governance, development, and poverty reduction – both nationally and internationally.

Target 13: Address the special needs of the least developed countries. Includes: tariff and quota-free access for least-developed countries' exports; enhanced programme of debt relief for HIPCs and cancellation of official bilateral debt; and more generous ODA for countries committed to poverty reduction.

Target 14: Address the special needs of landlocked countries and small-island developing states (through the Programme of Action for the Sustainable Development of Sm

all Island Developing States and the outcome of the twenty-second special session of the General Assembly).

Target 15: Deal comprehensively with the debt problems of developing countries through national and international measures.

Target 16: In cooperation with developing countries, develop and implement strategies for decent and productive work for youth.

Target 17: In cooperation with pharmaceutical companies, provide access to affordable essential drugs in developing countries.

Target 18: In cooperation with the private sector, make available the benefits of new technologies, especially information and communications.

Source: http://www.un.org/millenniumgoals/

growth is likely to be pro-poor is not seriously at issue: the question is, to what degree is it pro-poor and can its pro-poor effects be increased?[6]

The debate on how important growth is for poverty reduction has two opposing camps: those who contend that any kind of growth will help the poor and those who argue that growth is often accompanied by increasing inequality and that, despite growth, the poor may become even poorer.[7] This chapter takes the middle ground and reasons that growth will reduce poverty in most cases.

Poverty was the main theme when world leaders gathered at the Millennium Summit in 2000 to pledge their support for the Millennium Declaration. The first Goal adopted was to halve the share of extreme poor in the world by 2015 (see box 3.1). The underlying question with respect to the Millennium Development Goal on poverty is not whether growth reduces poverty but whether growth alone is sufficient to reach the goals. Two issues are at stake here. First, economic growth was slower in the 1990s compared to earlier decades in most developing economies so there is a need to enhance growth. Second, despite solid growth rates, some economies and regions have clearly performed below their potential in reducing poverty (see box 3.2). What occurred in

[6] See, for example, various works in http://www.worldbank.org/poverty/inequal/themgrp/index
[7] See Ahluwalia (1976), for an early account of the second viewpoint and, more recently, Lübker (2002).

these areas and how can we ensure that future growth will be translated into poverty reduction?

3.3. Poverty is a predominantly rural phenomenon

Even though many developing economies are becoming more and more urbanized, according to the UN Population Division, the rural population still comprised 59.5 per cent of the total population in less developed regions in 2000 (with an estimate of 56.8 per cent for 2005) and in the least developed economies the share was even higher at 74.8 per cent in 2000 and 72.3 per cent in 2005. Despite ongoing structural transformations in many of these economies, around 75 per cent of the poor still live in rural areas (IFAD, 2001). Figure 3.1 shows the positive correlation between poverty rates and percentages of rural populations.

Figure 3.1.   US$1 and US$2 a day poverty vs. rural population rates, 1978-2002

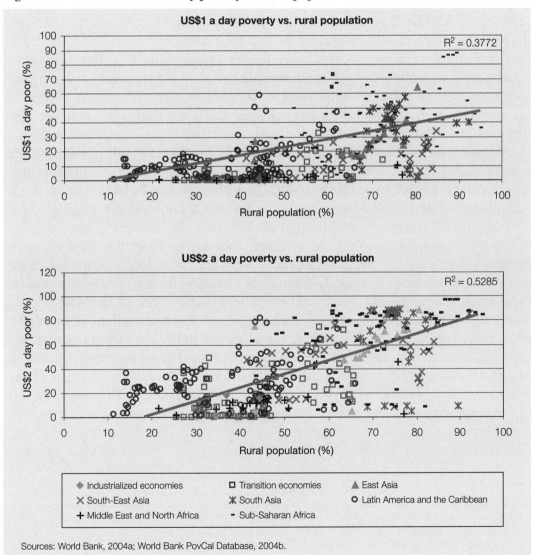

Sources: World Bank, 2004a; World Bank PovCal Database, 2004b.

Large shares of rural populations tend to be associated with higher poverty rates. While most of the rural poor (around 68 per cent) live in South and East Asia, sub-Saharan Africa is inhabited by 24 per cent of the world's rural poor. Locating where most of the poor live is the first step to finding solutions to reduce poverty.

In terms of employment, in 65 out of the 162 developing economies for which employment data are available by sector, the agricultural sector is still the main employer[8] (box 3.2 gives an empirical snapshot of the agricultural output and labour share by region over time). This is especially the case in sub-Saharan Africa, where on average more than six out of ten people work in this sector. In economies such as Gambia the agricultural share in employment is likely to be over 80 per cent. The share is also high in Asia where around five out of ten people work in agriculture. On the other hand, in the Middle East and North Africa only two out of ten people work in agriculture, and in Latin America and the Caribbean only between one and two out of ten people are employed in agriculture. In the Middle East and North Africa, this is mainly the result of the low share of agricultural employment in the oil-producing economies. In Latin America and the Caribbean, the figure masks a wide range of differently structured economies, but for many economies in the region agriculture still plays an important role in terms of employment. (For those economies with a share in agricultural employment larger than 40 per cent, see figure 3.2 and see also Chapter 1 of this Report.)

In addition to the fact that the poor live in rural areas and that agriculture is most likely the main source of employment in poor countries, it is obvious that jobs in rural areas are most likely in the agricultural sector. In India, for example, agriculture-related employment in the mid-1990s accounted for around 70 per cent of total rural employment (Fan et al., 1999; see also box 3.5 in section 3.4 of this chapter). Finally, although the available data are quite limited, there is some evidence that poor people living in rural areas are more likely to work in agriculture than non-poor people. In China, for example, 87 per cent of the poor in rural areas are employed in agriculture, whereas the share of the non-poor in rural areas working in agriculture is 72 per cent.[9] Another salient point is that women are typically more likely than men to work in the agricultural sector. For example, women in rural Africa produce, process and store up to 80 per cent of foodstuffs, while in South and South-East Asia they undertake 60 per cent of cultivation work and other food production (UNIFEM, 2000).[10] This might be one of the main reasons why poverty among women is higher than among men.

---

[8] There is a correlation between the availability of data and GDP per capita; the poorer an economy is, the less likely it is to report data. Given this fact, it is also likely that the share of agriculture-dominated economies would be much higher if data were available for all developing economies.

[9] Khan and Riskin, 1998.

[10] See ILO (2004) for more details on female employment in agriculture.

Figure 3.2.   Sectoral distribution of employment, economies with a share in agricultural employment > 40 per cent, latest available year

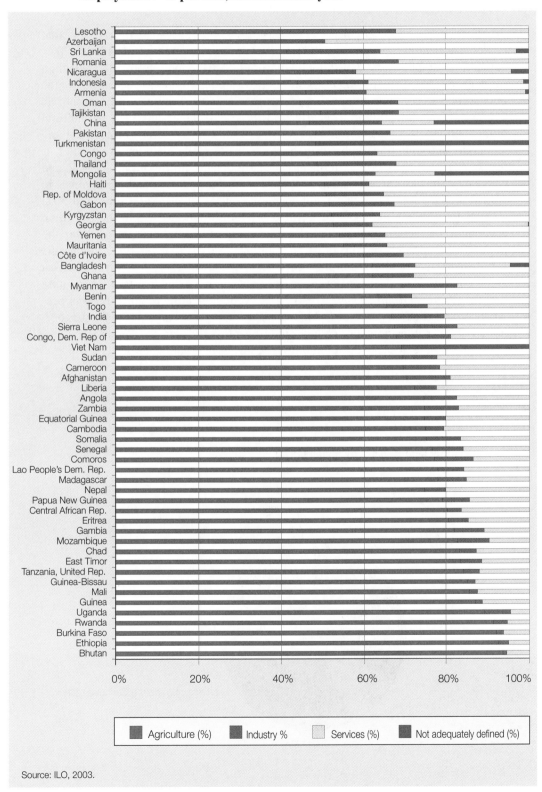

Source: ILO, 2003.

Box 3.2. Global shifts in levels and shares of agricultural output and labour, an empirical snapshot

What has happened to agriculture in the past three decades? An analysis of the state of global agricultural production and trends over time shows that from 1970 to 2000, agricultural output in the world doubled, from US$ 645.9 billion to US$ 1.3 trillion (in constant 1990 dollars). In the same period, labour input (as measured by the population of economically active persons in agriculture) increased by around 40 per cent – from 898 million to nearly 1.3 trillion persons in 2000. The agricultural output and labour shares of different regions in total agricultural world output and labour are shown in the graphs accompanying this box. The main feature of the pattern of change is the increase in the global share of agricultural output for Asia and China over the past three decades. At the same time, the shares of labour involved in agriculture in these areas have not increased by as much. Yet China and Asia account for a major share of the world's agricultural labour. Within the transition economies, the agricultural output share in the world has almost halved over the period and the labour share is down to one-third of its 1970 level. Even though the world share in agricultural output hasn't changed considerably for North America and accounted for 16 per cent of the world's output in 2000, it is interesting to note that the labour share in 2000 was below 1 per cent, indicating the high level of productivity in agriculture in North America. The same is obviously true for Europe. For all other regions no major changes in terms of world shares were observed during the past three decades, either in output shares or in labour shares.

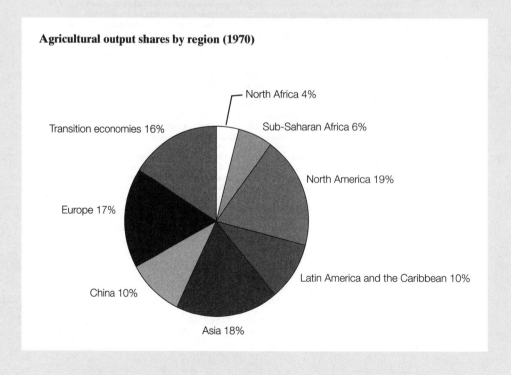

Agricultural output shares by region (1970)

North Africa 4%

Sub-Saharan Africa 6%

Transition economies 16%

North America 19%

Europe 17%

Latin America and the Caribbean 10%

China 10%

Asia 18%

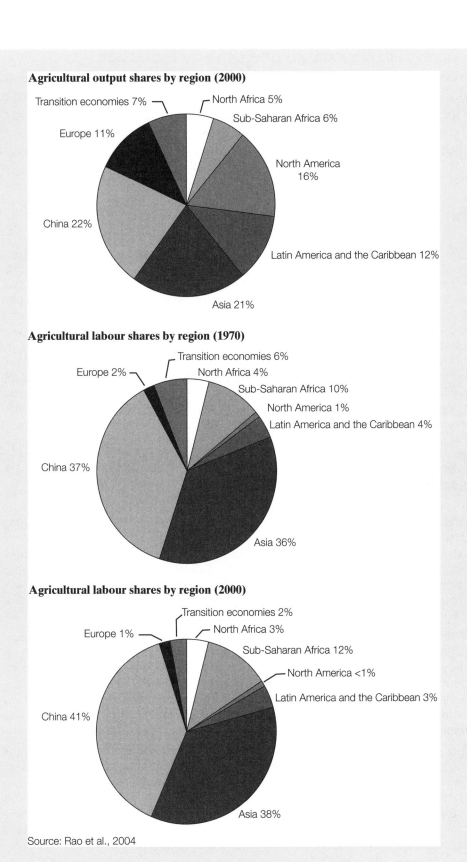

Agricultural output shares by region (2000)

Transition economies 7% — North Africa 5%
Sub-Saharan Africa 6%
Europe 11%
North America 16%
China 22%
Latin America and the Caribbean 12%
Asia 21%

Agricultural labour shares by region (1970)

Transition economies 6%
Europe 2% — North Africa 4%
Sub-Saharan Africa 10%
North America 1%
Latin America and the Caribbean 4%
China 37%
Asia 36%

Agricultural labour shares by region (2000)

Transition economies 2%
Europe 1% — North Africa 3%
Sub-Saharan Africa 12%
North America <1%
Latin America and the Caribbean 3%
China 41%
Asia 38%

Source: Rao et al., 2004

3.4. Growth in agriculture and poverty reduction

If poverty is largely rural and rural employment is mainly in agriculture, then it seems likely that the parts of the growth process that are linked to rural areas, and especially those related to agriculture, may have more immediate and direct effects on poverty reduction than would growth outside rural areas. Once this is established empirically – through a deconstruction of the growth process – it is

---

Box 3.3. Poverty measurements and the incidence of poverty around the world

World and regional poverty estimates vary greatly depending on the underlying methodologies employed in generating country-level poverty estimates. Three estimates of poverty are used throughout this chapter, each measuring US$1 and US$2 a day poverty rates and counts. The first set of estimates comes from the World Bank, as presented in Chen and Ravallion (2001). The second is an estimate done by the ILO that seeks to improve the former by detecting and correcting inconsistencies between survey and national accounts data (Karshenas, 2004). A third estimate based on work by Sala-i-Martin (2002) is also used in the analysis because it provides poverty figures for a wide selection of countries since the 1970s. Though the Sala-i-Martin data provide a longer period over which to measure trends in poverty, the methodology used to construct the data (which is exclusively national accounts-based) differs greatly from the methodology employed by the World Bank and ILO (which provide household survey-based estimates). This is the main reason why this box focuses on trends in poverty according to the World Bank and ILO figures. Whenever a longer-term perspective is needed for the analysis in this chapter, the Sala-i-Martin data are used.

There are differences between the ILO and World Bank estimates of overall poverty in the world. US$1 a day poverty was around 1.13 billion in 1987, which declined to 1.04 billion in 1998 based on ILO estimates. Comparative figures based on World Bank estimates are 1.18 billion in 1987 and 1.17 billion in 1998. So there has been weak decline in poverty on one estimate and a slightly more pronounced decline in the other. In terms of trends in poverty rates themselves, based on both data sets there has been a clear decline in the period from 1987 to 1998. The rate of decline has slowed in the more recent years.

While overall differences between the two estimates of poverty are not very large, regional estimates do vary. In this regard it is necessary to look at the distribution of the poor in the world. The salient difference between the regional distribution of the poor between the two sources is that in the ILO estimates the share of South Asia (29 per cent) in the global poor in 1998 is much lower compared to the World Bank estimates (44 per cent), while the share of China's poverty is higher in the ILO estimates (30 per cent) than in the World Bank estimates (18 per cent).

The ILO data suggest a decline in poverty rates in all regions except sub-Saharan Africa between 1987 and 1998. The South Asian sub-region however shows an increase in poverty rates between 1996 and 1998. In contrast the World Bank data show declining poverty rates in all regions except Latin America and sub-Saharan Africa over the period from 1987 to 1998. Overall both datasets are in agreement that, over the 1987 to 1998 period, poverty in sub-Saharan Africa has been increasing while China has realised the greatest amount of poverty reduction.

then essential to find out how to encourage growth in this sector and to identify the specific mechanisms through which growth can be linked to poverty reduction.

Deconstructing the growth process

Poverty rates, by and large, have fallen over the past three decades, though the decline in the 1990s has been more modest than in the two previous decades (see box 3.3 and Majid, 2004). It is clear that China is driving much of the poverty reduction in the developing world, while in sub-Saharan Africa poverty has increased. The overall slowdown in poverty reduction could jeopardize the poverty targets set forth in the Millennium Development Goals (see Chapter 1 of this Report). Moreover, although agricultural output growth was reasonably robust in the past three decades, it has been limited on a per capita basis in the developing world. As expected, the per capita output trends in China and sub-Saharan Africa are consistent with observed poverty trends: China's agricultural output per capita increased with decreasing poverty, while poverty in sub-Saharan Africa increased with decreasing agricultural output per capita.

There is clearly some evidence suggesting a linkage between poverty reduction and agricultural growth, but a further investigation is needed on the question of the relative importance of agricultural growth in comparison to other sectors in the economy for poverty reduction. Discussions on the importance of rural poverty and agricultural development are not new. These were preponderant in the development literature that emerged during and after the "green revolution" in the 1970s. The reason this primacy of agriculture argument is important to reiterate in the present policy environment of developing countries is precisely because agriculture has too often taken a secondary or tertiary role in development strategies. (For a summary of the arguments showing the linkages between agricultural development and development of the economy as a whole, see box 3.4.)

With increased data availability, some recent research[11] concentrates on the distributional effects of growth and shows fairly rigorously the immediate or short-run effects of growth on income distributions (which are not major) and the longer-run effect of growth on distribution, especially on the poor (which may be worsening) for developing countries. This research also shows that it is the structural features of an economy – and the importance of the agriculture sector in particular – which influence what happens to the poor in the long run. These findings have important implications for the sustainability of poverty-reducing growth strategies. In particular it has been shown that agricultural growth is more poverty-alleviating than non-agricultural growth in countries where the gap between the rich and poor is not extreme.[12]

---

[11] See Timmer, 1997.
[12] See Warr, 2002.

Box 3.4. The importance of the agricultural sector in the development process

For a long time, economists saw the main role of agriculture as the supply of labour for the industrialized sectors and, indeed, it is a necessary precondition for the development process. But by emphasizing this as the only important contribution, other significant functions of the agricultural sector tend to be overlooked.

Agriculture as provider of food

Just as important as providing the labour force for other sectors is that the agricultural sector has to be able to feed an expanding urban labour force. In other words, it must be capable of producing an agricultural surplus. This is only possible if productivity in the agricultural sector rises, as more food now needs to be produced by less people. In other words an "agrarian revolution" has to take place alongside the industrialization process. Developing countries cannot afford to become dependent on food imports (especially in early stages of development), as the imported goods are usually more expensive than those produced within the country (because of transportation costs and due to monopolistic market structures). The demand for agricultural goods increases with growing GDP per capita during the process of industrialization. Even if Engel's law (that the demand for agricultural commodities does not grow as fast as the demand for other goods with growing income) is taken into account, the demand does rise. The fast-growing population in most developing countries adds to the increasing demand for agricultural goods. If the agricultural sector is not capable of producing enough to meet rising demand, there is the risk of inflation, which can be a constraint for the development process itself (so-called structural inflation). Only if this risk is kept under control by supporting the agricultural sector as much as the modern sector can the process of industrialization be successful.

Agriculture as contributor to modern sector development or exporter

If the agricultural sector produces a commodity required as an input in other sectors, it should be supplied to these sectors when demand rises – which will be the case in the process of industrialization. If the agricultural sector produces an export commodity, its contribution to the development process is to provide the modern sectors with the imported capital goods that the agricultural sector receives for exporting its product.

Agriculture as demand sector

If one of the two above scenarios occurs, the agricultural sector also has the potential to become a market for goods produced in the modern sector. This is especially important for countries where the industrial sector does not (yet) produce for export markets. If the agricultural sector becomes a significant market for the modern sector, this guarantees that, further into the development process, the economy does not become as dependent on external markets as is the case for many developing countries. Such independence can protect an economy against vulnerabilities in the international environment.

Agriculture as contributor to financial sector

If the agricultural sector develops in parallel to the modern sector, it increases savings within this sector that can be offered to the industrial sector. It thereby contributes to the necessary accumulation of capital in the modern sector, again making it less dependent on foreign capital. This point might not seem very realistic for most developing countries, as the saving quota of the agricultural sector is rather low. But that can change if policies focus on institutional monetary deficits.

Agriculture as a last resort in times of crisis

Finally, in many developing countries without social safety nets, the agricultural sector is a last resort for those who seek work in times of economic slowdown. Even though the jobs people find during periods of economic stagnation might not be well paid (mainly because of low productivity), this should not be used as an argument against the sector's contribution during difficult periods. But it should be made clear that this can only be a short-term solution. In the long run, the focus should be on increasing productivity and thereby wages in agriculture.

Sources: Irz et al., 2001; Hemmer, 2000.

This point will now be illustrated at a broad macro level. Looking at decadal changes in poverty rates and sector value added for the three sectors (controlling for change in GDP per capita), it is clear that changes in agricultural value added have generally been significantly associated with poverty reduction in the 1970s and 1980s, when the greatest poverty reduction took place. These effects are represented graphically in figure 3.3.[13] This does not imply that one should ignore the many other possible factors that contributed to poverty reduction over this period, but rather that growth in agriculture appears to have been systematically important.[14]

The simple illustration on a regional basis for the Sala-i-Martin poverty data shows the strength of the agricultural coefficient more in the Asian and sub-Saharan Africa cases. In sub-Saharan Africa, a 1 percentage point increase in agricultural output was associated with a reduction in poverty of 0.2 percentage points in the 1970s and 0.13 percentage points in the 1980s (figure 3.3c). In Asia, it was almost 0.6 percentage points in the 1970s and slightly over 0.1 percentage points in the 1980s (figure 3.3d). On the other hand, based on this empirical work, no conclusive case can be made for an agricultural growth and poverty reduction linkage in Latin America. Rather, in the Latin American case, growth in the service sector during the 1970s was most associated with poverty reduction (figure 3.3b). The large land distribution inequalities in Latin America could be the main reason for this result (see figure 3.4).

In no case does manufacturing growth show a direct, significant association with poverty reduction. This also makes sense: growth in manufacturing is more likely to be capital- and not labour-intensive. For this reason, manufacturing-led

---

[13] The same is also true of services growth in the 1970s.

[14] The results of the following analysis differed depending on the poverty measure used but overall the results were consistent, whether Sali-i-Martin or the ILO or World Bank poverty data were used. The results for the estimates with World Bank poverty data are not shown in this chapter as they were very similar to those of the ILO poverty estimates.

**Figure 3.3.   Change in poverty associated with 1 percentage point increase in sector value
added growth rate, selected years**

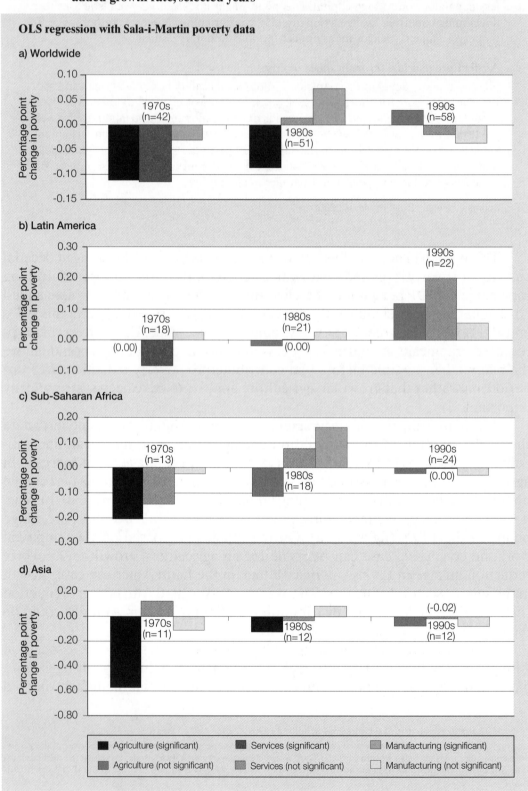

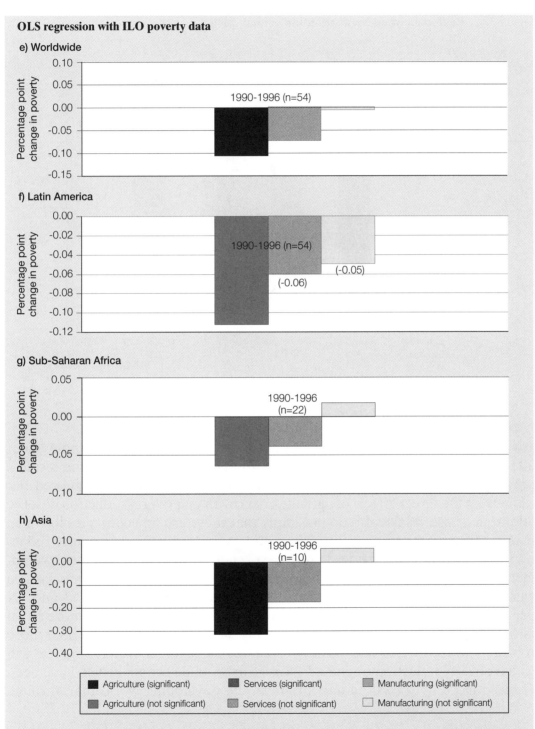

OLS regression with ILO poverty data

e) Worldwide

f) Latin America

g) Sub-Saharan Africa

h) Asia

Legend:
- Agriculture (significant)
- Services (significant)
- Manufacturing (significant)
- Agriculture (not significant)
- Services (not significant)
- Manufacturing (not significant)

Note: Figures a) b) c) and d) are for various years in the 1970s, 1980s and 1990s. Figures e) f), g) and h) are for various years in the 1990s. Dark colours (as compared to light colours) represent statistically significant coefficients at less than 10 per cent. As an example of how to read these figures, figure a) shows that in the 1970s growth in both agriculture and services were negatively associated with poverty, that is, poverty tended to decrease with an increase in output in agriculture and services. The magnitude of the effect was slightly larger in the case of services than in agriculture. Manufacturing output growth was also negatively associated with poverty, but the result was not statistically significant. N is the number of countries for which data were available. All regressions use ordinary least squares (OLS) techniques, which are used in this case to provide the best "fit" to the data in determining the relationship between poverty and growth in different sectors.

Figure 3.4.   Regional ownership distribution of land, 2000

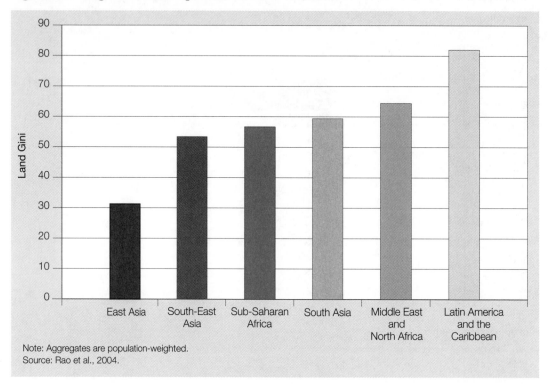

Note: Aggregates are population-weighted.
Source: Rao et al., 2004.

growth is unlikely to have large first-order employment effects. If employment effects are indeed the most direct way to lift people out of poverty, the result is not surprising. This is not to say that manufacturing can or should be ignored, but rather that the direct effects of agricultural growth on poverty reduction deserve attention. These results also do not imply that there are no economies in which manufacturing growth contributed to employment growth and poverty reduction. This can and indeed does happen, especially at later stages in the development process when agriculture becomes less important for the economy as a whole. Nevertheless, taken together, the results shown in figures 3.3 and 3.4 demonstrate that growth in agriculture does indeed matter and that more equal initial distributional conditions make the impact of this growth on the poor more robust. [15] Moreover, the ILO poverty estimates suggest that even for the 1990s in which poverty reduction stagnated, a case can be made for poverty to have been reduced more by growth in agriculture in the developing world than through

---

[15] The land distribution inequality is most dramatically illustrated with the case of Brazil. Rural workers include independent small farmers, sharecroppers, tenant farmers and agricultural day labourers, who are the country's poorest and most vulnerable sector, depending on the land to produce the crops that are their livelihood. Yet, at last count, 40 per cent of farmers shared 1 per cent of the land, while the richest 20 per cent owned 88 per cent of the land. Despite an attempt at land reform during the 1990s, land tenure has not become more equitable over the last two decades. The Landless Workers' Movement (MST) estimates that there are 20 million landless people in Brazil (4 million families), while 7 million more barely survive as squatters, sharecroppers, and migrant workers (Cassel and Patel, 2003).

growth in other sectors. This result is driven by Asia and more specifically China (see also box 3.7). This chapter therefore suggests that if there is a specific type of sectoral growth that will best directly assist in the achievement of the Millennium Development Goals on poverty reduction, it is through the agricultural sector. [16]

Major factors determining agricultural output growth

The importance of land, labour and technical investment (such as fertilizers and tractors) for growth in agriculture is clear, and an empirical snapshot of what happened to these factors during the last decades is helpful in understanding overall trends in agriculture. Figures 3.5 to 3.9 show trends in output and factor use indices for the developing regions of the world, estimated on a five-year basis from 1970 to 2000. The input indices shown for land, labour, fertilizer and tractors display growth normalized to one in 1970, and do not reflect levels of factor use. Clearly, as these are technical factor indices, they also do not show the institutional and societal contexts of output growth.

For China, the results indicate a spectacular growth performance since 1980. Output grew more than 400 per cent over this period, or roughly twice the growth of the total world agriculture index. The rest of Asia also shows an increase, while a more modest increase took place in other regions (figure 3.5).

Breaking down output growth into the components in the Chinese case, it is clear that land, labour and fertilizer use have all shown marked, sustained growth (although the latter two showed slower rates of growth more recently) while growth in tractor use tapered off after the mid-1980s. Carefully interpreted, this might give an indication that China's agricultural development during the past two decades was not purely led by shedding labour and replacing it with machines. It is also interesting to look at sub-Saharan Africa, whose very modest growth in output was coupled with a clear stagnation or worsening in land, fertilizer and tractor use and a massive increase in labour use. The increase of labour in the context of stagnating complementary inputs and low output growth suggests a worsening employment situation for agricultural workers in the region.

From figures 3.5 to 3.9 it might appear that output growth in agriculture has been very large in the past three decades. However, in reality the growth in agricultural output and also in the value of crops measured per person has been rather modest in most parts of the developing world. It has stagnated in sub-Saharan Africa (figures 3.10 and 3.11).

---

[16] Importantly, this broad-level analysis does not directly address the key issue of the composition of agricultural growth – that is, whether it is productivity- or employment-led growth that matters most for poverty reduction. This is discussed in section 3.5.

Figure 3.5.   Output by region, 1970-2000

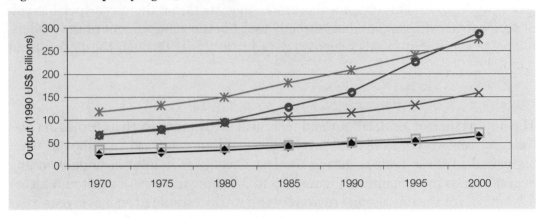

Figure 3.6.   Land index by region, 1970-2000

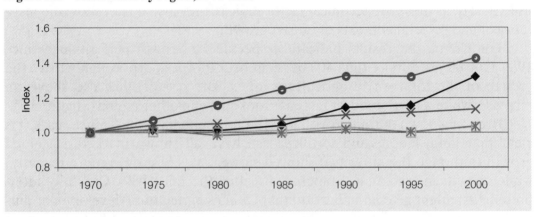

Figure 3.7.   Labour index by region, 1970-2000

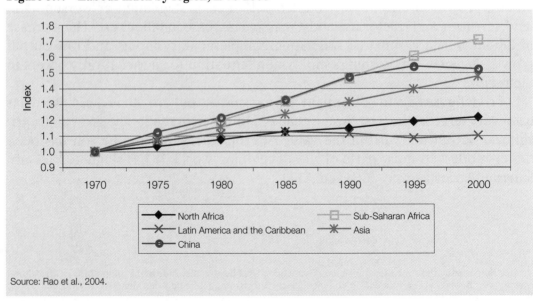

Source: Rao et al., 2004.

Figure 3.8. Fertilizer index by region, 1970-2000

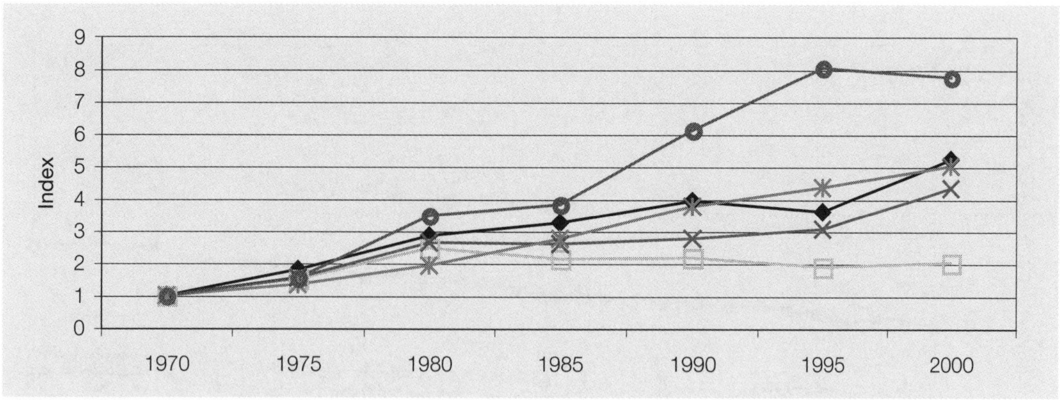

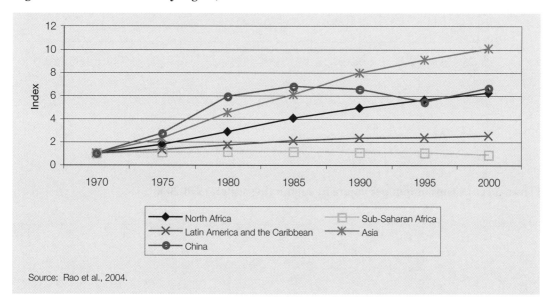

Figure 3.9. Tractor index by region, 1970-2000

Source: Rao et al., 2004.

Some linkages between agricultural growth and poverty reduction: The availability of food and rural non-farm-activities

Whereas the previous section showed that growth in agriculture is the result of a combination of inputs – labour being one of them – this section now looks at two major links between growth and poverty reduction. For sound development strategies, it is important to understand precisely how growth in output can lead to improvements in living standards for the poor. There are both direct and indirect ways in which growth in agriculture can help reduce poverty. This section discusses the direct effects of increased food production and changes in food prices on poverty, as well as the poverty-reducing indirect effects that agricultural growth can potentiate, by stimulating the creation and expansion of new non-farm income-generating activities in rural areas.

Figure 3.10. Agricultural output per capita by region (log scale), 1970-2000

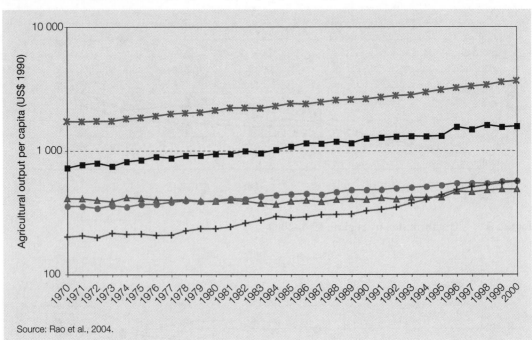

Source: Rao et al., 2004.

Figure 3.11. Crops output per capita by region (log scale), 1970-2000

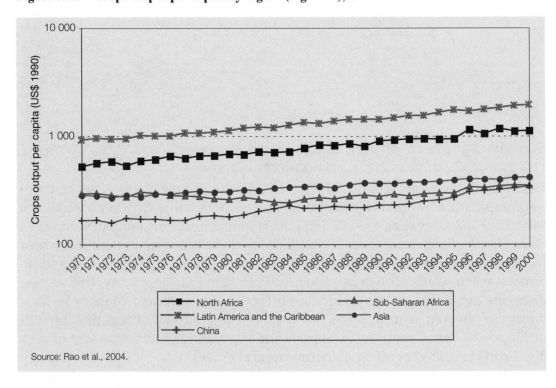

Source: Rao et al., 2004.

Box 3.5. A favourable monsoon contributes to the economic boom in India

While the share of India's agricultural sector in total output has declined substantially over the past 30 years, agriculture still comprises over 20 per cent of GDP, compared with only around 2 per cent of output in the OECD countries. As a result, overall economic growth in the world's second most populous country is greatly influenced by the performance of its agricultural sector. India's current economic boom highlights this fact: the more than 10 per cent GDP growth rate the country is now experiencing comes on the heels of a record monsoon which has fuelled a substantial rise in agricultural output.

Given the structure of employment in the country, India's prospects for reducing poverty are directly linked to the performance of the agricultural sector: an estimated 70 per cent of the country's population, comprising mainly the lower range of the income spectrum, relies on agriculture for a living. Several studies have found that among a range of government expenditures which all had a positive impact on poverty reduction, productivity-enhancing investments in agriculture have had a particularly strong and significant impact on reducing extreme US$1 a day poverty in the country. Spending on agricultural research and development (R&D) designed to increase agricultural productivity has been 2.5 times more effective than spending on education, ten times more effective than spending on irrigation, and over 3 times more effective than general rural development expenditures in terms of reducing poverty. Overall in South Asia, the World Bank estimates that it costs on average about US$179 in additional agricultural R&D to raise yields sufficient to lift one person out of US$1 a day poverty. The only type of investment with greater overall poverty-reducing effects has been road infrastructure, which is also linked with productivity in the country's agricultural sector.

Productivity-enhancing investments have translated into income gains among the country's poor farmers. The World Bank estimates that average real incomes of small farmers and landless labourers in southern India increased by 90 per cent and 125 per cent respectively during 20 years of the "green revolution". The country's current monsoon-led agricultural boom is forecast to boost rural incomes further and aid in reducing poverty. For sustainable poverty reduction to continue in the long run, however, productivity in India's agricultural sector must continue to rise.

Sources: World Bank, 2000; Byerlee and Alex, 2002.

A central result of agricultural growth, namely the greater amount of food produced per person, is particularly relevant for poverty reduction. Because the rural poor have very few assets and usually work as casual labourers, sharecroppers or very small-scale operators, a greater availability of food output is indicative of a better potential position of the rural poor, particularly when the poor themselves have to purchase food.[17] Consequently the supply of food within a country, which admittedly reflects cropping patterns and price-driven incentive structures, can also be seen as a measure of greater proximity to food for the poor who work within the agricultural sector. To this end, there have been dramatically different regional trends in the index of food production per capita as

[17] IFAD, 2001.

Figure 3.12.   Food per person index (1990=100), 1970-2000

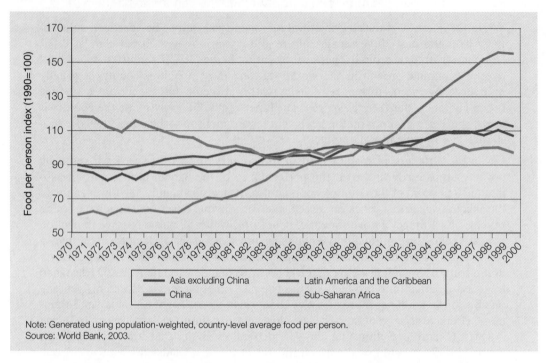

Note: Generated using population-weighted, country-level average food per person.
Source: World Bank, 2003.

Figure 3.13.   Regional population-weighted food price index (1995=100), 1980-2000

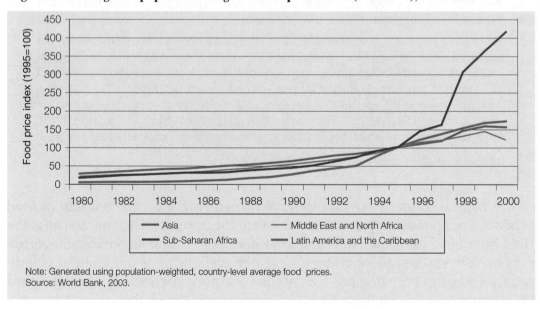

Note: Generated using population-weighted, country-level average food prices.
Source: World Bank, 2003.

figure 3.12 shows. Asia's position has continued to improve on this indicator and much of this improvement is based on results in East Asia, particularly in China. Moreover, given the worsening poverty trends in sub-Saharan Africa, the stagnation in food per person visible in this region suggests that food supply per capita is a reasonable indicator of vulnerability to poverty.

Looking in addition at the food price index across the regions in figure 3.13, important trends become clear. Asia has had a gradual increase in food prices yet these have not outstripped the per capita food supply trend. In this case (and particularly in China), rural income has steadily increased, pushing food prices upwards. There is a slightly greater rise in the food price index in the Latin American region. This could be due to the very high rural-to-urban migration, which has put pressure on the food supply for the increasingly urban population. In sub-Saharan Africa the food price increases in the 1990s have been extremely high. This fact, in conjunction with the deteriorating trends in food availability per capita, indicates the strong likelihood of anti-poor agricultural trends in the region. Finding the right balance between food price increases and food price stability has to be of concern for policy-makers. If prices grow too quickly, those poor people who consume these goods might suffer. If on the other hand prices do not rise, producers might have no incentive to invest, which can have negative impacts on employment creation. This is especially true for those who export their goods.

While food output and prices are special policy foci within a pro-poor agricultural growth strategy, the case for agricultural growth for poverty reduction also has some forceful supporting arguments. While poverty is largely rural, and agriculture is a major part of the rural economy, other activities within the rural economy can be stimulated by agricultural growth. Rural non-farm activities (NFA) are often included in the income-generating activities of households, and this is also true for poor households engaged in agriculture.[18] Examples of these activities include own-account (domestic) services, construction, education, food processing and sales, public administration and manufacturing, among others. It is estimated that non-farm sources account for 40 to 45 per cent of average rural household income in sub-Saharan Africa and Latin America, and 30 to 40 per cent in South Asia.[19] In India the range is from 25 to 35 per cent of rural income, according to IFAD (2001). Non-farm activities also account for a substantial share of employment among the rural population.[20] On average in developing countries, around 30 per cent of total rural employment is found in NFA. In Asia, NFA employment accounts for 44 per cent of rural employment and is growing twice as fast as farm employment in some countries, according to IFAD (2001). Non-farm activities represent at least 30 per cent of rural employment in Latin America. Looking at some economies also illustrates the importance of NFA employment in developing countries. For example, in China 34 per cent of the employment in rural areas was outside the agricultural sector in 2000.[21] In India, the share of employment in NFA has also increased

---

[18] Chuta and Liedholm, 1981; Saith, 1992; Lanjouw and Lanjouw, 1995.

[19] Start, 2001.

[20] Rural employment in NFA may be underestimated, since employment in most cases refers only to agricultural employment. In addition, jobs common among female labourers (clothing production, food processing, and education for the household) are not remunerated in most developing countries and therefore not included in employment figures.

[21] Johnson, 2002.

considerably, representing 29 per cent for males and 15 per cent for females in 2000.[22] In Viet Nam in 1993 the share was even higher, with 70 per cent of total rural employment being in NFA.[23]

The NFA sector can promote growth and improve rural welfare in several important ways. In a situation in which the rural workforce is increasing at a rate higher than employment in agriculture, non-farm activities can lower rural unemployment and underemployment and reduce pressures associated with rural-to-urban migration. Apart from the sector itself being a large market for agricultural output, growth in agriculture in the presence of a supported NFA sector can allow for the consumption of commodities and services produced in the NFA sector, thereby potentially providing important multiplier effects, both for rural employment and rural welfare overall.

Yet a survey of the issue done for the 1995 *World Development Report*[24] argued that support to this sector is undertaken largely within the context of an overall policy framework that is biased against the sector. Given the diversity of the rural non-farm sector, it is difficult to give a broad policy perspective. While independent efforts to support the sector may have dividends in themselves, it is important to recognize that the role of the sector in poverty reduction is likely to come into proper play when there is reasonable growth in agriculture. An important question when considering the potential contribution of NFA to development is whether such activities are efficient – in a local context – in terms of converting resources into output. Some non-farm activities may provide workers with low returns in relation to casual agricultural wage labour. Nevertheless, these new employment opportunities may be the starting point for people beginning to work themselves out of poverty and enhance their economic security.

3.5. The impact of productivity and employment on poverty reduction

The discussion so far has shown that agricultural development and growth is crucial for immediate and sustainable poverty reduction and that it is often even more important than growth in other sectors of the economy; that this growth also has supplementary multipliers within the rural areas; and that the role of food production and food price trends within agricultural development may be of particular focus within an agricultural growth-driven poverty reduction strategy.

Besides these factors, two other components contribute to growth: productivity and employment. It is often falsely argued that there is a negative trade-off between the two but, as shown in Chapter 2 of this Report, this is not necessarily the case. In fact, it is the complementary character of these two components on the aggregate level that drives growth in the long run. But is this also the case for

---

[22] Kundu et al., 2003.

[23] Lanjouw and Lanjouw, 2001.

[24] ibid.

the agricultural sector by itself? To answer this question, the focus now shifts to the relationships between productivity and employment creation in agriculture and poverty reduction.

Productivity in the agricultural sector: Is there a linkage with poverty?

Productivity – whether labour productivity or total factor productivity – is about how efficiently resources are used to generate economic growth. Given that growth reduces poverty and productivity contributes to growth, it is worthwhile to look closer at productivity in general and – for the specific focus of this chapter – at productivity in the agricultural sector and how it relates to poverty reduction. [25]

Figure 3.14 gives a systematic view of labour productivity in agriculture by region (see also Chapter 1 of this Report). The figure is not only informative with respect to growth trends in labour productivity but also with respect to labour productivity levels. Latin American levels of labour productivity are the highest in the developing world, followed by the Middle East and North Africa and the transition economies. East Asia, South Asia and sub-Saharan Africa all have considerably lower average labour productivity figures (for specific details on sub-Saharan Africa, see box 3.6). At the same time, these are the regions in which the largest number of the world's poor live.

Looking at the labour productivity trends from 1992 to 2001, there have been small increases in all regions, with Latin America and the Caribbean showing fairly sizeable gains in recent years. In terms of percentage gains, however, China leads these groups, as its agricultural labour productivity grew by over 36 per cent from 1992 to 2001 (although its overall labour productivity still remains quite low). China's growth is followed by Latin America (26.6 per cent), the Middle East and North Africa (20.7 per cent), South Asia (16.3 per cent) and sub-Saharan Africa (5.4 per cent).

On the other hand, total factor productivity (TFP) [26] in agriculture shows consistent increases in all developing economy groups even after the early 1990s (figure 3.15). The regional differences in total factor productivity growth are also apparent in the developing world. It is noteworthy, however, that TFP growth has been somewhat more accentuated than labour productivity growth, especially in the 1990s.

In other words, while there is no evidence of enhanced regional labour productivity from the mid-1990s onward, when poverty reduction began slowing down, TFP still grew in each of these developing regions. The most impressive region was again China, and the region with the lowest TFP growth performance

---

[25] Despite the vast literature on the connection between agricultural growth and poverty reduction, much less has been written on the specific relationship between productivity and poverty reduction. When researchers have investigated this relationship it was often with a specific country focus: India by Ahluwalia (1978) and Datt and Ravallion (1996, 1998), Kenya by Rangarajan (1982) and Block and Timmer (1994), Philippines by Coxhead and Warr (1991), Bolivia by de Franco and Godoy (1993), and Bangladesh by Wodon (1999). These studies in general demonstrate that agricultural growth through productivity growth is important in reducing poverty.

[26] For a discussion on the different measurements of productivity see box 1.2 in Chapter 1 of this Report.

**Figure 3.14.   Labour productivity in agriculture by region, 1992-2001,
                  and labour productivity levels in 1992 and 2001 (index 1992=100)**

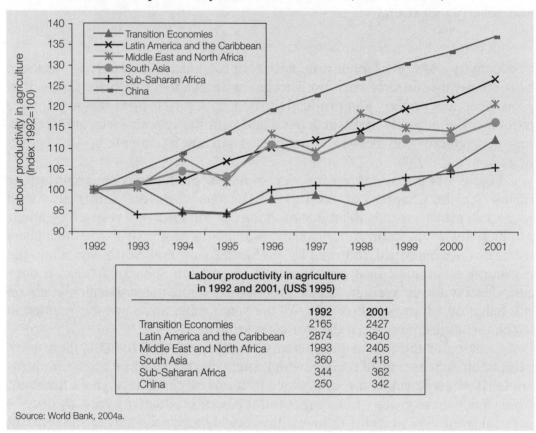

Labour productivity in agriculture in 1992 and 2001, (US$ 1995)		
	1992	**2001**
Transition Economies	2165	2427
Latin America and the Caribbean	2874	3640
Middle East and North Africa	1993	2405
South Asia	360	418
Sub-Saharan Africa	344	362
China	250	342

Source: World Bank, 2004a.

**Figure 3.15.   Weighted average annual growth in total factor productivity in agriculture
                  by region, 1970-2001 (index 1970=1)**

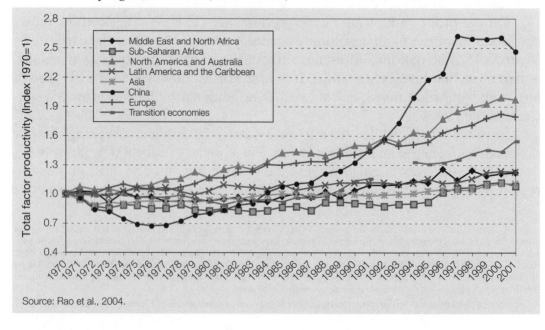

Source: Rao et al., 2004.

was sub-Saharan Africa. It can also be seen that China, with an average TFP performance until the mid-1980s, suddenly gathered momentum, with TFP growth accelerating rapidly in the 1990s. The Chinese agricultural sector's performance appears to have matched the performance of its manufacturing sector and its overall GDP growth in the 1990s. This significant fact is not given sufficient attention. The dramatic declines in poverty in China are often related to its spectacular overall growth (especially in manufacturing). The point is that the country's general growth performance has been very balanced, with agriculture playing a key role in terms of both TFP and labour productivity growth.[27] The Chinese case[28] is probed further in box 3.7.

In terms of explicit linkages between agricultural productivity and poverty reduction, the empirical analysis conducted for this chapter (explained in detail in appendix 3.1) strongly supports the anecdotal evidence presented so far. In sum, it shows a strong and positive relationship between agricultural productivity growth and poverty reduction.[29] The results indicate that increases in agricultural labour productivity appear to have a more significant direct effect on poverty reduction than increases in TFP. One of the main reasons for this is most likely the relationship between higher labour productivity and higher wages. Thus, a relatively stronger case can be made for the importance of labour productivity growth in terms of directly reducing poverty versus the direct poverty-reducing effects of TFP growth. Yet, in all cases studied that were not characterized by extreme inequality, TFP and labour productivity were found to be complementary in terms of poverty reduction.[30]

The empirical analysis also highlights important indirect effects of agricultural productivity (both in terms of TFP and labour productivity) and poverty reduction. Since agricultural productivity impacts both on food production and food prices (as higher productivity allows for expanded food production and lower food prices), increases in agricultural productivity can also indirectly impact on poverty through these channels. The empirical analysis in appendix 3.1 points to a strong, negative relationship between food production per capita and poverty: as food production increases, poverty declines. The analysis also shows a positive, significant relationship between food prices and

---

[27] For a discussion of China's institutions and agriculture, see Hussain et al. (1999).

[28] In India, on the other hand, the cumulative growth factor in total factor productivity between 1970 and 2000 was fairly low, resulting in only a 0.3 per cent average annual growth. Partly, the low TFP growth appears to be due to the high base in 1970, which was followed by significant declines in TFP.

[29] One of the most recent works on this debate on agricultural productivity and poverty reduction was conducted by Thirtle et al. (2003). Via an econometric approach they first identify the importance of labour productivity in the agricultural sector for overall poverty reduction. In a further investigation they include and endogenize many of the relevant variables that affect poverty in a system of equations. The results show that investment in agricultural R&D raises agricultural value-added sufficiently to give very satisfactory rates of return within the agricultural sector, both in Africa (22 per cent) and Asia (31 per cent), but much less in Latin America (10 per cent). Thus agricultural productivity growth gives rise to sufficient growth to pay for R&D, with a substantial effect on poverty reduction. These authors find that a 1 per cent increase in yield reduces the numbers living in under US$1 a day poverty by over 6 million, 95 per cent of them being in Africa and Asia. They also find that the per capita cost of poverty reduction through agricultural productivity growth in Africa is US$144, for Asia US$180, but US$11,400 for Latin America.

[30] Earlier in this chapter, Latin America was identified as the one region where a high inequality was found to be the reason that high levels of labour productivity were not translated into poverty reduction.

Box 3.6. Challenges and potential in sub-Saharan Africa's agricultural sector

Sub-Saharan Africa has the highest regional poverty rate in the world, with over 45 per cent of its population living on less than US$1 a day. While this figure alone is alarming, more worrying still is that the share of the extreme poor in the region has actually been rising. Meanwhile, the number of people falling below the poverty line has climbed sharply to around 325 million, up nearly 65 per cent from two decades earlier.

The region is highly dependent on agriculture – two-thirds of its inhabitants live in rural areas, the majority of whom are engaged in small-scale, subsistence farming. Not surprisingly, there are clear and convincing indications that the region's poverty problems are strongly linked to the poor performance of its agricultural sector, which itself has declined primarily as a result of insufficient gains in productivity. Value added per worker in agriculture has actually declined over the past 25 years, from US$425 in 1980, to US$368 in 1990, to US$362 in 2001. (For more details, see Chapter 1 of this Report). This is partially the result of falling agricultural prices and also of low agricultural productivity. One clear cause of this low productivity is inadequate farming inputs; fertilizer use in the region in 2001 was 30 per cent less than in 1981, while the number of tractors per unit of land also declined over the period. One likely cause of the declines in these inputs is that the inputs themselves tend to have a smaller beneficial effect on productivity in sub-Saharan Africa than in most other parts of the world, largely because of the poor irrigation systems in the region.

Not surprisingly, agricultural output has not been sufficient to meet the needs of the region's growing population. The 1990s have witnessed a further increase in food production, yet population growth has also increased. As a result of these trends, the region is highly dependent on food imports, which were valued at US$18.7 billion (nearly 28 per cent of the value of the region's total agricultural output and 5.7 per cent of total GDP) in 2000. Even with these expensive imports, sub-Saharan Africa does not have enough food – over 200 million chronically hungry people live in the region, an increase of over 30 million in the past decade. This shapes the vicious cycle of hunger, low productivity and poverty: workers suffer from malnutrition and poor health, which leads to low productivity, which then results in low growth and continued poverty. In addition, workers have neither the strength nor the resources to invest in their human capital.

Yet despite sub-Saharan Africa's many poverty-related challenges and its history of agricultural stagnation, there are several reasons to remain hopeful that growth in the agricultural sector can be improved and used as a tool for poverty reduction, given the right mix of policies and donor support. The region has an abundance of land: sub-Saharan Africa has nearly 8 times as much land as India, yet only two-thirds the number of people to feed. The vast supply of land is also relatively equitably distributed and predominantly farmed by small shareholders. This implies that yield-enhancing productivity gains will have equitable growth consequences, and that growth in agriculture will likely reach those who need it most. Finally, contrary to general opinion, sub-Saharan Africa has enough water resources to increase agricultural output. The UN Food and Agriculture Organization estimates the amount of water withdrawn for agricultural irrigation as a percentage of all renewable water resources was only 3 per cent in 2000.

Yet in order for productivity improvements to take place, progress must be made in several areas. First, policy-makers need to encourage *appropriate* research and development (R&D) initiatives in the region. Whereas much of the world's agricultural R&D is conducted with a focus on the needs of the developed world, in which large-scale production is the norm, agricultural R&D in sub-Saharan Africa must be locally relevant and therefore acknowledge the region's smallholder farming structure. Given sub-Saharan Africa's rapidly growing labour force, agricultural research should also explore the best ways to foster labour-intensive production methods. Second, governments and donors need to focus on raising agricultural yields in the region, particularly vis-à-vis food crops. This requires expanded use of irrigation and greater investment in inputs such as fertilizer. Governments in the region should also adopt more production-friendly policies. This includes removing taxes on agricultural production (again, particularly for food crops). Finally, rural infrastructure in sub-Saharan Africa needs substantial improvement. Without adequate roads and ports, there is little hope for the region to progress beyond agricultural subsistence. The challenges for improving agriculture and reducing poverty in sub-Saharan Africa remain considerable, but well-designed agricultural policies and greater and better-targeted assistance from donor countries could foster real poverty reduction in the region.

Sources: World Bank, 2004a; Hazell, 2002; Cleaver and Donovan, 1995.

poverty. In other words, if developing economies manage to increase the amount of food produced per person and thereby decrease the overall cost of food, poverty is expected to decline. Since agricultural productivity increases lead to greater food output and lower prices, the indirect effects of productivity gains vis-à-vis poverty reduction are clear. Taken together, these direct and indirect effects provide strong support for the notion that both labour productivity and TFP increases are needed to maximize the impact of agricultural growth on poverty reduction.

Determinants of productivity in the agricultural sector

Given the clear linkages between agricultural productivity growth and poverty reduction, devising how to increase both TFP and labour productivity is an essential first step in synthesizing a poverty-oriented development strategy in the agricultural sector. Appendix 3.2 provides the empirical results of an analysis of these determinants. In terms of the determinants of TFP in agriculture, several key relationships appear from the analysis. First, measures of economic openness, such as trade and foreign direct investment are consistently positively associated with higher levels of total factor productivity. Along similar lines, geographic isolation tends to negatively impact on TFP. Human capital appears important to TFP: as literacy rates improve, so does TFP. Next, adverse health conditions negatively affect TFP, as shown by the systematic negative relationship between malaria prevalence and total factor productivity. Inequality is also negatively related to TFP. Finally, the proportion of land under irrigation positively and significantly impacts TFP.

While there are many factors that determine TFP, given that the quantities of land and labour and geography are relatively fixed, these results imply that

Box 3.7. China's experience with agricultural productivity and poverty reduction

China is one of the few countries in the developing world to make substantial progress in reducing its total number of poor in the past two decades. Official documents indicate that the number of poor in China started declining from 1978 onwards. There were 250 million rural poor (33 per cent of the rural population) in 1978. This changed dramatically after the rural reforms, which started in the same year. By 1984 only 11 per cent of the rural population was living below the poverty line, decreasing to 8 per cent in 1994 and 3.7 per cent in 2000, representing only 30 million people. Even by taking the more conservative World Bank figures (which are generally higher), there was a reduction of rural poverty from 31 per cent in 1990 to 11.5 per cent in 1998. A reduction in poverty on this scale and within such a short time is unprecedented in history. Contributing to this success were policy and institutional reforms, promotion of equal access to social services and production assets, and public investment in rural areas.

Agricultural reforms were introduced by Deng Xiaoping in 1978 in order to raise the living standards of the people and to eliminate poverty by 2000. These reforms consisted in dismantling the commune system, granting farmers decision-making power, introducing the contract responsibility system, and raising producer prices. These reforms created a mixed economy where central planning coexisted with markets. The introduction of the "household production responsibility system", for example, allowed farmers to retain a certain proportion of outputs after fulfilling a production quota. Grain output increased dramatically as did per capita income, which increased on average at a rate of 15 per cent a year between 1978 and 1984, but at a much slower pace of 3 per cent between 1985 and 1989 (mainly because of stagnation in agricultural production after the reforms). Much of the success in raising per capita agricultural income – and thereby reducing poverty – was attributed to productivity improvements. With crop prices stagnating, rural income gains had to come from increased productivity in agriculture or from employment outside of agriculture.

Agricultural productivity grew rapidly between 1979 and 1984, the early stages of agricultural reform. Productivity growth continued but at a lower pace from 1984 onwards. This slow rate is mainly the result of opening up the rural industrial sector and the rapid growth of China's township-village enterprises, which drew higher quality labourers (over 28 per cent of the rural labour force in the 1990s in certain rural areas) away from traditional agriculture. In sum, growth in agricultural productivity came through:

- Improvements in technology (machines and fertilizer)
- Research and development
- Increased production (extension)
- Better infrastructure (irrigation, roads, etc.)
- Institutional reforms
- Better education

Other, parallel measures were also taken to reduce poverty, such as instituting higher agricultural wages, increasing non-farm employment opportunities, rural reforms, public investments, and targeted poverty investment programmes. It should also be mentioned that progress in reducing poverty has generally occurred during periods of rising rural incomes in China. In the past twenty years, China showed a strong economic growth rate, averaging over 11 per cent a year in the 1990s, a phenomenal growth that would not have been possible without agricultural productivity growth. In sum, agricultural productivity increased, leading to higher rural incomes through changes in the marketing system and employment structure and encouraging the outflow of workers from agriculture into rural non-farm activities.

Sources: Fan et al., 2004; Mead, 2003.

sustainable rural development will arrive through increases in the quality of labour and land, and through decreasing transport costs through better infrastructure. In particular, the results suggest several avenues for developing countries to increase total factor productivity in the rural sector. Investment in human capital through education and health outlays is one avenue, improving physical infrastructure for the rural sector is another. Both ways are clearly dependent on the constraints and sector biases that a country faces with regard to public investment. While a more open trade regime appears to be associated with higher agricultural productivity, it is essential to examine more specifically what open trade regimes really mean in an agricultural policy context in a given economy. Land ownership distributions are relevant and better distributional conditions appear to have a beneficial impact on TFP. Improving institutional conditions such as the extent of democracy, political stability, and conflict reduction are important goals in themselves, but based on the empirical work done for this chapter, they cannot be proposed as factors that cause improvements in productivity in the agricultural sector. The reasons for this may indeed be that the quantitative notion of "institutional" improvement itself carries representational biases reflected in indicators, and more participatory agrarian environments may not be linked to the extent of political freedom, as is commonly understood.

In terms of the determinants of agricultural labour productivity, the vast majority of the results are consistent with many of the correlates of TFP. This implies that well-designed policies can positively impact both sources of productivity in agriculture at the same time. The empirical results show that using better quality fertilizers, more (or better) tractors, and widespread irrigation are good examples of technical-input quality improvements that have direct influences on labour productivity. Openness also appears to be favourable in the labour productivity context, offering some evidence of the benefits that global markets can provide to agricultural workers. As box 3.8 shows, it comes as little surprise that health status appears very important in determining labour productivity. A healthy agricultural workforce is crucial to expanding output on a sustainable basis. The data also show that income inequality is negatively related to labour productivity in agriculture. Thus, improving land ownership distributions in those countries that have not had proper land reform is a significant policy intervention to consider on grounds of poverty reduction as well as on grounds of equity.

Productivity and food prices: An important link to poverty reduction

Section 3.4 of this chapter argued that food price development provides an important linkage between growth and poverty reduction. A closer look shows that it is often productivity changes that drive changes in prices. Demand for most agricultural goods, particularly staple foods, is very inelastic (that is, consumers are not very responsive to changes in price). In the short run, the supply of agricultural goods is also highly inelastic (producers cannot and do not immediately change the amount of agricultural goods they supply because of changes in price). As a result, when technological improvements raise agricultural productivity and the supply curve shifts outward (the same amount of output can be produced with less input), the prices of goods typically fall considerably. In the developed world, where there are relatively fewer producers of agricultural goods, and where no single agricultural commodity typically makes up more than 5 to 10 per cent of consumer budgets, high variability in prices in agriculture does not seriously threaten society's overall welfare. In developing economies, however, in which large segments of the population typically rely on agricultural production for their income, and where budget shares of food staples are very large, high variation in agricultural products can have serious negative consequences on living standards (Gabre-Madhin et al., 2003).

The impact of productivity improvements in the agricultural sector on poverty can vary considerably. It depends on the structure of the market for the given commodity and also on the nature of production in terms of whether producers themselves rely on their product for consumption. The following points provide some examples of the different ways in which productivity improvements can impact on prices and poverty:

- In a closed economy, when demand for an agricultural product is highly insensitive to price changes and producers themselves do not consume a large portion of their product, the benefits of productivity improvements accrue to consumers through lower prices. The basic notion is that only the early adopters of a new agricultural technology will benefit from the increased revenues associated with more production. As more and more producers adopt the production-expanding technology, total production increases and prices drop, benefiting consumers but hurting producers. Because the poorest producers are also the least likely to be able to afford adopting the new technology, they will be most likely to face falling prices without production increases, and thus their overall welfare will fall.

- When the same conditions exist as in the previous point but producers themselves consume a large portion of their product, the benefits of productivity improvements accrue to both producers and consumers. The larger the quantity of home consumption, the higher the consumer surplus that accrues to producers. This is more the case of a closed developing economy.

- In a small open economy, in the case of export crops, the benefits of productivity improvements accrue primarily to producers. Here the assumption is

Box 3.8. The impact of HIV/AIDS on productivity in agriculture

'The family has been talking over their problems since the sun went down. The young ones move in and out of the hut, anxious but not able to sit still. The father lies on a string bed, coughing, unable to speak for long. Their oldest son moved to the city and helped by sending money home, but the payments stopped some weeks back. They are worried about him, and about how they will manage. John says they must stop cultivating the far field – it takes too much time. Young Thomas offers to take the goats there to graze, but Rose bursts out, "How can you do that, and weed the maize, and go to school? If you stop school, how will you make progress when you're an adult?" Then, more quietly, "Anyway, I think we have to sell the goats. We don't have Peter's money, and the medicine is so expensive". Mary suggests, "If we take in one of your brother's children, he can help work the middle field, and grandmother will have one less mouth to feed". "But we'll have one more. I don't know. We need help with caring for father, and with the farm, but if we take one of your cousins we may not have enough food. Whatever happens, Mary, you and I must keep tending the vegetables, and look after the chickens well. Without them we'll be eating only mealy porridge and that isn't good, especially for the young ones." But Rose was afraid that even this wouldn't be possible for long. She had started to feel sick and weak herself. She wouldn't tell them until she had to, but she knew that soon it would be up to Mary to look after all of them.' (Citation from Leather, 2003.)

This distressing story portrays the human impacts of HIV/AIDS. It also illustrates the economic impacts involved, not only for this family but for the economy overall. The epidemic mainly affects those between 15 and 45 years of age, the most productive workforce and the financial mainstay of families and communities. As a result, the more labour-intensive the economic activity, the more it is at risk in high-prevalence countries. And the more an activity depends on the labour of women, the more it is also at risk – over half of all new HIV infections are among women, and 60 per cent of those infected in Africa are women.

AIDS was long perceived as a largely urban, rather than rural, phenomenon. This view has now changed, given the complex pattern of dependency between rural and urban areas, the rural poverty that propounds lack of access to information and health services, and the greater hold of tradition and customary law in rural areas. Current statistics bear this out, with many countries reporting a more rapid increase in new cases in rural areas.

The only way poor households can react to the epidemic is to reduce their farming hours or switch to less labour-intensive – but probably also less productive or lucrative – crops. Tasks which yield more benefits in the long term tend to be neglected in favour of more immediate returns. A particular issue, which will have repercussions for generations to come, is that children are taken out of school to help with the jobs that need doing, or because school costs too much, or because they lose their parents. The next stages were described by UNAIDS Director, Peter Piot: "People are obliged to adopt survival strategies that may put their lives in danger. Some of them emigrate, often to shanty towns that lack health and education services; women and children may be forced to prostitute themselves in exchange for food, work or other essentials…." The HIV/AIDS epidemic thus has a negative impact on productivity – not only in the present but also for the future – making it almost impossible to use the potential of agriculture for the overall development of an economy.

Source: Leather, 2003; Dromeel, 2003.

that prices do not fall as a result of increased production, as export demand is growing as well, so producers benefit greatly from expanding production. The same case applies when producers consume a portion of their output.

Since the overall welfare effects of agricultural productivity improvements are typically positive (and are strictly so for consumers), and because welfare-reducing effects for agricultural producers stem from the price mechanism, policy-makers concerned with reducing poverty should pay close attention to agricultural pricing policies. There is no single way for governments to address the multitude of needs of the poor members of society. But those economies with large segments of the population involved in agriculture that have been successful in fostering sustained economic growth and reducing poverty have very often instituted policies that provided price supports to producers (for some examples, see box 3.12).

Wages and employment in agriculture and poverty reduction

As mentioned earlier and also discussed in other chapters of this Report, growth is not only a function of productivity but also of employment. This holds true for all sectors: if more people work, it is likely that more will be produced. At the same time, the more people earn (through their work), the more they can either save or consume – the former having an indirect effect on growth via interest rates and investment, the latter having a direct growth effect. As simple as this seems, many development initiatives fail to focus on employment, thereby reducing the likelihood of having a sustainable impact on poverty reduction.

Often, the only asset poor people have is their potential to work. The link between employment and poverty reduction is even more obvious than the link between growth and poverty reduction or productivity and poverty reduction. If people have a job in which they earn money, they have a chance to get out of poverty. It then becomes a question of how much they earn and whether they can lift themselves and their families above the poverty line. While this is certainly true for all sectors of the economy, since the poor are mainly found in rural, agriculture-producing areas, it is specifically true in the present context. The next question is, how can poor agricultural workers earn enough to escape poverty? This is where productivity enters the picture. Even if there are cases in which higher productivity does not automatically and immediately lead to higher wages, in the long run these two variables go hand in hand. This is true for the economy as a whole, but also for each sector. Therefore the policies to raise labour productivity in agriculture outlined in the previous section should also have positive impacts on wages and thereby on poverty reduction.

But there is also another, very human dimension to raising productivity. By not only giving people any kind of job – even if they are well paid – but rather decent jobs, productivity will rise in the long run. A healthy mother with a satisfying job where she can work in freedom and dignity, where she may voice her opinion and where she has some type of security if she becomes sick or loses her job, will be more able to work herself and her family out of poverty. She will also make sure that her children will have the same chances later on in life. She will send them to school, provide them with health care, and be able to better tend to their other needs. As a result, expanding decent and productive work sets the stage for poverty reduction, and also for future growth in the economy as a whole. Box 3.9 offers an interesting example of employment creation and box 3.10 looks at the lack of decent jobs in agriculture. One argument is that the price paid for decent work for some people is that fewer people will be able to find a job, but this is very unlikely to happen. A person out of poverty will consume more goods and services and thereby contribute to growth, which creates further employment opportunities. Poor people without jobs or with low-paid jobs simply do not have this capacity. Poverty itself inhibits employment growth and, without growth in decent employment, one important source for overall growth and poverty reduction is neglected.

There is no doubt that some sources of labour productivity growth, especially capital-intensive technologies such as tractors, may increase productivity but could also be employment-reducing – especially in the short and medium run. Yet output growth is unlikely to be sustainable unless it is also underpinned by technological change. If this is not the case, agricultural labour productivity might not rise fast enough or may even stagnate, and employment will subsequently be less likely to make a significant dent in poverty. At the same time, employment reduction in agriculture can have serious, adverse implications for poverty in the short run. To minimize these effects, adequate social safety nets must be in place unless other sectors are able to absorb the surplus labour.

The empirical evidence underscores the fact that employment growth and productivity growth in the agricultural sector can go hand in hand. Figures 3.16 and 3.17 show that both labour productivity and employment in agriculture grew in many economies in the period from 1980 to 2001 and in the period from 1990 to 2001 (China is one of the economies in this quadrant). Figures 3.16 and 3.17 also show a large number of economies that have experienced declining employment coupled with increasing productivity. Even though on first sight this seems to emphasize the view that rising labour productivity means the loss of jobs, a careful examination reveals that in most cases these economies have gone a step further in the development process – in which structural change has started attracting labour away from the agricultural sector. This reinforces the argument advanced in this chapter: many economies have seen growth in agricultural output per person employed in parallel with structural change, making the point that the development process ideally has to be supported by a healthy agricultural sector.

Figure 3.18 adds to this argument. It shows the average change in poverty for all countries within each of the quadrants from figures 3.16 and 3.17. Whether taking the US$2 or US$1 a day poverty line and whether the past ten years or 20 years is the period chosen, the economies with increases in productivity and increases in employment in agriculture have had the highest decreases in poverty. Economies with an increase in productivity but a decrease in employment

Box 3.9. Women in agriculture: Fresh cut flowers in Colombia and Ecuador

The cut-flower industry

With an estimated value of US$30 billion, the global market for fresh flowers has rapidly become an important source of income for several developing economies, which now supply over 30 per cent of the world market. Favourable growing conditions in southern countries, cheaper labour and low relative transport costs of flowers are increasing developing economies' comparative advantages for production. In Colombia, the industry has grown from a mere US$20,000 in the 1970s to US$580 million in 2000, or over 3 per cent of total export earnings. At the present time, Colombia is the world's second largest producer of flowers after the Netherlands. In Ecuador, the industry is now the country's fourth largest in terms of exports. Together, these two economies currently achieve around US$775 million in export earnings annually from cut-flower sales. For developing countries participating in the industry, this new source of income is providing an increasingly important supplement to the often declining revenues earned from traditional commodities.

Industrialized countries consume the vast majority of cut flowers sold in the world, with consumers in the United States alone spending over US$16 billion each year. As the base of production in developing countries is typically found in rural areas, the cut-flower market provides a direct and important link between the rural poor and these global markets. This is particularly the case for poor women living in rural areas. In Colombia, some 70,000 to 75,000 people are employed in the cut-flower business, 60 to 80 per cent of whom are women, and another 50,000 people are employed in related industries. In Ecuador, around 50,000 people are employed in the industry, between 50 and 60 per cent of whom are women. The large and growing number of jobs it is providing to rural parts of developing countries raises hopes that this industry might serve as a force for poverty reduction, particularly among women, who bear a disproportionate share of the global poverty burden.

Profile of women cut-flower workers

Women workers in the cut-flower industry tend to be young. One study estimated that 86 per cent of women working in flower-packing operations in Ecuador were between 15 and 29 years of age. Many of the women workers are single and often have children. In Colombia, some 80 per cent of households that depend on the cut-flower industry are headed by women. Female workers in the industry tend to have very little education, few tangible assets, and little in the way of employment alternatives aside from domestic work and textiles, which typically pay lower wages. Taken together, the characteristics of women workers in the industry reveal a poor and vulnerable workforce, lacking alternative employment and educational opportunities and struggling to rise out of poverty.

While jobs in the cut-flower industry are providing women with new and often better income-generating options than those previously available to them, much work remains to be done to translate the industry's poverty-reducing potential for women into a reality. Most noticeably, the large gender disparities in employment positions clearly work against women workers. In Colombia, for example, women comprise only 5 per cent of top managers, 9 per cent of managers, 10 per cent of mid-professionals and 48 per cent of lower rank supervisors in the industry. In addition, the majority of the jobs women hold lack employment benefits such as health insurance and pensions. The widespread use of temporary, seasonal, and other insecure work arrangements provides additional barriers to reducing poverty among workers in the industry.

In order for the cut-flower industry to become a sustainable poverty-reducing force in the developing world, the employment status of workers in the industry, particularly among women, needs to improve. Effective training programmes could raise worker productivity and foster greater tenure among workers. Companies should also strive for greater gender equality in management positions throughout the industry. Finally, enforcement of national and international labour protection and codes of conduct is needed to ensure that the most basic and essential labour standards are being met.

Sources: Dolan and Sorby, 2003; World Bank, 2003b.

also showed a reduction in poverty over the past 20 years, but less so than those economies in the northeast quadrant. Over the past ten years, the reduction in poverty has been higher on average in economies with productivity increases and employment decreases in agriculture – again as a result of the structural transition process.

Box 3.10. Decent work deficits in agriculture

Decent work for all is one of the principal goals of the ILO. Decent work reflects the aspiration of men and women everywhere to obtain productive work in conditions of freedom, equity, security and human dignity. Decent work encompasses respect for basic rights, access to employment, safe and healthy working conditions, and social security. Decent work comes about through social dialogue.

Unfortunately, decent work deficits are pervasive in the agricultural sector. They are expressed in the widespread denial of rights at work, in poor quality employment and high levels of unemployment, in unsafe working conditions and lack of income security, and finally in the inadequate representation of agricultural workers in the social dialogue which could improve their working lives.

The ten ambitious Millennium Development Goals set by the world community aim at reducing poverty and hunger, at increasing access to safe drinking water, to health care, to education and at implementing national strategies for sustainable development. All of these goals are of direct interest to those who live and work in rural areas. Indeed, ensuring rural workers' access to secure employment and decent working and living standards are critical steps in reducing poverty and achieving sustainable livelihoods.

Providing decent jobs for people in agriculture is not "doing them a favour". It is the only possible way to guarantee sustainable future development, because it gives these people the opportunity to work themselves out of poverty, not just in the immediate future but for the long run.

Source: http://www.ilo.org/public/english/dialogue/sector/sectors/agri.htm

Figure 3.16.   Productivity vs. employment changes in agriculture, 1980-2001

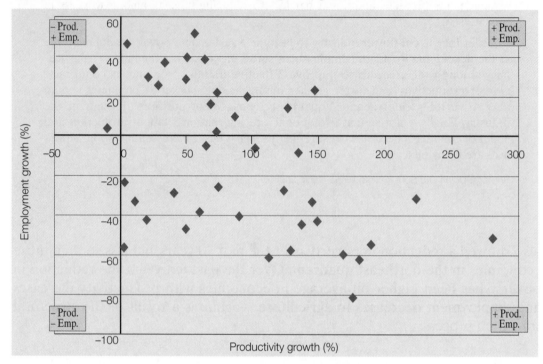

Figure 3.17.   Productivity vs. employment changes in agriculture, 1990-2001

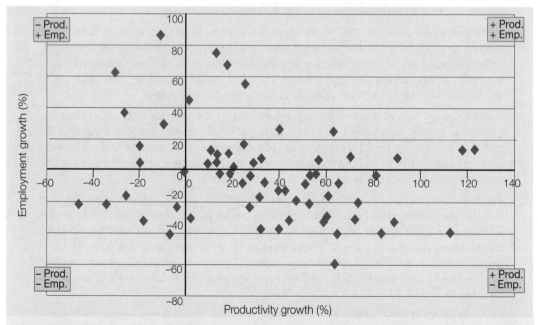

Source: Calculation based on ILO, 2003, series 4a: Employment by sector (percentages); series 18e: Labour productivity, agriculture. Figures 3.16 and 3.17 are interpreted as follows: economies in the upper left quadrant experienced a decline in agricultural productivity and an increase in agricultural employment over the period in question. Economies in the upper right quadrant experienced an increase in both agricultural productivity and agricultural employment over the period. Those in the lower right quadrant experienced an increase in agricultural productivity and a decrease in agricultural employment, and economies in the lower left quadrant experienced a decline in both agricultural productivity and agricultural employment over the period analysed.

Figure 3.18.   Average percentage point change in poverty rates, different productivity and employment trend groups, 1980-2001 and 1990-2001

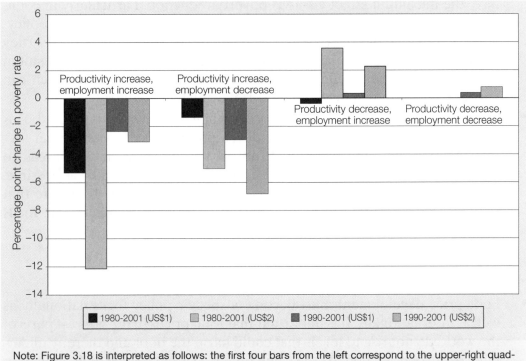

Note: Figure 3.18 is interpreted as follows: the first four bars from the left correspond to the upper-right quadrant in figures 3.16 and 3.17. The first of these bars shows that on average between 1980 and 2001, the economies in this quadrant reduced US$1 a day poverty by 5 per cent. The second of these bars shows that, on average, economies in this quadrant reduced US$2 a day working poverty by just over 12 per cent. The third and fourth bars show that between 1990 and 2001, economies in the upper-right quadrant of figures 3.16 and 3.17 reduced US$1 and US$2 a day poverty by between 2 per cent and 3 per cent, respectively.

Source: Estimates based on the Global Employment Trends model. For additional information on the model and sources, see the ILO Employment Trends web site for world and regional estimation on http://www.ilo.org/public/english/employment/strat/wrest

3.6. Policy recommendations

While poverty has been decreasing in the world, the rate of decline slowed in the 1990s – a trend that occurred in parallel with declining interest in the agricultural sector among policy-makers. There has also been a large divergence in global poverty trends, in particular with poverty rates falling throughout much of the world, but surging in sub-Saharan Africa. This is likely to seriously jeopardize the Millennium Development Goals on poverty. This chapter has shown that agricultural growth is critical for poverty reduction, largely because poverty has a very significant rural and often agricultural dimension. To attack poverty effectively in countries whose poor are largely dependent on agriculture, an explicit agricultural growth strategy is needed. To achieve the maximum impact of growth in agriculture for poverty reduction, the following points need to be emphasized in development strategies.

Focusing policies on labour productivity and decent employment creation

- Agricultural growth that is led by growth in labour productivity appears to have the maximum effect vis-à-vis poverty reduction. Particularly in countries with large segments of the population working in agriculture, policy-makers should avoid overemphasizing mechanization in agriculture. They should also exercise caution vis-à-vis granting subsidies that could result in over-generous credit policies and over-valued exchange rates, which can encourage sub-optimal use of labour-replacing technologies.[31]

- Poverty reduction is most likely to occur when employment is created. This is at least true for the period in the development process where other sectors do not yet have the capability to absorb surplus labour in rural areas. To this end, agricultural policies should be as employment-friendly as possible, particularly in countries with surplus labour in rural areas. To ensure that the overall gains from agricultural development are sustainable, the focus needs to be on the creation of decent jobs.

Laying the ground for poverty reduction by focusing on processes, institutions and infrastructure

- Food price development must become a specific policy focus nationally as well as internationally. It is important that food prices in the poorest parts of the world do not rise to levels that could harm the poor and thereby undermine poverty reduction. At the same time prices have to be high enough to ensure that food-exporting economies can earn enough to foster an attractive investment environment and earn enough foreign exchange to meet domestic development objectives.

- While a more equal income distribution is generally better for poverty reduction, in particular better distribution of land ownership in agriculture will facilitate both output growth and accelerate poverty reduction.

- Investments in water supply (see box 3.11), infrastructure and health not only have a positive impact on productivity growth but also on employment creation and poverty reduction.

- The same holds true for investment in education, agricultural research and development and other institutional reforms, even though the impacts on these kinds of investments might not immediately pay dividends.

- Non-farm activities should be fostered as an additional source of employment creation, adding further to the poverty reduction potential of the agricultural sector.

As with every set of policy recommendations, there is no "one size fits all" solution with regard to agricultural policies: advising developing countries to focus on agricultural development could potentially lead to the adoption of flawed and inappropriate policies. Whether a focus on agricultural productivity,

---

[31] ILO, 2002; Khan and Lee, 1995.

Box 3.11. Water as a source of success: How it can contribute to productivity growth, employment creation and poverty reduction

In many cases the supply of water and timely irrigation facilities is the most important starting point for productivity, output and employment growth, and thereby for poverty reduction in rural areas:

- In dry areas the supply of water raises output per hectare as well as the availability of fertile land.

- The use of fertilizers often only makes sense if there is enough water to keep the growing output per hectare alive.

- Healthy water is the precondition for healthy workers, and a healthy workforce can produce more. For example, by being able to wash one's hands with soap and water can reduce diarrhoea by 35 per cent in the world (2.2 million people die every year from diarrhoea.)

- Implementing and containing water supply systems and water management projects can be used as a means of employment creation.

- In many developing countries with a shortage of water, the task of collecting water often falls on women, who sometimes must walk long hours to fetch it. Their productive potential might be more profitably utilized.

A successful Food and Agriculture Organization (FAO) project provides one example of how easy and effective it can be to provide people with water. In the early 1980s, thousands of farmers in Bangladesh began using a revolutionary new device – a simple, inexpensive human-powered water pump to irrigate crops. The FAO was convinced that this technology would help African farmers if it could be adapted to local conditions and manufactured locally. In Zambia, a recent joint project of the FAO's Special Programme for Food Security and the International Fund for Agricultural Development demonstrated the benefits of the pump. Then, with assistance from International Development Enterprises, an NGO, local manufacturers were trained to produce and sell the pumps. Soon a network of retailers had spread across the country, and more than 1,000 pumps were sold at a cost of US$75 to 125. Instead of lugging heavy buckets of water to their small plots of beans, sweet potatoes and cassava, farmers pumped more water in less time with the treadle pump. Growers doubled their land area under crops and introduced new varieties such as tomatoes, cabbage, rapeseed and onions. Women in particular profited from the technology, being able to better feed their families while generating additional income. Similar ventures with local manufacturers have started in Burkina Faso, Malawi, Mali, Senegal and the United Republic of Tanzania.

Today, 70 per cent of water used in the world is in agriculture (with 22 per cent for industrial use and 8 per cent for domestic use). It is important to make sure that this scarce resource is not wasted. The success of sustainable water management should include the support of local people and their knowledge, effective information policies to raise awareness, and training on how to make the best use of water.

Given the advantages water brings to people's lives, investment in the water supply is one of the most effective ways to support productivity growth at the same time as employment growth.

Sources: Bowden, 2002; UNEP, 2002; FAO, 2003a.

Box 3.12. Some successful examples of agricultural policies

The following are some examples of ways in which agricultural policies have been fostered in some economies:

1) **Maintaining stable and profitable prices received by producers**

- India established minimum agricultural support prices.
- The Republic of Korea established a price stabilization fund for cash crops.
- In Taiwan (China), the Government maintained stable rice prices by actively intervening in this economy's rice market.

2) **Delivering modern, productivity-enhancing inputs to small, poor farmers**

- In India, the Government offered profitable prices for crops for which new technologies were available and announced their policies before the sowing season, in order to encourage production.
- The Republic of Korea provided extensive subsidies to producers and established a nationwide campaign to distribute high-yield rice varieties among farmers.

3) **Strengthening and expanding rural credit institutions**

- Taiwan (China) provided rent in kind for use of government-owned land for production.

employment and growth is appropriate for a country depends on its stage in the development process, and on the potential of the agricultural sector in terms of natural resources and human resources. It also depends on international commodity prices and the market situation for specific products. Economies have to find their niche in terms of where they can compete with other economies inside and outside the developing world. They also have to make sure that the path they choose is sustainable in terms of environmental constraints.

But success not only depends on the right choice of each individual country (for some successful examples of agricultural policies on the country level, see box 3.12). It depends on the behaviour of the world community as a whole. Without collective action taken to achieve a fair globalization, national activities in agriculture are bound to fail. Global rules and policies on trade and finance must allow more space for policy autonomy in developing countries. This is essential for the development of policies and institutional arrangements best suited to specific-country levels of development and specific circumstances. The policies of international organizations and donor countries must also shift more decisively away from external conditionality to national ownership of policies.[32]

Some region-specific issues must be taken into account when formulating development strategies for the agricultural sector. For example, in sub-Saharan Africa, the majority of agricultural output is from poor smallholders who consume a large portion of their output. Here, the direct effects of productivity

---

[32] World Commission on the Social Dimension of Globalization, 2004. The development of the agricultural sector in the light of trade barriers for many commodity goods is one of the key issues of the Commission's report.

improvements – such as greater production and revenues, increased home consumption and increased nutritional value of food – are very important in terms of poverty reduction. Encouraging technological innovations among these poor farmers will have direct benefits vis-à-vis reducing poverty. In much of Asia, to take another example, most of the poor are landless and live in rural areas. Here, the indirect effects of agricultural growth – reduced food prices and positive employment and wage effects – are most important for poverty reduction. The best mechanism in this case is targeting technological improvements towards employment creation for alleviating poverty.[33] A third example is Latin America, where poverty is mainly urban and large farmers own a majority of the land. Here, the best way to reduce poverty with productivity improvements is through reductions in the prices of the types of food that the poor most often consume. In all cases it is important to focus on a stabilization of the prices of export goods.

3.7. Concluding remarks

For too long policy-makers have ignored the agricultural sector's potential to foster poverty reduction and to promote economic development. The reasons for this neglect are manifold and should be addressed so that agriculture can resume its significant role. Some of the typical concerns and fears of policy-makers include:

- Many of the positive impacts of productivity and employment work best in a small-farm agricultural environment, whereas modern development (increased rural to urban migration and growing globalization) seems to call more for large farm structures. Even if this is the case in the longer run, for the time being there are many economies in which small farms are still dominant, especially in Asia and sub-Saharan Africa. These economies would still benefit from a sharpened focus on agriculture. In addition, the fact that small farms cannot always successfully compete with larger farms could often be overcome by coordination among farmers and by higher investment in human and social capital.

- The long-term fall in global agricultural commodity prices and declining terms of trade in economies in which agriculture has a large share in total output has undermined the profitability of agriculture as a business. Although this has been true, the picture can be improved. By reducing agricultural subsidies in developed economies and by fostering developing economies' access to the developed world's markets, agriculture can be profitable. In addition, public investment in rural areas can lower production costs in agriculture and make the sector more competitive (see box 3.13).

- Focusing on agriculture runs the risk of exacerbating problems related to natural resource constraints, particularly with regard to soil and water. But this limitation is not only true for agriculture and sustainable agricultural

---

[33] For a detailed analysis of the specifics of the Asian agricultural sector and its potential for productive employment, see Khan and Lee, 1995; Ishikawa, 1978.

Box 3.13. Risk and reward in agricultural trade

International trade in agricultural goods has received a great deal of attention from policy-makers, researchers and the media recently, particularly regarding the controversy surrounding the World Trade Organization's Fifth Ministerial Conference held in Cancún, Mexico in September 2003. The meeting in Cancún was set up with the goal of moving forward agriculture-related trade reforms proposed in the 2001 Doha Declaration. In general terms, this meant phasing out export subsidies and reducing other forms of domestic supports to agriculture. Most analysts have since declared the Conference a disappointment, as developing and industrialized economies ultimately failed to reach consensus as to how to move agricultural trade reforms forward. A July 2004 meeting at WTO headquarters in Geneva appears to have successfully restarted the debate, as broad consensus was reached on how to begin to move Doha forward again. This series of events begs the question as to what exactly makes trade in agriculture so controversial.

To start with, it is important to note that agriculture is one of the most heavily protected economic sectors in the world. Average agricultural tariffs in the OECD countries are around 40 per cent, and in the developing world tariffs average more than 20 per cent. As a result, tariffs on agricultural goods are as high today as industrial tariffs were in 1950. Many economists surmise that liberalization of these markets would have a large, positive impact on total output in the world. One study estimated that a decline in agricultural support of 50 per cent could add over US$50 billion in annual output by 2010. Yet the same study estimates that this reduction in agricultural support runs the risk of a negative impact on terms of trade (the ratio between export prices and import prices) throughout much of sub-Saharan Africa, China, India, the Philippines and elsewhere, as all of these economies are net-importers of food and import prices are likely to rise quicker than export prices in a liberalized world. Given that changes in the world's agricultural trade regime will inevitably leave both winners and losers, it is important to ensure that agricultural trade reforms – at the national as well as the international level – seek to maximize economic gains. It is also important that the policies are pro-poor. While the full scope of what is needed vis-à-vis trade reform in agriculture cannot be outlined here, some key points merit attention.

1) **Food security must be the first priority** – Ensuring that the world's poor receive adequate nutrition is absolutely essential in terms of promoting decent and productive work, fostering rural development and, ultimately, reducing poverty. To this end, policy-makers must be mindful of both prices and productivity. It is important that food prices in the poorest parts of the developing world do not rise to levels that could harm the poor. At the same time prices for export goods from developing countries need to have a certain level to make investment in the agricultural sector attractive. Continued agricultural productivity also needs to be fostered. Given scarce resources and rising populations, particularly in the developing world, agricultural productivity gains are needed to maintain adequate food supplies.

2) **Trade reforms must address commodity dependence in the developing world** – Many developing countries rely heavily on one or two agricultural commodities for export earnings, with sugar and coffee being the most commonly cited examples. Volatility in the prices of these commodities can translate into large swings in living conditions in developing countries, particularly for poor workers

engaged in the production of the commodities. Indeed, as coffee and sugar prices reached historically low levels between 1999 and 2001, rural wages declined and poverty rose sharply in countries dependent on these goods. Future trade reforms must address the potentially harmful effects of global markets on the world's poor agricultural workers.

3) **Developing economies need market access** – Market access is the only possibility for developing economies to ensure sustainable development and decent and productive employment in rural, agricultural-producing regions in the long run. This implies greater openness in the industrialized world, tariff reductions and lower subsidies so that agricultural workers will be able to benefit more fully from globalization.

Sources: FAO, 2003b; UNDP 2003.

development – it is a question of investing in the right environment-friendly technologies.

- Policy-makers often fear that concentrating on agriculture may slow down the structural transformation process. The present chapter has demonstrated that this is not the case. A balanced development of all sectors seems to be the most favourable for overall development and, for many of the least developed economies, a focus on the agricultural sector will be a step forward in the development process and the fastest and surest way out of poverty.

This chapter in no way denies that there are other ways to reduce poverty. Nor does it wish to argue against the process of structural change as the one and only long-run development path. But in the many cases in which the agricultural sector employs a large share of the population in developing economies – and more specifically in sub-Saharan Africa and much of Asia – it is essential to use this sector to support the development process and to make progress in terms of reducing poverty.

The international community can and should have an impact on helping the poorest countries find their way out of poverty. Each international agency must focus on their relevant mandate and field of expertise and, at the same time, exchange knowledge and experience to guarantee coherence in policies. In terms of the ILO's mandate, the Organization will focus on decent employment creation by concentrating on four key challenges: making decent work a global goal, making the ILO a global player in shaping globalization, mobilizing tripartism for global action and making the Organization as a whole a "truly global team" in the quest for fair globalization.[34] Overall, the report of the World Commission on the Social Dimension of Globalization can be taken as a guideline for new, more coherent policies on globalization.

---

[34] For details, see World Commission on the Social Dimension of Globalization (2004). See also ILO press release, 7 June 2004 (ILO/04/27). For a summary of selected ILO activities concerning the agricultural sector, see appendix 3.3.

References

Ahluwalia, M.S. 1978. "Rural poverty and agricultural performance in India", in *Journal of Development Studies*, Vol. 14, pp. 298-323.

—. 1976. "Inequality, poverty and development", in *Journal of Development Economics*, Vol. 3, No. 3, pp. 307-342.

Bardhan, P. 1999. *Democracy and development: A complex relationship* (University of California at Berkeley).

Block, S.; Timmer, T.P. 1994. *Agriculture and economic growth: Conceptual issues and the Kenyan experience* (Cambridge, Harvard Institute for International Development Development), Discussion Paper No. 498, Nov.

Bowden, R. 2002. *Water supply: Our impact on the planet 2002* (London, Hodder Wayland).

Byerlee, D.; Alex, G. 2002. *Designing investments in agricultural research for enhanced poverty impacts* (Washington, DC, World Bank).

Cassel, A.; Patel, R. 2003. *Agricultural trade liberalization and Brazil's rural poor: Consolidating inequality* (Oakland, Food First/Institute for Food and Development Policy), Policy Brief No. 8, Aug.

Chen, S.; Ravallion, M. 2001. "How did the world's poorest fare in the 1990s?", in *Review of Income and Wealth*, Vol. 43 (3), pp. 283-300.

Chuta, E.; Liedholm, C. 1981. *Rural non-farm employment: A review of the state of the art* (East Lansing, Michigan State University).

Cleaver, K.; Donovan, W. 1995. *Agriculture, poverty and policy reform in sub-Saharan Africa* (Washington, DC), World Bank Discussion Paper 1995/02/28.

Coxhead, I.; Warr, P.G. 1991. "Technical change in agriculture and the distribution of income: A general equilibrium analysis for Philippine agriculture", in *American Journal of Agricultural Economics*, Vol. 73, No. 2, pp. 345-360.

Datt, G.; Ravallion, M. 1998. "Farm productivity and rural poverty in India", in *Journal of Development Studies*, Vol. 34, No. 4, pp. 62-85.

—. 1996. "How important to India's poor is the sectoral composition of economic growth?", in *World Bank Economic Review*, Vol. 10, pp. 1-26.

De Franco, M.; Godoy, R. 1993. "Potato-led growth: The role of agricultural innovations in transforming Bolivian agriculture – A macroeconomic perspective", in *Journal of Development Studies*, Vol. 29, No. 3, pp. 561-587.

Dolan, C.S.; Sorby, K. 2003. *Gender and employment in high-value agriculture industries* (Washington, DC, World Bank), Agriculture and Rural Development Working Paper No. 7.

Dollar, D.; Kraay, A. 2004. "Trade, growth and poverty", *Economic Journal*, Royal Economic Society, Vol. 114, No. 127, pp. F22-F49.

Dorward, A.; Kydd, J.; Morrison, J.; Urey, I. 2001. *A policy agenda for pro-poor agricultural growth* (London, Imperial College of Science, Technology and Medicine).

Dromeel, M.P. 2003. "AIDS and hunger", in *Labour Education*, Vol. 2-3, No. 131-132 (Geneva, ILO).

Fan, S.; Hazell, P.; Thorat, S. 1999. *Linkages between government spending, growth and poverty in rural India* (Washington, DC, International Food Policy Research Institute), Research Report No. 110.

Fan, S.; Zhang, L.; Zhang, X. 2004. "Reforms, investment and poverty in rural China", in *Economic Development and Cultural Change*, Vol. 52, No. 2, pp. 395-421.

Food and Agriculture Organisation (FAO), 2003a. AQUASTAT, Land and Water Development Division, available at: http://www.fao.org/ag/agl/aglw/aquastat/main/index

—. 2003b. *World agriculture: Towards 2015/2030 – An FAO perspective* (Rome).

Gabre-Madhin, E.; Barrett, C.; Dorosh, P. 2003. *Technological change and price effects in agriculture: Conceptual and comparative perspectives* (Washington, DC, International Food Policy Research Institute), MTID Discussion Paper No. 62.

Hazell, P. 2002. *Challenges and opportunities for agriculture in African agriculture* (Washington, DC, International Food Policy Research Institute) (http://www.ifpri.org/themes/ieha/workshops/200204/hazell0402.pdf).

Hemmer, H.R. 2002. *Wirtschaftsprobeleme der Entwicklungsländer*, 3rd ed. (Munich, Vahlen).

Hussain, A.; Stern, N.; Stiglitz, J. 1999. "Chinese reforms from a comparative perspective", in P. Hammond and G. Myles (eds.): *Incentives, organization and public economics*, paper in honour of Sir James Mirrlees (New York, Oxford University Press).

International Fund for Agricultural Development (IFAD). 2001. *Rural poverty report 2001: The challenge of ending rural poverty* (Rome), p. 102.

International Labour Organization (ILO). 2004. *Global employment trends for women*, Employment Strategy Paper 2004/8 (Geneva).

—. 2003. *Key Indicators of theLabour Market*, 3rd ed. (Geneva); also available on CD-ROM.

—. 2002. *Global employment agenda* (Geneva).

Irz, X.; Lin, L.; Thirtile, C.; Wiggins, S. 2001. "Agricultural productivity growth and poverty alleviation", in *Development Policy Review*, Vol. 19, No. 4, pp. 449-466.

Ishikawa, S. 1978. *Labour absorption in Asian agriculture* (Bangkok, ILO).

Johnson, G.D. 2002. "Can agricultural labour adjustment occur primarily through creation of rural non-farm jobs in China?", in *Urban Studies*, Vol. 39, No. 12, pp. 2163-2174.

Kapsos, S. 2004. "Estimating growth requirements for reducing working poverty: Can the world halve working poverty by 2015?" (Geneva, ILO), Employment Strategy Paper 2004/14. Background paper prepared for the *World Employment Report 2004-05*, available on the CD-ROM version.

Karshenas, M. 2004. *Global poverty estimates and the Millennium Goals: Towards a unified framework* (Geneva, ILO), Employment Strategy Paper 2004/5.

Khan, A.R.; Lee, E. 1995. "The expansion of productive employment in Asian agriculture: The lessons of the East Asian experience", in J. Cameron (ed.): *Poverty and power: The role of institutions and the market in development* (New Delhi, Oxford University Press).

Khan, A.R.; Riskin, C. 1998. "Income inequality in China: Composition, distribution and growth of household income, 1988 to 1995", in *China Quarterly*, Vol. 154, pp. 221-251.

Kundu, A.; Sarangi, N.; Dash, B.P. 2003. *Rural non-farm employment: An analysis of rural urban inter-dependencies* (London, Overseas Development Institute), Working Paper No. 196.

Lanjouw, J.O.; Lanjouw, P. 1995. *Rural non farm employment – A survey* (Washington, DC, World Bank), Policy Research Working Paper No. 1463.

—. 2001. "The rural non farm sector: Issues and evidence from developing countries", in *Agricultural Economics*, Vol. 26, pp. 1-23.

Leather, S. 2003. "AIDS and agriculture: A threat to rural workers and food production", in *Labour Education*, Vol. 2-3, No. 131-132 (Geneva, ILO).

Lipton, M. 1998. *Successes in anti-poverty* (Geneva, International Institute of Labour Studies).

Lübker, M. 2002. *Assessing the impact of past distributional shifts on global poverty levels* (Geneva, ILO), Employment Paper No. 2002/37.

Majid, N. 2003. *Globalization and poverty* (Geneva, ILO), Employment Paper No. 2003/54.

—. 2004. "Reaching Millenium Goals: How well does agricultural productivity growth reduce poverty?" (Geneva, ILO), Employment Strategy Paper No. 2004/12. Background paper prepared for the *World Employment Report 2004-05*, available on the CD-ROM version.

Mead, R.W. 2003. "A revisionist view of Chinese agricultural productivity", in *Contemporary Economic Policy*, Vol. 21, No. 1, pp. 117-131.

Park, A.; Wang, S. 2001. "China's poverty statistics", in *China Economic Review*, Vol. 12, No. 4, pp. 384-398.

Rangarajan, C. 1982. *Agricultural growth and industrial performance* (Washington, DC, International Food Policy Research Institute), Research Report No. 33.

Rao, D.S.; Coelli, T. J.; Alauddin, M. 2004. "Agricultural productivity growth, employment and poverty in developing countries, 1970-2000" (Brisbane, University of Queensland), Centre for Efficiency and Productivity Analysis. Background paper prepared for the *World Employment Report 2004-05*, available on the CD-ROM version.

Saith, A. 1992. *The rural non-farm economy: Processes and policies* (Geneva, ILO), World Employment Programme.

Sala-i-Martin, X. 2002. *The world distribution of income (estimated from individual country distributions)*, (Washinton, DC, National Bureau of Economic Research), Working Paper No. 8933, May.

Start, D. 2001. "The rise and fall of the rural non-farm economy: Poverty impacts and policy options", in *Development Policy Review*, Vol. 19, No. 4, pp. 491-505.

Thirtle, C.; Lin, L.; Piesse, J. 2003. "The impact of research-led agricultural productivity growth on poverty reduction in Africa, Asia and Latin America", in *World Development* (SSCI. Impact Factor: 1.056. ECONLIT), Vol. 31, No. 12, pp. 1959-1975.

Timmer, C. P. 1997. *How well do the poor connect to the growth process?* (Cambridge, Harvard Institute for International Development), CAER (Consulting Assistance on Economic Reform) Discussion Paper No. 178.

United Nations Development Programme (UNDP). 2003. *Making global trade work for people* (New York).

United Nations Environment Programme (UNEP). 2002. *Global Environment Outlook 3* (London, Earthscan).

United Nations Development Fund for Women (UNIFEM). 2000. *Progress of the World's Women* (New York).

United Nations Economic and Social Council. 2003. *Draft Ministerial Declaration*, E/2003/L.9.

Warr, P.G. 2002. *Poverty incidence and sectoral growth: Evidence from Southeast Asia* (Helsinki, World Institute for Development Research, WIDER), Discussion Paper No. 2002/20.

Wodon, Q.T. 1999. *Micro determinants of consumption, poverty, growth and inequality in Bangladesh* (Washington, DC, World Bank), Working Paper No. 2076.

World Bank. 2004a. *World Development Indicators 2004* (Washington, DC).

—. 2004b. *PovCal Datase 2004*. Available at: http://www.worldbank.org/lsms/tools/povcal

—. 2003a. *Land policies for growth and poverty reduction* (Washington, DC).

—. 2003b. *World Development Indicators 2003* (Washington, DC).

—. 2002. *Globalization, growth and poverty: Building an inclusive world economy* (Oxford and New York, Oxford University Press).

—. 2001. *World Development Report 2001: Attacking poverty* (Washington DC).

—. 2000. *India: Reducing poverty, accelerating development* (Washington, DC), World Bank Country Study 2000/01.

World Commission on the Social Dimension of Globalization. 2004. *A fair globalization: Creating opportunities for all* (Geneva, ILO).

Yao, S. 2000. "Economic development and poverty in China over 20 years of reforms", in *Economic Development and Cultural Change*, Vol. 48, No. 3, pp. 447-474.

Appendix 3.1 [35]

In table A3.1, each of the two poverty data sets (Sala-i-Martin and ILO) for the selected years are pooled and the relationship between the two measures of productivity and poverty are examined in regressions 1 to 4. The standard variable of per capita income is excluded in the regressions because the productivity measures are themselves related to per capita national income.

Having established broad contours of the agricultural productivity and poverty relationship controlling for the distribution of populations and incomes, the exercise proceeds in models 5 to 8 by qualifying some of the poverty-relevant dimensions of agricultural growth. For this purpose the variable capturing food production per person (food production per capita index), as well as food price (food price index) is introduced. Since land ownership distribution may be particularly linked to rural dimensions of poverty, a variable on this (LANDGINI) is also introduced.

One important result is that the agricultural labour productivity indicator appears to be more strongly associated with poverty reduction than TFP. The agricultural labour productivity indicator is negatively and significantly related to poverty for both data sets. On the other hand, the TFP variable has a negative sign in the Sala-i-Martin data set and a positive sign in the ILO data in the one case in which it is statistically significant. The variable on rural population has a positive sign in the cases in which it is significant. While the income distribution is consistently positive and significant, land ownership distribution is always positive and in two cases also significant. This suggests that intervention in the distribution of land is still an important policy to consider today when the objective is the reduction of poverty, especially in rural settings. As far as the food production index is concerned, it is significant in three cases and in each of these it has a negative sign. Therefore, as a qualifier to the focus on agricultural growth itself, the results suggest that growth in agriculture would be better for poverty reduction if food production per capita also grows. The positive, significant coefficients on the food price index imply that higher food prices tend to hurt the extreme poor, a likely reflection of the very high proportions of income spent on food among these members of society.

---

[35] The analyses in appendices 3.1 and 3.2 are based on Rao et al., 2004.

Table A3.1. Results based on regressions of poverty on labour productivity and TFP (US$1 a day poverty)

	Sala-i-Martin	ILO	Sala-i-Martin	ILO	Sala-i-Martin	ILO	Sala-i-Martin	ILO
	pooled 1970-2000	pooled 1987-2000	pooled 1970-2000	pooled 1987-2000	pooled 1970-2000	pooled 1987-2000	pooled 1970-2000	pooled 1987-2000
	1	2	3	4	5	6	7	8
Log of TFP	--	--	– NS	+ ***	--	--	– NS	+ NS
Log of agricultural output/labour	– ***	– ***	--	--	– ***	– ***	--	--
Log of rural population %	– NS	+ NS	+ ***	+ ***	– NS	– NS	+ ***	+ ***
Log Gini	+ *	+ ***	+ NS	+ ***	+ ***	+ ***	+ ***	+ ***
Food production per capita index	--	--	--	--	– NS	– ***	– **	– ***
Food price index	--	--	--	--	+ ***	+ NS	+ ***	+ **
Log of LANDGINI	--	--	--	--	+ **	+ ***	+ NS	+ NS
Constant	+ **	+ NS	– ***	– ***	+ NS	– NS	– ***	– ***
R² (adjusted)	0.36	0.49	0.24	0.41	0.55	0.64	0.42	0.53
N	195	180	200	185	97	124	101	129

Notes: – sign is negative, + sign is positive, -- not applicable, NS not significant, *significant at 10%, **significant at 5%, ***significant at 1%.

Appendix 3.2

This appendix provides the results of econometric models used to identify the determinants of total factor productivity and labour productivity across countries and over time. Independent variables used in the analysis include measures of non-labour agricultural inputs, such as irrigation prevalence, the number of tractors and quantity of fertilizer used; macroeconomic policies, such as government investment and consumption; economic openness, including trade policies and measures of foreign direct investment; education, as measured by literacy rates; quality of governance, as measured through polity and institutional quality variables; health status, for which a malaria-prevalence variable is used as a proxy; geography, which is measured by a tropics variable, rural population, an isolation indicator and through regional dummy variables; inequality, which is measured using a land Gini variable; and finally political stability, which is measured through a war indicator variable.

The results of this analysis are presented in a qualitative form. Table A3.2 reports the signs and significance of the coefficients. The research has used a general to specific modelling approach, in which the "general model" includes all of the independent variables. Regression 1 presents this general model, while regression 2 is the reduced or specific model in that it includes only those variables whose coefficients prove to be significant at the 10 per cent level or higher. In regression 3, a model is run in which continental dummy variables for sub-Saharan Africa (SSA), East Asia (EASIA), South Asia (SASIA) and Latin America and the Caribbean (LATAM) are included. In regressions 4 to 6 the approach of the previous three regressions is repeated, but with the inclusion of the Gini coefficient for the ownership distribution of land (LANDGINI). This model was run separately since the LANDGINI variable is only available for approximately 70 per cent of the countries in the sample; thus it significantly reduces the sample size. A comparable model is examined in regression 7 with the more standard labour productivity measure as the dependent variable. Additional explanatory variables used in regression 7 are tractors per thousand workers (TRACTORS) and fertilizers per million workers (FERTILIZERS).

1. Determinants of total factor productivity in agriculture

In general, the regressions perform quite well for yearly data of this nature, explaining 32 to 47 per cent of the variation in total factor productivity levels for agriculture. In regressions 1, 2 and 3 the variable indicating the proportion of land that is irrigated is positive and significant. TRADE and FDI, which can be said to constitute a proxy for openness, enhance TFP. This is a result, especially with respect to trade/GDP ratios, that is sometimes also found for poverty.[36] The signs on government investment (GDI) and government consumption as percentage of GDP (GOVCON) are negative. While at first sight this seems counter-intuitive, it might reflect urban biases in state allocation and funding agriculture.

---

[36] Dollar and Kraay, 2004; Majid, 2003.

Table A3.2. Results based on regressions of agricultural TFP and labour productivity

Dependent Variable	TFP	TFP	TFP	TFP	TFP	TFP	Labour Productivity
Regression No.	1	2	3	4	5	6	7
Observations	1450	1497	1497	1023	1023	1023	1023
R^2	0.33	0.32	0.35	0.36	0.36	0.47	0.91
R^2_a	0.33	0.31	0.35	0.3¬5	0.35	0.46	0.91
TRADE	+***	+***	+***	+*	+*	+***	+***
ILLITERACY	–***	–***	–***	–***	–***	–***	+ NS
ICRG3	–**	–***	– NS	– NS	--	– NS	– NS
GDI	–***	–***	–***	–***	–***	–***	+ NS
GOVCON	–***	–**	–***	–***	–***	–***	– NS
FDI	+***	+***	+***	+***	+***	+***	+***
TROPLAND	+***	+***	+ NS	+***	+***	–***	+***
DMALARIA	–***	–***	–**	–***	–***	–***	–***
RURAL	–***	–***	– NS	–***	–***	+ NS	– NS
DISTANCE	–***	–***	–***	–**	–***	–***	--
IRRIGATED	+***	+***	+***	+***	+***	+***	+***
POLITY	+ NS	--		–**	–***	–**	+***
WAR	– NS	--		+**	+***	+***	– NS
AGEDEPEND	+ NS	--		+***	+***	+**	+***
LANDGINI	--	--	--	–**	–**	–***	–**
TRACTORS							+***
FERTILIZERS							–***
SSA	--	--	+**	--	--	+***	
EASIA	--	--	+**	--	--	+***	+***
SASIA	--	--	– NS	--	--	+***	+****
LATAM	--	--	+***	--	--	+***	+***
CONSTANT	+***	+***	+***	+***	+***	+***	–***

Note: – sign is negative, + sign is positive, -- not applicable, NS not significant. *significant at 10%, **significant at 5%, ***significant at 1%.

On the other hand, this may also be reflective of fiscal constraints that developing countries face in the context of structural reforms.[37] While such discrimination can be traced to early development thinking, it is also a result of biases inherent in political systems as well as the fiscal straightjackets normally associated with reforms. The broad point is that government policy may discriminate against the rural sector both implicitly and explicitly. Human capital (ILLITERACY) and health (ΔMALARIA) indicators both show expected negative signs: a healthier and more educated workforce is associated with greater TFP. This is a policy area in which things can be done; it is also one that is directly related to poverty, since health and education are known correlates of poverty. Physical and geographical isolation (DISTANCE), also show a negative relationship with

---

[37] This correlation holds net of the effect of other variables in the model such as illiteracy rates, which are largely also a function of government expenditure.

TFP. The regression shows that the proportion of land in the tropics is positive and significant (TROPLAND). The positive coefficient on TROPLAND, though perhaps counter-intuitive in that tropical soils are generally less fertile, may be explained by perhaps beneficial effects of greater rainfall or other meteorological conditions.[38] The indicators of basic political participation (POLITY) or extent of political stability (WAR) do not show significant relationships to TFP. Moreover, regressions 4, 5 and 6 present several apparent anomalies. POLITY and WAR are, respectively, negatively and positively correlated with TFP levels, both of which can be construed as somewhat counter-intuitive results. In this context it needs to recognized that many of the best performers in terms of agricultural TFP do not perform well on these institutional and indices of political participation. Many countries that performed well in agricultural TFP have performed poorly in terms of increasing political freedom, corruption indices, and macroeconomic policy reform. The point, however, is that it is necessary to deconstruct democracy much more in order to meaningfully examine its relationship to agricultural growth.[39] Similarly the indicator of institutional quality (ICRG3) shows a negative sign in regressions 1 and 2. Once again, while the relationship may appear counter-intuitive, it is likely that this measure captures non-agrarian institutional conditions.[40] The variable that is likely to best capture "institutional conditions" in agriculture is probably the distribution of ownership holdings (LANDGINI) because it is the distribution of assets that reflect social relations and property rights best in an agrarian context. As expected, this variable is significantly and negatively correlated with TFP levels. The inclusion of LANDGINI renders the institutional quality variable insignificant (regression 4).

2. Determinants of labour productivity in agriculture

Regression 7 shows that the TRACTORS variable is highly significant but the FERTILIZERS variable has a negative sign, which is difficult to explain. The inclusion of these variables results in several changes to other non-technical coefficients in the model. In particular, the coefficients on illiteracy, GDI and GCON (which were negatively correlated with TFP) are no longer significant. This may suggest that urban biases in resource allocation may apply more to TFP-led growth. DISTANCE is no longer significant, POLITY has a positive sign and the institutional variable is not significant. LANDGINI is negative, suggesting that for both TFP and labour productivity more equal land distributions may be beneficial. The results on labour productivity suggest that the number of tractors per 1,000 workers appears to account for about 50 per cent of the variation in labour productivity observed across the developing countries in this

---

[38] Furthermore, when fixed effects are included in regression 6, the TROPLAND variable becomes negatively correlated with TFP levels.

[39] Bardhan et al., 1999.

[40] The addition of fixed effects (continental dummies; regression 3) appears to consistently render the coefficients on RURAL and ICRG3 insignificant.

data set. The remainder of the variation is largely explained by geographical and geological factors, as well as FDI flows. The overall fit of the regression on labour productivity is better than the TFP models.

Appendix 3.3

Selected ILO activities in the agricultural sector

The ILO has long recognized the potential of the agricultural sector to contribute to economic development and to alleviate decent work deficits (see also box 3.10). A selection of ILO activities in agriculture is listed below.

International labour Conventions related to agriculture

Many of the ILO's Conventions are directly or indirectly related to working conditions in the agricultural sector. These include:

- Convention No. 184 on Safety and Health in Agriculture (adopted in 2001 and so far ratified by three countries).
- Convention No. 182 on Worst Forms of Child Labour (147 ratifications).
- Convention No. 129 on Labour Inspection (Agriculture) (41 ratifications).
- Convention No. 141 on Rural Workers' Organisations.
- Conventions No. 97 and No. 143 on Migrant workers (42 and 18 ratifications, respectively).

(For a more complete list, see "Safety and health in agriculture", Report VI (1), International Labour Conference, 88th Session, 2000, http://www.ilo.org/public/english/standards/relm/ilc/ilc88/rep-vi-1.htm)

Clearly, there is no lack of instruments to tackle decent work deficits in agriculture; what are lacking are more ratifications and implementations.

"Jobs for Africa"

Jobs for Africa is an ILO flagship programme to support the creation of decent and productive employment for poverty reduction in Africa. The programme provides the framework for regionalizing the Global Employment Agenda in the context of the New Partnership for Africa's Development (NEPAD) and for supporting the formulation processes of the Poverty Reduction Strategy Papers (PRSPs) with the ultimate objective of reducing the decent work deficits in Africa. Recognizing the importance of a parallel development of all sectors, the idea is first to develop a conceptual framework for comprehensive and sectoral policies on employment creation for poverty reduction; second, to identify policy tools and operational systems to implement employment creation for poverty reduction; and third, to design a comprehensive regional programme to support country-level employment promotion programmes. The programme has two main parts: concentrating public investment on labour-intensive infrastructure projects that employ the poor and are located in poor areas, and reforming capital markets to provide sufficient credit to the poor to finance self-employment and micro-enterprises in both urban and rural informal sectors.

ILO's Global Campaign on Social Security and Coverage for All

Efforts by the ILO to help improve social protection for agricultural workers are placed within the broader framework of the ILO's Global Campaign on Social

Security and Coverage for All, which was launched in 2002 following the conclusion of the general discussion on social security at the 2001 International Labour Conference. The ILO global programme on Strategies and Tools against Social Exclusion (STEP) is a key operational instrument in this campaign. Among other activities, STEP seeks to develop innovative mechanisms for the inclusion of agricultural workers and farmers within social protection mechanisms.

Tripartite Meeting on Moving to Sustainable Agricultural Development through the Modernization of Agriculture and Employment in a Globalized Economy

The purpose of this meeting in September 2000 was to exchange views on the agricultural sector in the twenty-first century: to gauge its contribution to employment, incomes and prospects for productivity gains; to adopt conclusions that include proposals for action by governments, by employers' and workers' organizations at the national level and by the ILO; and to adopt a report on its discussion. (For more details see: http://www.ilo.org/public/english/dialogue/sector/techmeet/tmad00/tmadr.htm#_Toc488568316)

International Workers' Symposium on Decent Work in Agriculture:

In September 2003, the ILO Bureau for Worker's Activities organized an International Workers' Symposium on Decent Work in Agriculture. The goal was to raise awareness and to promote the ILO's mandate in the context of the rapid globalization of agriculture throughout the world. In particular, the Symposium addressed the problems workers in agriculture face, such as social exclusion, poverty, and lack of fundamental rights. It also focused on sustainable agriculture and development, food security and decent work in agriculture. The final conclusions summarizing the findings of the Symposium are available at: http://www.ilo.org/public/english/dialogue/actrav/new/agsymp03/concl.pdf For more details on this Symposium, see http://www.ilo.org/public/english/dialogue/actrav/new/agsymp03/ index.htm

Technical assistance

Advisory services and technical assistance are available and provided regularly to member States in the areas of rural farm and non-farm employment promotion, rural poverty alleviation, technology, training, wage policy, occupational safety and health, labour administration, social security, and rural workers' organizations.

Research in the area

The agricultural sector has long been a research focus in the ILO. Previous related ILO research topics range from detailed country analyses of specific agricultural products to regional analyses of the agricultural sector as a whole. For a selection of related ILO papers, see http://www.ilo.org/public/english/dialogue/sector/sectors/agri/publ.htm

4. A stable workplace? A mobile workforce? – What is best for increasing productivity?

4.1. Introduction

Globalization and the pace of technological change have fuelled the long-running debate over labour market flexibility. Both, it is argued, increase competitive pressures and the speed with which enterprises need to react to change, thereby putting a premium on flexibility. The corollary of this argument is that, when labour markets are flexible, structural transformation can occur more rapidly, since both capital and labour can shift to newer, higher value-added sectors. The growth of the ICT service sector in the United States is offered as an example, as is the (labour-saving) use of ICT in process innovations or, indeed, in outsourcing. Flexibility, therefore, is said to favour inter-sectoral mobility, and, in turn, inter-sectoral mobility favours productivity and employment growth.

Curiously, however, this macro-view of structural transformation in relation to flexibility differs from the micro-view. As this chapter discusses, there is substantial evidence that stability of employment (tenure) is positively related to productivity gains. Many reasons exist for this positive relationship. Most prominently, tenure not only increases the gains of learning by doing, but is also an inducement for firms to invest in training (as they will be able to reap the rewards of their investment). The objective of the present chapter is to address the "flexibility versus stability" paradox of productivity growth.

Section 4.2 of this chapter looks at "structural transformation", or the mobility of labour and capital between sectors. Section 4.3 examines the opposite – the relative "fixity" or stability of capital and labour at the micro-level. Both are then set in relation to their implications for the future of labour market institutions and regulations, in Section 4.4. In particular, balancing flexibility and stability is addressed through the policy of protected mobility. The foregoing sections mainly consider industrialized countries. Section 4.5 poses the question of whether the conclusions for industrialized countries also apply to developing countries.

4.2. The mobility of labour and capital between sectors

Fifty years ago, in 1954, the Nobel laureate economist Sir Arthur Lewis wrote an article still considered an influential classic in the development economics literature. Lewis's central insight was that development occurs when labour and capital move from lower value-adding sectors, such as agriculture, into the more dynamic, higher value-adding manufacturing sector. When workers move from low productivity to high productivity sectors, overall productivity increases and so does economic growth. His view of the process is discussed in box 4.1.

Box 4.1.   Arthur Lewis, a pioneer of development economics

Arthur Lewis (1915-1991) was a leading figure in research on developing countries. His ground-breaking works[1] in the mid-1950s – *Economic development with unlimited supplies of labour* and *Theory of economic growth* – have been followed by a series of other important works. The experience he gained from his numerous assignments, as an economic adviser and as the administrator of a large development bank, gave him great insight into evolving political guidance for countries during the development process. Lewis tackled issues that were basic to the causes of poverty and to the unsatisfactory rate of economic growth in the developing world. His work, designed to describe and explain the intrinsic problems of underdevelopment, won great acclaim and gave rise to widespread scientific debate which has resulted in a series of variations and additions to Lewis's original premises.

The model of interest for this chapter is based on the dual nature of a developing economy. Lewis wrote: "One day in August, 1952, walking down the road in Bangkok, it came to me suddenly ... throw away the neoclassical assumption that the quantity of labour is fixed. An 'unlimited supply of labour' will keep wages down... The result is a dual (national or world) economy, where one part is a reservoir of cheap labour for the other. The unlimited supply of labour derives ultimately from population pressure, so it is a phase in the demographic cycle." He referred to an agricultural sector functioning on traditional lines, primarily based on self-support, which engages the labour of the greater part of the population. This sector is characterized by low productivity and value added. The other sector is modern, market-oriented, primarily engaged in industrial production and characterized by high productivity and value added. The driving force in the economy stems from the industrial sector, which expands with the support of unlimited supplies of cheap labour by migration from the agricultural sector. People migrate from agricultural areas because of lack of work and because they are forced to take any income opportunity given to them (the problem of hidden unemployment in the agricultural sector). The modern sector is able to pay slightly higher wages because of higher productivity. Profits in the modern sector create the growing savings which finance the capital formation for expansion.

[1] Lewis, 1954; 1955.

Source: "Sir Arthur Lewis – Autobiography", http://www.nobel.se/economics/laureates/1979/lewis-autobio.html

While Lewis's article is a discussion of development, the general message is that inter-sectoral mobility is important for productivity growth and, consequently, employment and output growth. This resides in turn on the mobility with which capital and labour move to the most dynamic growth sectors. Yet all economies have limits on such mobility. Product market regulations – for example, commercial taxes or zoning laws, the costs or bureaucratic hurdles to be overcome in starting a new business – can be such that they discourage entrepreneurship. Similarly, deficiencies in the education and skill formation systems can impede labour mobility.

Although admittedly suggestive rather than conclusive, figure 4.1 appears to make intuitive sense. It relates inter-sectoral mobility to productivity growth

Figure 4.1. Change in employment by sector and annual productivity growth, selected industrialized countries (1980-2000)

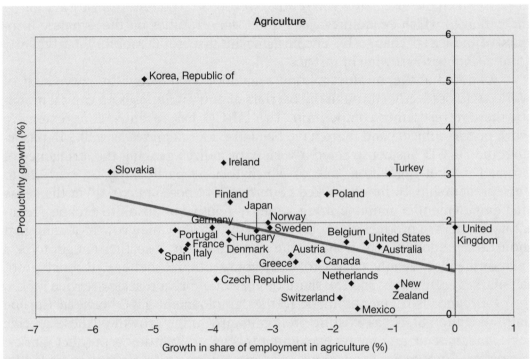

Note: Change in the agricultural share of employment, productivity growth (%).
Source: ILO, 2003a.

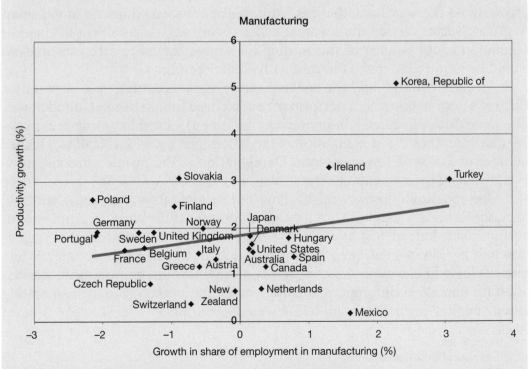

Note: Change in the manufacturing share of employment, productivity growth (%).
Source: ILO, 2003a.

and, as predicted in the Lewis argument, the relationship is indeed positive. While innovation and productivity improvements *within* industries are important (to which the discussion will return) so, too, is "structural transformation" – the extent to which economies can exploit opportunities on the dynamic frontiers of industrial change by encouraging inter-sectoral mobility, particularly from declining to growing industries.

As noted above, product market regulation could slow the movement of workers across sectors through the barriers of entry it imposes on capital mobility, thereby restricting competition. The OECD has recently done extensive work on this subject[1] and there have been previous analyses as well.[2] In particular, the OECD has constructed a variety of indices gauging the stringency of product market regulation, one of which focuses particularly on barriers to entrepreneurship. In industrialized countries (or "post-industrial" in the sense that employment in manufacturing stands in relative or absolute decline), regulatory barriers in product markets could plausibly slow the growth of emergent industries, predominantly in the private, service sector. If so, there ought to be a relationship between the degree to which competition is sheltered through product market regulations, and the share or growth of private-sector service jobs.

Reference is frequently made to the "employment gap" between Europe and the United States as existing predominantly in the growth of these specific jobs. And, indeed, arguments explaining this gap rely little on product market regulation. Europeans, for example, consume many more services provided by the public sector – particularly health – which Americans, in contrast, purchase privately. At the very least, there is a difference between countries in the share of private-sector service employment and, as figure 4.2 suggests, product market regulation could be part of the reason. Of course, far more rigorous analysis would be required to make the case with greater certainty.

An earlier study[3] held European product market regulation to account for Europe's poor employment performance compared to that of the United States. The same study relegated labour market rigidities to a subsidiary role in explaining this difference:"... deregulation in the labour market will ... lead to a higher number of low-skill, low-wage jobs. Deregulation in the product market, however, will lead to job creation across the board."[4]

One conclusion to draw might therefore be that labour market "rigidities" turn out to be less significant as an explanation for differences in employment performance. Indeed, just how much weight to assign to labour market regulation and institutions has been a subject of debate for over two decades. While there is logic in elevating the constraints on the product market as an explanation for important differences in employment and output growth, exonerating labour market regulation completely would seem facile. The situation is more

---

[1] OECD, 2002.

[2] McKinsey Global Institute, 1994.

[3] ibid.

[4] ibid., cited in ILO, 1995, p. 158.

Figure 4.2.   Share of private-sector employment in services vs. the entrepreneurship barrier index, selected industrialized countries, late 1990s and early 2000s

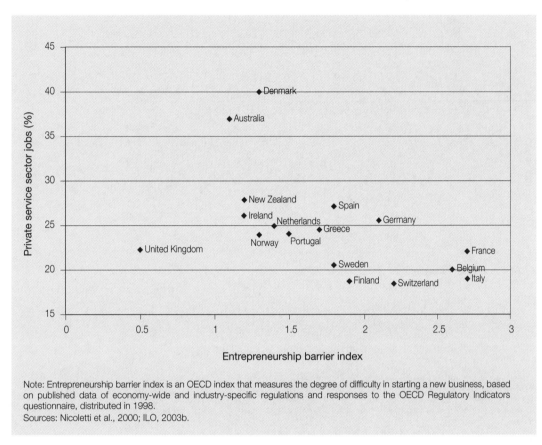

Note: Entrepreneurship barrier index is an OECD index that measures the degree of difficulty in starting a new business, based on published data of economy-wide and industry-specific regulations and responses to the OECD Regulatory Indicators questionnaire, distributed in 1998.
Sources: Nicoletti et al., 2000; ILO, 2003b.

complex, as there are important interdependencies in product and labour market regulation.

Research by the OECD[5] found a significant and positive relationship between the strictness of product and labour market regulation, with labour market regulation proxied by an index of the stringency of employment protection legislation (EPL). In one hypothetical interpretation of this relationship, limiting product market regulation could allow a country to have tougher laws on employment protection, since reducing competition in product markets could enhance the employment stability of those with work. Alternatively, the hypothesis could be argued with the reverse causality: the social choice of legislating greater employment protection could require that product market competition be circumscribed. Figure 4.3 reveals that the share of workers with long tenure (greater than ten years) is quite clearly related to the degree of stringency of product market regulation. Taken together, this implies a third relationship: the likelihood that the stringency of EPL is positively related to employment tenure. It is, and discussion will return to this point.

---

[5] Nicoletti et al., 2000.

**Figure 4.3. Strictness of product market regulation vs. share of workers with long tenure,
selected industrialized countries, late 1990s and early 2000s**

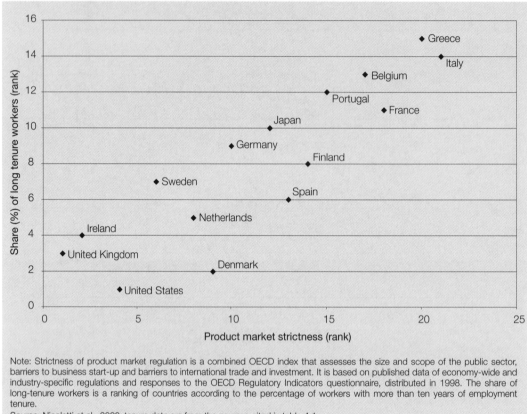

Note: Strictness of product market regulation is a combined OECD index that assesses the size and scope of the public sector, barriers to business start-up and barriers to international trade and investment. It is based on published data of economy-wide and industry-specific regulations and responses to the OECD Regulatory Indicators questionnaire, distributed in 1998. The share of long-tenure workers is a ranking of countries according to the percentage of workers with more than ten years of employment tenure.
Source: Nicoletti et al., 2000; tenure data are from the sources cited in table 4.1.

National governments regulate product and labour markets differently. Increasing globalization, however, generally implies more pressure on both markets to respond to change arising from external competition. In the European Union, for example, with the accession of ten new Member States, greater competitive pressure is anticipated. As figure 4.4 suggests, the degree to which competition can be curtailed through product market regulation bears some relation to the degree of economic openness (measured here as the log of the share of imports and exports in GDP). A plausible hypothesis is that regulatory regimes that seek to shelter product and labour markets from the full gales of competitive pressures are able to do so with less openness to the external economy.

Yet the winds of change are such that product markets will likely yield to greater openness, and, indeed, regulatory reform of product markets in Europe is advancing.[6] In view of the close relationship between product and labour market regulation, the question is whether labour markets, and the institutions and regulations that support them, will also need to yield to greater openness. The

---

[6] Blanchard, 2004.

Figure 4.4. Degree of openness vs. barriers to entrepreneurship, selected European countries, 1970-2000

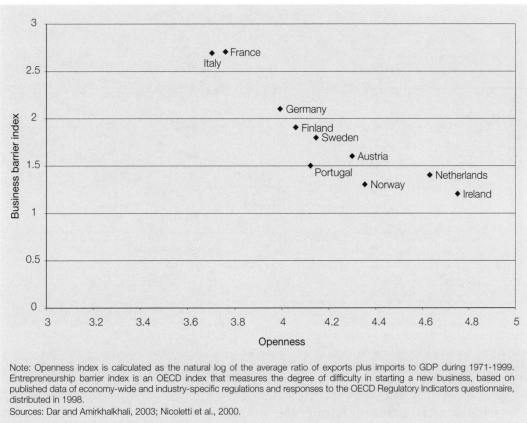

Note: Openness index is calculated as the natural log of the average ratio of exports plus imports to GDP during 1971-1999. Entrepreneurship barrier index is an OECD index that measures the degree of difficulty in starting a new business, based on published data of economy-wide and industry-specific regulations and responses to the OECD Regulatory Indicators questionnaire, distributed in 1998.
Sources: Dar and Amirkhalkhali, 2003; Nicoletti et al., 2000.

answer is likely to be in the affirmative, but with an important difference: whereas openness and a tendency to product market deregulation are apparent, openness and labour market deregulation are decidedly not.

In fact, if spending on labour market policies can be taken as a proxy for labour market intervention, then the more open an economy is, *the more such intervention occurs*, as is clearly apparent in figure 4.5.

Money spent is nonetheless a crude indicator of policies and programmes. What should the nature of such intervention be? To answer this question requires an understanding of the economics – not of capital and labour mobility – but of employment stability, to which discussion now turns.

4.3. Employment stability and productivity

First, the term "tenure" is defined, with some descriptive observations on differences in tenure between countries. The reasons for such differences are presented, with a focus on two labour market institutions in particular. Thereafter, the relation between employment tenure and productivity is reviewed, and also the theoretical and empirical literature on whether or not tenure is good for productivity growth.

**Figure 4.5. Spending on labour market policies increases with openness,
selected industrialized countries, 1970-2000**

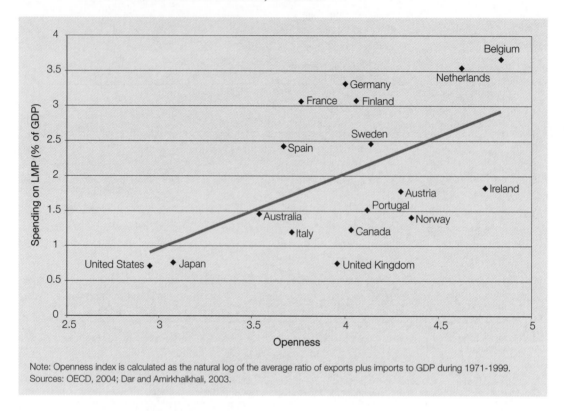

Note: Openness index is calculated as the natural log of the average ratio of exports plus imports to GDP during 1971-1999.
Sources: OECD, 2004; Dar and Amirkhalkhali, 2003.

Employment tenure is simply the amount of time that a worker has spent working for the same employer, even if the worker's job within the firm has changed. In short, "employment" tenure and "job" tenure are not synonyms. In fact, short job tenure in the context of long employment tenure with the same firm possibility reflects "functional" flexibility, or the extent to which firms adjust internally to changes in labour demand, rather than through the external labour market. As table 4.1 shows, average aggregate employment tenure varies – often quite substantially – across countries. In general, European and Japanese workers have longer tenure than those in the United States, and the latter have longer tenure than workers in Latin America.[7]

What explains differences in employment tenure?

A variety of factors accounts for differences in the length of employment tenure. An initial observation is that – whatever these factors are – the differences themselves appear to change negligibly over time. Thus, the rather stark difference in employment tenure between the United States and the European Union remains the same today as 15 years ago. On the one hand, this is a reflection of

---

[7] A salaried or dependent worker is an employee, thus the data include persons who are employed by large, small and micro-enterprises as well as workers employed as domestic servants. Self-employed workers are not considered dependent and are excluded from the data.

Table 4.1.   Average tenure and tenure distribution, selected OECD and Latin American countries, various years

	Average tenure (years)	Workers with < 1 year tenure (%)	Workers with > 10 years tenure (%)
Greece	13.6	9.8	52.1
Japan	12.2	8.3	43.2
Italy	12.2	10.8	49.3
France	11.2	15.3	44.2
EU-14*	10.6	14.8	41.5
Germany	10.6	14.3	41.7
Denmark	8.3	20.9	31.5
United Kingdom	8.2	19.1	32.1
Argentina	6.7	27.5	21.2
United States	6.6	24.5	26.2
Peru	6.3	29.0	20.1
Chile	5.5	34.5	18.8
Brazil	5.3	37.2	16.4
Honduras	3.9	51.4	10.1

*Excludes Austria.

Sources: Data for Europe from 2002 based on Eurostat; US data from 1998 based on national sources; Latin American data from IADB (2004) based on household surveys of the late 1990s and 2000s.

just how deeply rooted – and durable – are the different characteristics of national labour markets. On the other hand, this durability itself considerably qualifies the popular assumption that employment security has eroded everywhere.[8]

Beyond this observation is the clear presence of cultural, economic, institutional, and purely demographic factors that explain differences in tenure. For example, demographic factors matter in a rather straightforward manner, as figure 4.6 illustrates. The younger a country's population, the lower its average tenure will be, for the simple reason that a greater share of the working-age population will have lived less long (a distinguishing feature between developing and industrialized countries). Younger people also change jobs more frequently than older people. The latter, with time, will have perhaps found the job match that suits both them and their employer, have family responsibilities which increase the fixed costs of mobility, have invested more in firm-specific skills, or have attained a level of income and benefits difficult to replace in the external job market.

Differences in GDP growth can also influence tenure. A country with sustained, higher levels of GDP growth is likely to be one in which employment is increasing as well. New entrants to the employed workforce reduce the average aggregate tenure of the workforce as a whole. Good economic times can also

---

[8] Auer and Cazes, 2003. See Neumark (2000) for an in-depth analysis of changes in job stability and security in the United States in the 1990s.

Figure 4.6. Average tenure vs. median age, selected European and Latin American countries, Japan and the United States, late 1990s and early 2000s

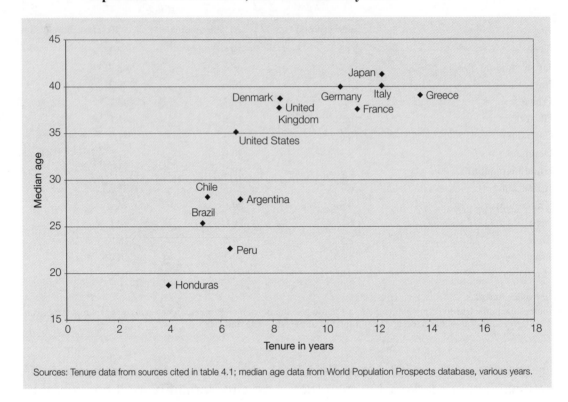

Sources: Tenure data from sources cited in table 4.1; median age data from World Population Prospects database, various years.

encourage greater voluntary transitions between jobs. Economic growth's influence on tenure applies at more disaggregated levels as well: a growth sector is likely to have lower average tenure than a mature one. Another economic factor to which discussion returns below is that of differing economic structures. An economy with a relatively higher share of small firms is likely to have lower average tenure duration than one whose share of large firms is greater, since small firms are characterized by a higher rate of market entrances and exits than large firms. While it hardly proves the point, this may be one reason why a small-firm economy such as Denmark, for example, also has tenure duration substantially lower than the EU average. A speculative point is that a small-firm economy may *require* a higher degree of micro-flexibility than one in which large firms predominate.[9]

Institutional and regulatory factors

Labour market "institutions", whether formal or informal, are an expression of underlying social and economic relations and cultural preferences in a society. Broadly understood, institutions can be of many sorts. Formal institutions

---

[9] Several other economic factors (some of which were described by Alfred Marshall in the nineteenth century) plausibly affect tenure. For example, if labour costs are a small share of total costs, tenure is often longer.

include the regulations that govern hiring and dismissal (i.e. employment protection legislation), collective bargaining negotiations that concern job retention and dismissal, or set the wage/employment trade-off, as well as social protection policies such as unemployment insurance, which can influence mobility and hiring decisions.

Numerous informal institutions also affect tenure. Certain customs may be embedded in a society to encourage job retention on the part of both employers and workers. Such preferences can be codified: Malaysia's social partners, for example, have agreed to a code of conduct whereby a first response to a business downturn ought to be through an across-the-board cut in earnings affecting both managers and workers. The point is that any restrictions on numerical flexibility (whether formal, as through EPL, or simply through custom) create the incentive that alternatives to adjustment through dismissals be found. Society's expectations also matter. For example, beliefs regarding childcare and work may influence a worker's decision to remain in the labour market or not.

Two institutions in relation to employment tenure

Among the myriad factors that affect employment tenure, two labour market institutions – employment protection legislation and collective bargaining – are key influences.

Employment protection legislation (EPL) and job stability

Employment protection legislation has played a prominent role in the debate over labour market flexibility and employment creation. The arguments are well-rehearsed and need no recalling here.[10] Of note in the present discussion is the relationship between EPL and extended tenure in OECD countries, evident in figure 4.7, which shows the share of long-tenured workers (defined as greater than ten years) relative to an index of the stringency of EPL. The two are clearly related: the more stringent EPL is, the greater the share of workers with long tenure.

Unionization, social dialogue and employment stability

The stability or flexibility of an employment relationship is also influenced by the level of unionization that exists in a country, as well as the characteristics and aims of social dialogue. The nature of this relationship, in turn, has important effects on productivity. At an aggregate level, union presence does seem to be related to longer average tenure, as figure 4.8 illustrates. A comparison of Europe, Japan, Latin America and the United States shows a positive relationship between average employment tenure for salaried workers and the percentage of salaried workers covered by collective bargaining agreements. As with the relationship to employment protection legislation, the continental European countries – with collective bargaining coverage rates ranging from 55 to 95 per cent – have much higher tenure than either Latin America or the United States,

---

[10] OECD, 1994; ILO, 1995; IMF, 2003.

Figure 4.7. Strictness of employment protection legislation vs. percentage of workers with long tenure, selected industrialized countries, 1998

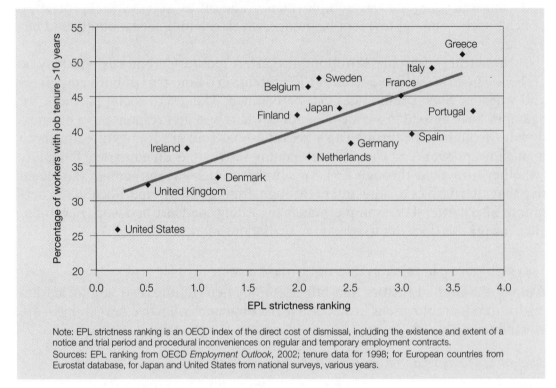

Note: EPL strictness ranking is an OECD index of the direct cost of dismissal, including the existence and extent of a notice and trial period and procedural inconveniences on regular and temporary employment contracts.
Sources: EPL ranking from OECD *Employment Outlook*, 2002; tenure data for 1998; for European countries from Eurostat database, for Japan and United States from national surveys, various years.

where collective bargaining coverage is low (mainly under 20 per cent). Japan is an outlier, with a 20 per cent collective bargaining coverage rate but the highest average tenure – perhaps a good example of how other less formal labour market institutions, in this case the *nen-ko* security-based earnings and promotion system, can play an important role in promoting employment stability.

Because these data cover all salaried workers, the direct effect of unions on employment tenure is not readily apparent. Further breakdown of the analysis in order to compare unionized versus non-unionized workers in the United States reveals sharp differences: 48 per cent of unionized workers have long tenure (employment tenure greater than ten years) compared with only 22 per cent of non-unionized workers.[11] The average tenure for unionized workers in the United States approaches the European average. Explicit employment security provisions in collective bargaining agreements no doubt explain some of this difference, but are not the only factor. In many countries, unionized workers tend on average to be older than those who are non-unionized; and organized workplaces are often in more established firms, where average tenure may be longer. It also matters whether the data relate to the public sector, where unionization rates (and tenure) are often higher than in the private sector.

---

[11] Data prepared by the American Federation of Labor-Congress of Industrial Organizations, based on the 1998 US Current Population Survey (see http://www.aflcio.org).

Figure 4.8. Collective bargaining coverage and average tenure in selected European and Latin American countries, Japan and the United States, late 1990s and early 2000s

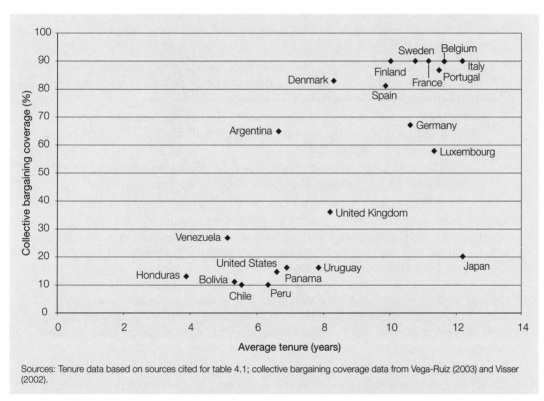

Sources: Tenure data based on sources cited for table 4.1; collective bargaining coverage data from Vega-Ruiz (2003) and Visser (2002).

While it cannot be asserted that unionized workplaces are always more productive than equivalent non-union ones, there remains substantial evidence of the beneficial effects of unions on productivity growth. Recent evidence for the United States, for example, concludes that "the unionized firms that ... adopted ... workplace innovations had higher productivity than even the non-unionized firms with those innovations. This finding may be due in part to the job security unions provided that enabled the workers to speak freely about potential improvements in the production process without fear of losing their jobs."[12] The organization of work as a powerful source of productivity growth is a subject to which discussion will return. The more general effects of unions on productivity-enhancing employment stability are described in box 4.2.

Unions and training

A major conduit for improving productivity is through training, and here unions play a salient role. Dialogue with workers' representatives regarding training can reduce information asymmetries by identifying those areas where workers' skills are weakest. Furthermore, when their representative participates in the development of a training programme, workers are more likely to accept the

---

[12] Black and Lynch, 2004, p. 3.

Box 4.2. How do unions promote employment stability?

Unionization and social dialogue can promote employment stability both at the micro- or firm-level as well as the macroeconomic level. At the firm-level, unions promote stability in three ways.

- Higher wages associated with unionism deter workers from switching jobs on the supply side and, on the demand side, wage pressure could force employers to seek productivity improvements to offset it.

- Institutional mechanisms available through unions give workers a "voice," allowing them to channel the grievances of the "median" worker for resolution, rather than opt for "exiting" the job.

- Many collective bargaining agreements include provisions that limit lay-offs, again inducing cost-adjustment solutions through other channels.

As is commonly discussed in the literature on the economic effect of unions, union workers earn on average more than their equivalent non-union counterparts as a result of their bargaining power with employers. This is known as the union-wage differential, and depending on the country, the industry, the bargaining power of workers, and the socio-economic characteristics of the workforce, the differential can amount to 15 per cent above the wages of similar non-unionized workers. Because a worker in a unionized firm risks losing this differential upon quitting, there is greater incentive for workers to stay with their employers, thus increasing tenure. The lower quit rate, in turn, implies greater overall employment stability among union members.

As there is an association between trade unionism and a significant reduction in quit rates, it is clear that trade unions do more than just raise the wages of their members. They also provide an institutionalized form of communication that gives workers the ability to voice dissatisfaction – the "voice mechanism". Such a mechanism allows workplace problems to be solved, rather than having workers simply "exit" the firm. Worker and employer representatives can establish grievance procedures and other forums for worker-manager dialogue that facilitate worker participation, thereby encouraging greater stability in the employment relationship.

Both higher wages and improved communication encourage union members to stay on the job, but another compelling reason for the relatively higher employment stability among unionized workers are union efforts to ensure employment security. Unions can promote employment stability by negotiating collective bargaining agreements that include provisions against worker dismissal, in exchange for other concessions. Indeed, "job security has emerged as the primary trade-off under flexibility bargaining".[1] A review of bilateral and trilateral flexibility negotiations in 22 countries found that unions traded employment security in exchange for concessions on wages, contingent work, cuts in working time, and employee ownership programmes.

At the macroeconomic level, unions also promote stability through social dialogue with government and employers' representatives. In these instances, agreements are made on national wage policies. For example, the setting of the minimum wage or the development of wage policies which ensure wage increases match productivity growth, can help to establish macroeconomic conditions that facilitate job growth. In times of economic change or uncertainty, social dialogue can be instrumental in making job retention and job creation a priority for governments and social partners.

Having an effective mechanism in place for social dialogue at the national level can prove a competitive advantage for countries, particularly during economic restructuring or downturn. Singapore's relatively rapid adjustment to the Asian financial crisis with minimal job loss is a case in point. Rather than lay-offs or wage cuts, the solution of choice was to relieve employers of a share of their non-wage labour costs. Enterprises thereby received some relief in their labour costs, yet the retention of jobs and earnings propped up aggregate demand in the economy.

In Europe in the 1990s, many countries engaged in national social dialogue to develop policies for increasing competitiveness without compromising on social protection. The issues were wide-ranging and included monetary policy, taxation, wage increases, social welfare reforms, and the enhancement of workplace collective rights. In Ireland, Denmark and the Netherlands, the government and social partners agreed on social pacts aimed at solving the countries' economic problems through a concerted approach based on wage moderation and a boost in economic competitiveness. The policies resulted in strong employment creation. Similarly, national social dialogue in Barbados in the 1990s focused on surmounting economic crises while minimizing lay-offs and social hardship. The social partners and government agreed to focus on competitiveness and productivity, to accept wage freezes until corresponding productivity gains were achieved, and to retain jobs.

[1] Ozaki, 1999, p.127.
Sources: Freeman, 1980; Ozaki, 1999; Auer, 2000; Campbell, 2001; Ishikawa, 2003.

programme, potentially improving its effectiveness. Employers' organizations can also be instrumental in encouraging training, as they can persuade individual firms to provide general training for an industry's workers. Without this joint commitment of firms within a given industry to provide training, the industry may develop an incentive problem: firms would be hesitant to train a worker out of fear that she or he may leave the firm or be poached by a competitor.[13]

The relationship between unions, training and employment stability runs both ways. By ensuring that workers' skills are deepened and kept up to date through training, unions have an instrument to attain employment security for their workers. At the same time, firms are more willing to invest in training their workers if they have some assurance that they will stay. This assurance has been instrumental to the success of high-performance work systems, as box 4.3 explains. Since union members are characterized as having lower turnover, union-covered firms may train a greater proportion of their workers, as firms are more likely to receive the returns from this investment.

Research findings support this theory. A recent study of the relationship between union coverage and training, based on a sample of male workers from household surveys in the United Kingdom between 1991 and 1996, reports a training incidence among union-covered men that was ten percentage points higher than non-union-covered men.[14] The authors then estimate an econometric

---

[13] Soskice, 1990.

Box 4.3. Tenure, productivity, and the new organization of work

The emergence of "high-performance work systems" has renewed attention on the use of tenure as a policy to induce workers to improve their performance. High-performance work systems (HPWS) involve a reorganization of work, away from the Taylorist model of direct supervision of employee tasks, to autonomous teams focused on problem-solving or quality improvement. The purpose of HPWS is to increase the participation of workers in decision-making. Workers make assessments about job tasks and methods of work and then communicate their insights with other workers, managers and experts. Active participation of workers in problem-solving committees is believed to raise productivity and numerous studies indicate that high-performance work systems increase productivity.

This conclusion is borne out in a study of the manufacturing sector.[1] The authors found that workers assigned most importance to job security, measured in the study as the existence of an explicit employment security agreement or trust in management to do its best to avoid lay-offs in the case of a decline in company sales. In the steel industry, for example, employee security's influence on "uptime" (the amount of time a factory is running) was nearly double that of incentive pay. Given that line delays are extremely costly in steel production, assuring security proved beneficial for output. In the garment industry, the authors also found similar productivity benefits among low-skilled workers, who traditionally receive little investment from firms. Employment security, it would seem, is relevant not only in white-collar or knowledge-intensive industries.[2]

Guaranteeing job security is imperative in HPWS in order to induce workers to discuss their ideas about productivity improvements. In the absence of security, workers will fear that they may innovate themselves out of a job: "Since high-performance companies consider workers as one of their key investments, they view layoffs as an option of last resort, offering instead an explicit commitment to employment security. Some firms adopt no-layoff policies; others send employees for training during 'slow' periods or redeploy workers to other jobs within the company. Still others turn to employee ownership as a way to avoid job losses. High-performance companies also respond to business downturns with various employment arrangements, including part-time, contract, temporary full-time, and work-sharing. When companies support employment security policies, workers reciprocate with greater flexibility and commitment."[3]

[1] Applebaum et al., 2000.

[2] Indeed, the European Commission (2002) found that low-skilled workers who receive on-the-job training have a risk of unemployment comparable to that of high-skilled workers, similarly benefiting from jobs with training.

[3] US Dept. of Labor, 1994, p.11.

Sources: OECD, 1999; Applebaum et al., 2000

model that accounts for differences in workers' traits, including motivation and ability. They find that among similar workers, union-covered workers have a five percentage-point greater chance of receiving training. In the sample, this amounted to four extra days of training for union versus non-union workers.[15]

---

[14] Booth et al., 2003.

[15] ibid. The extra training also resulted in a 7 per cent wage increase for union workers.

The foregoing discussion thus offers support for the positive relationship between employment tenure and employment protection legislation and the institution of collective bargaining. Such stability in the workplace is likely to be favourably perceived by the employees who benefit from it. The question remains, however: Are the benefits of stability at odds with economic performance, as reflected in trends in productivity growth? Discussion now turns to this issue.

The productivity benefits of stability: The evidence

Economic studies of the benefits of tenure on wages consistently show that an increase in tenure will increase a worker's real wages. Typically, it is estimated that (controlling for other characteristics such as the worker's education, gender, occupation and industry) an additional year on the job increases a worker's wage by about two per cent. [16] But do the economic benefits that workers receive from tenure translate into benefits for a firm or an economy? In other words, does a firm, or an economy, increase its rate of productivity as tenure increases?

Many economists have propounded on what firms gain in having a more tenured workforce. The most common explanation invokes the theory of "firm-specific human capital", in which tenure is a mechanism that allows firms to invest in workers over time, since it minimizes the risk of the employee leaving. Firms invest in on-the-job training that is firm-specific and that results in an increase in worker productivity. Because the training is firm-specific, its value in the external labour market is less, thus reducing the risk of costly labour turnover. Yet the worker does not immediately receive all of the wage gains from the increased productivity. By delaying some of the returns to increased productivity, firms structure the incentives as another means to discourage workers from leaving. Workers are then less inclined to leave, as they would forsake these earnings. [17]

Those workers who receive firm-specific training have skills that are not available on the external market. Moreover, firms are limited in their supply of available, trained and experienced workers, since only past entrants to the firm have received this training. The external workforce does not have this internal training and cannot therefore substitute for the firm's more experienced workers. [18] As one economist noted, "experienced workers are produced by passing young workers through the seniority system" of an internal labour market. [19] Based on the firm-specific capital model, tenure induces firms to train their workers, while the structure of compensation induces commitment by workers. The result is an increase in the worker's productivity and the firm's output.

Research on industrialized countries supports theoretical work on the beneficial relationship between tenure and productivity. An early and important

---

[16] Farber, 1998.

[17] Lazear, 1979.

[18] Lichtenberg, 1981.

[19] See Oswald, cited in Blakemore and Hoffman, 1989.

empirical study of the tenure-productivity relationship in the United States found that for every 1.0 per cent increase in the median year of job tenure in the manufacturing sector, labour productivity increased by 0.39 per cent.[20] This could be attributed to the on-the-job training that workers with longer tenure receive and would offer support to the argument that seniority rules are consistent with increased productivity.[21] Box 4.4 shows similar results for a study of the private sector in France, supporting the hypothesis that employment stability and productivity growth go hand-in-hand.

The ILO has also recently explored the link between tenure and productivity using productivity and tenure data measured at the sectoral level for 13 European countries for the years 1992 to 2002.[22] Based on 822 observations, and controlling for differences in countries and sectors, the study measures labour productivity against average tenure by sector.[23] The results prove a positive and significant association between tenure and labour productivity, with a 1.0 per cent increase in the average rate of tenure increasing productivity by 0.16 per cent.

Focusing only on average tenure can mask patterns in the labour market, such as countries that have a stable core of long-term workers and many less stable workers. Because of this, an important policy concern is whether greater segmentation in class of tenure affects productivity. The ILO study estimates how different groups of tenured workers affect productivity: short-tenure workers (workers with less than one year with the same employer), long-tenure workers (more than ten years of tenure) and very long tenure workers (more than 20 years). The results in figure 4.9 show that increasing the share of workers with short, long and very long tenure will have a negative effect on productivity. In particular, a 1.0 per cent increase in the share of long-tenure workers will cause productivity to fall by 0.02 per cent; a 1.0 per cent increase in the share of very long tenure workers has a greater negative effect, causing a productivity drop of 0.09 per cent. For short-tenure workers, the effect on productivity is also negative and significant, with a 1.0 per cent increase in the amount of workers with less than one year of tenure causing productivity to decline by 0.04 per cent.

The negative effect of an abundance of workers on short-term contracts confirms the findings of other studies. In France, the study cited in box 4.4 found that a doubling in the number of short-term workers will cause productivity to

---

[20] Blakemore and Hoffman (1989) merged output data from the US manufacturing sector between 1963 and 1981 with aggregate tenure data from the Current Population Survey, yielding 63 observations. They argue that in the short run only firm-specific skills (training) will affect labour productivity, because the other variables affecting it are long-run – ability and general training (education). Thus, their model is designed to measure short-run productivity as a function of the share of workers with different levels of tenure, since workers with longer or shorter tenure have received different amounts of firm-specific skills training.

[21] An alternative hypothesis is that seniority rules are the only impersonal and transparent (i.e. "fair") criterion for promotion.

[22] See Auer, Berg and Coulibaly, 2004, for methodology used.

[23] As the model controls for sector, the average capital-intensity of a given sector in relation to other sectors is controlled. It is important to control for the capital-intensity of production, since it can have an influence on tenure to the extent that, if labour costs are a small share of total costs, firms might be less inclined to adjust labour demand through dismissals. As in Blakemore and Hoffman (1989), it is assumed that in the short run only firm-specific skills affect labour productivity.

Box 4.4. Employment stability and productivity in the private sector in France

A study of the French private sector also supports the hypothesis that stability in employment is good for productivity. To estimate the effects of tenure on firm productivity, the authors grouped workers according to how long they remained in the job ("stayers"). The four groups of stayers are less than one year, 1-4 years, 4-10 years and more than 10 years (with more than 10 years used as a control). The study found that employing workers with 4-10 years of tenure has the most beneficial effect on productivity: a 1.0 per cent increase in the share of this group increases firm productivity by 0.36 per cent, as the graph accompanying this box shows. On the other hand, a 1.0 per cent increase in the proportion of workers with less than one year of tenure has a negative effect on productivity, lowering productivity by 0.02 per cent. The productivity effect of increasing the 1-4 year tenure group by 1.0 per cent is a positive although modest 0.05 per cent. Thus, in relation to workers with more than 10 years of tenure, the greatest gains in productivity would come from an increase in the proportion of workers with medium tenure (4-10 years). The study also concludes that a low turnover rate is associated with higher labour productivity.

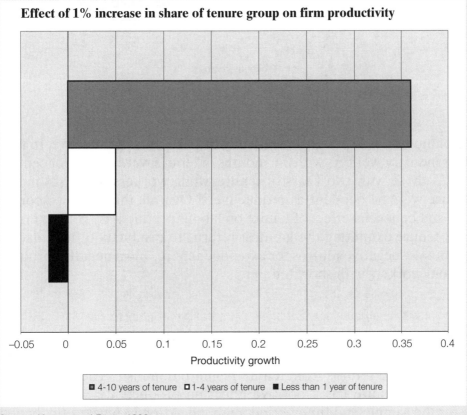

Effect of 1% increase in share of tenure group on firm productivity

Productivity growth

■ 4-10 years of tenure   □ 1-4 years of tenure   ■ Less than 1 year of tenure

Source: Kamarz and Roux, 1999.

fall, a result not found for the other tenure groups. A study of the manufacturing sector in the United States also found that short-tenured workers were less productive. Workers with 0-6 months of tenure in the durable goods industries were only 24 per cent as productive as workers with over two years of tenure; workers

Figure 4.9. Effect on productivity of a 1.0 per cent increase in the share of workers in three tenure groups, 13 European countries, 1992-2002

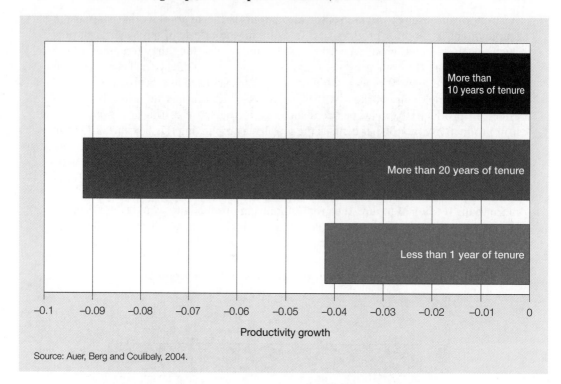

Source: Auer, Berg and Coulibaly, 2004.

with 7-24 months of experience were only 65 per cent as productive. In the non-durables industry, workers with 0-6 months of tenure were only 5 per cent as productive as those with two years of tenure, while workers with 7-24 months of experience were 54 per cent as productive.[24] Overall, the evidence points to a positive and beneficial effect of tenure on labour productivity with intermediate levels of tenure exhibiting the greatest returns to productivity, with decreasing and eventually negative returns for extended tenure, and a negative productivity effect from workers with short tenure.

At what point is tenure no longer productive? Is there an "optimal tenure"?

The negative effect of increasing the share of workers with more than ten years of tenure and those with more than 20 years begs a second question. Is there a point at which the returns from tenure begin to diminish? The ILO study finds that aggregate tenure has a positive effect on productivity, at least until 13.6 years, for the sample and time period analysed. After 13.6 years, the benefits of increased average tenure on sectoral productivity begin to decrease, as figure 4.10 shows. Nonetheless, although the productivity benefits are decreasing, the

---

[24] Lichtenberg, 1981.

Figure 4.10. Life cycle of tenure–productivity, 13 European countries, 1992-2002

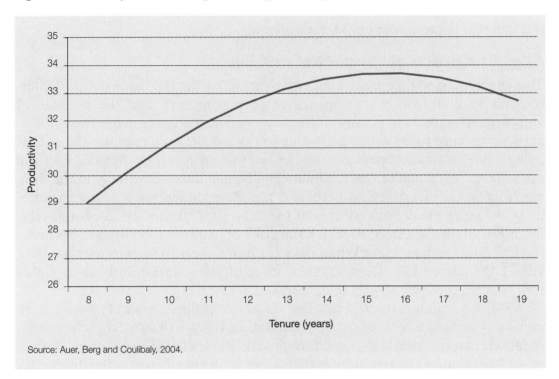

Source: Auer, Berg and Coulibaly, 2004.

firm still benefits from retaining these workers past 13.6 years, as long as the total wages paid to workers are less than their output.

It is important to note that the finding above refers to aggregate, average tenure. Per occupation, sector or country, these estimates would vary. More importantly, at the individual level, it should not be predicated as the appropriate length of time to retain a worker. In other words, while an "optimal tenure" may exist, at what point it arrives for a particular worker is not known. The most that can be concluded from the empirical exercises reviewed here is that, in general, short tenure (less than one year) and long tenure (more than ten years, but particularly above 15 and 20 years) can have negative productivity affects. Medium tenure, between one and ten years, but particularly between five and ten years, would seem optimal for productivity growth.

There are other grounds, in any case, on which optimal tenure ought not to imply that workers who exceed that level should leave the firm. Not only would this contravene a worker's right to be protected against age discrimination, it would likely also be a prescription for age-related structural unemployment. In addition, it would place further strains on social security systems which are already under pressure. Finally, it would be a curb on growth expansion, as many developed economies face increasing labour shortages. This is precisely why European Union policy on older workers runs in just the opposite direction, by attempting to reduce the use of early retirement programmes and to increase the employment-to-population ratios of women and older workers. The macroeconomic costs of not doing so are likely to greatly outweigh the microeconomic productivity effects of workers with tenure over the optimal level. There is a solution to the latter, and it is inherent in the concept of lifelong learning.

4.4. The policy of "protected mobility"

This chapter has so far emphasized two issues in particular: the benefits of inter-sectoral mobility for increasing aggregate productivity and the benefits of employment stability in pursuit of the same ends. Clearly, it is a question of balance – a balance to be struck according to diverse national circumstances. That being said, economic openness implies a growing need for flexibility at the micro-level. Yet much of this flexibility can be generated internally in the firm, via "functional" flexibility. Nonetheless, the more difficult it is to adjust internally, the more likely firms will resort to "numerical" flexibility. Economies differ, however, in the extent to which the risks of external mobility are borne by the individual or by society. When risks are more likely to be borne by the individual, the perception of employment insecurity is greatest and can arguably spill over negatively into aggregate demand.

This leads to a further point. The reform of product markets would seem inevitably to carry a component of deregulation. It is not obvious that the reform of labour markets needs to come through the channel of deregulation. Rather, an optimal route to labour market regulatory reform and greater flexibility may require that flexibility be traded against greater security – with more investment in labour market policies, the more open an economy becomes. "Flexicurity" is the composite word that describes these dual needs. It is a policy concept considerably more evolved than the earlier monolithic debates over flexibility through deregulation alone.

The interdependent economy of the future will require labour market institutions that promote micro-flexibility in all its senses, including to facilitate and to protect the mobility of people in an ongoing context of restructuring – or structural transformation. What is needed, in short, are approaches to a concept of "protected mobility", by recognizing the value of stable, but adaptable internal labour markets as well as simultaneously acknowledging that external mobility will occur and that better governance of transitions is preferable to the absence of such governance. This conclusion derives from what might be called the macroeconomics of security.

Micro-flexibility and macro-stability: The macroeconomics of security

The stability of employment conveys macroeconomic benefits, as a strong incidence of stability bolsters confidence and ensures the continuity of aggregate demand. In other words, the perception of employment security influences consumption behaviour. Workers who feel insecure about the future of their job may hold back consumption, as evidenced, for example, in the United States, where a recent study found that households will respond to an increase in the probability of future job losses by reducing their food consumption in the year prior to a job loss by 5 per cent.[25] Similarly, during the economic recession that affected Switzerland in the 1990s, increased job insecurity negatively affected consumer spending, which then compounded the negative effects of the economic downturn.[26] The study's author estimates that, as a result of the fall in consumption, GDP growth rates were further reduced by half.

Of course, a host of factors condition whether employees feel secure in their employment prospects. Two are especially relevant in the present discussion – the micro-level perception of security, and the perception of security in the event of job loss. The former rests on the likelihood of a long-term employment relationship. After all, the best source of economic security is a job, and the longer an employee is in a job, the more secure the employee generally feels. It is also the case that the probability of job loss falls substantially as tenure increases.[27] Employment protection at the micro-level clearly has a role to play but, as will be seen, it does not fully account for perceptions of security. The second has to do with a sense of "security of transition" in the labour market in the event of job loss. A measure of such security is whether the transition is from worse to better jobs, or the "trap" of transition from one low-quality job to the next (or no job at all).

Data for perceptions of transition into the external labour market exist for the European Union, and the perception that one low-quality job will lead to another is positively related to a sense of insecurity. The European Commission defines transition rates as those from *low-quality jobs* ("dead-end" or low-paid jobs/low-productivity jobs) to *high-quality jobs* (good jobs and jobs of reasonable quality). Jobs are grouped in these four categories depending on pay, productivity, job security, training opportunities and career prospects. Thus, workers who believe that they will replace their current dead-end job with another dead-end job will report relatively high perceptions of job insecurity. This is one explanation of the relatively high insecurity ranking in Spain. Another important dimension to job security, however, is the social protection provided by governments in case of job loss. Insecurity can be mitigated with labour market policies, as several European countries have done. Social protection is therefore important in increasing security and creating a productivity-enhancing environment. Having greater opportunity to transition from low-quality jobs to high-quality jobs lessens insecurity, as figure 4.11 shows.

Noteworthy here is the empirical point that, while longer tenure reduces the risk of job loss, countries with the longest records of employment tenure (and the most stringent protection of the same) are not necessarily those with the lowest perception of employment insecurity. Perceptions of security, it would seem, depend more on what will happen in the event of job loss. Here, again, a crude

[25] Stephens, 2001.

[26] Wolter, 1998.

[27] The fall in probability of job loss will depend on the country-specific labour market. Valetta (2000) finds that five additional years of tenure reduces the dismissal probability by nearly one-half for the average male worker in the US Panel Study on Income Dynamics conducted between 1976 and 1992; Farber (1998) summarizes similar findings for the United States.

Figure 4.11. Quality of job prospects and insecurity, selected European countries, 1995-2000 (percentage)

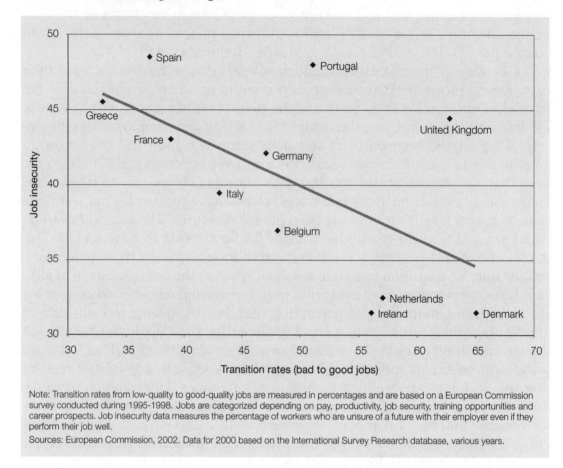

Note: Transition rates from low-quality to good-quality jobs are measured in percentages and are based on a European Commission survey conducted during 1995-1998. Jobs are categorized depending on pay, productivity, job security, training opportunities and career prospects. Job insecurity data measures the percentage of workers who are unsure of a future with their employer even if they perform their job well.

Sources: European Commission, 2002. Data for 2000 based on the International Survey Research database, various years.

proxy shows a convincing relation between the perception of employment insecurity and the amount of money governments spend on labour market policies. In figure 4.12, it is apparent that perceptions of employment security bear some relation to insurance against the risk of job loss.

In short, perceptions of employment security do not necessarily depend upon the micro-level. Instead, they appear to depend upon the extent to which the risk of external mobility can be alleviated. And that risk has both a quantitative and a qualitative dimension. For example, in the United States – despite the increase in long-term unemployment over the past several years – the risks of external mobility appear to be less in terms of job-to-job mobility than in the quality of the transition. A recent study noted: "Job creation, to the extent that it is happening, is taking place in lower-wage industries. In 48 of 50 American states, jobs in higher-paying industries have given way to jobs in lower-paying industries since the recession ended in November 2001. Nationwide, industries that are gaining jobs relative to industries that are losing jobs pay 21 per cent less

Figure 4.12. Job insecurity and spending on labour market policies, selected OECD countries, 2000

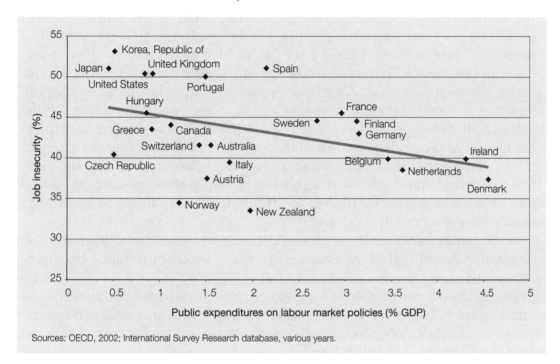

Sources: OECD, 2002; International Survey Research database, various years.

annually."[28] Employment security in the United States appears to have a more qualitative than quantitative dimension.

Labour market policies increase perceptions of job security, and this helps to boost economic performance. As the OECD explains, "more generous unemployment insurance benefits and higher union density do cause workers to report greater satisfaction with job security, perhaps because their families' incomes are better protected, should they lose their jobs".[29] Denmark provides an interesting case in this analysis, since it combines low tenure (8.3 years on average in 2001) with high levels of social protection and low levels of insecurity. Danish expenditures on labour market policies are the highest in the European Union, at about 5 per cent of GDP. Benefit replacement rates in the Danish system average 60 to 70 per cent of the lost wage, although low-income recipients receive roughly 90 per cent of their past income. Labour market indicators show that the labour market functions well, with a high rate of labour force participation (65.6 per cent) in 2002 and a low unemployment rate (4.3 per cent), and a very low long-term unemployment rate (0.8 per cent). The level of perception of insecurity in Denmark is in sharp contrast with the United Kingdom, which has a similar average tenure (8.2 years), yet reported insecurity of 50.5 per cent in 2000 compared with Denmark's 37.5 per cent.

---

[28] Economic Policy Institute, 2004.

[29] OECD, 2002, p. 268.

Activation of labour market policies

What conclusions may be drawn here? First, spending on labour market policies is the hallmark of open economies in a globalizing world, in which labour market adjustments are becoming more profound and more frequent. Here, the role of "traditional" labour market policies of the passive type consists of providing income in the event of job loss through unemployment insurance. The macro-economic benefits are clear. An effective unemployment insurance system will operate as a stabilizing mechanism for the economy while providing for the needs of laid-off workers. In the United States, it is estimated that the unemployment insurance programme mitigated the loss in real GDP by approximately 15 per cent during the five recessions that occurred between 1969 and the early 1990s. The programme exhibited a substantial and significant counter-cyclical effect on changes in real GDP over the three decades, resulting in an average annual peak saving of 131,000 jobs.[30]

A household-level analysis of the effect of unemployment insurance on consumption found that in the absence of unemployment insurance, becoming unemployed would be associated with a fall in consumption of 22 per cent, compared with the 6.8 per cent drop for unemployment insurance recipients in the United States.[31] Moreover, if the replacement rate of income under the unemployment insurance programme were above 84 per cent – compared with the current rate of approximately 50 per cent – unemployment insurance would fully smooth consumption across the unemployment spell. In comparison with other stimulus measures, such as income tax cuts, one study shows that the United States unemployment insurance system is at least eight times as effective as the tax system as a whole in offsetting the impact of a recession.[32]

The trend now, however, is toward the "activation" of labour market policies – combining income replacement (with its proven consumption-smoothing advantages) with a greater emphasis on and commitment to labour market reinsertion. In 1998, the European Union adopted employment guidelines that emphasized an "activation strategy". This requires unemployment beneficiaries to participate in job training and educational programmes after 12 months of receiving benefits, or six months if the worker is under the age of 25. In the case of Denmark, the passive component of unemployment benefits was reduced for adults from four years in 1994 to two years in 1998 and to one year in 2000.[33] Activation strategies, while more costly, have the benefit of improving workers' skills and also reducing the disincentive effects typically associated with unemployment insurance.

---

[30] Workers covered in the unemployment insurance system in the United States pay a tax of approximately 0.5 per cent of earnings and receive in benefits approximately half of their income, according to their level of earnings and in which state they reside. Despite its economic benefits, the system has become less effective over time as only full-time, long-term workers are eligible – but their share in employment has fallen (Chimerine et al., 1999).

[31] Gruber, 1997.

[32] Orszag, 2001.

[33] Madsen, 2003.

The present analysis yields the following conclusions.

- Both stability and mobility contribute to productivity growth, although arguably with different employment consequences.
- With increasingly open economies, it is likely that there will be further product market deregulation and greater competitive pressures. This in turn is likely to put pressure on the close relation between curbs on competition and regulated employment protection at the micro-level.
- Perceptions of employment security matter at the macroeconomic level for the stability of aggregate demand, which fuels productivity and employment growth. Yet, such perceptions appear to be unrelated to the degree of employment protection at the micro-level.
- Instead, they appear to be related to workers' perceptions of security in the event of labour market transitions – of moving from job to job.
- Passive measures through unemployment insurance to insure against the risk of job loss make individual and macroeconomic sense. But, if used alone, passive measures carry with them the risk of moral hazard or disincentive effects and they do not guarantee labour market reinsertion, or reinsertion on the most favourable terms.
- Insuring people against employment loss is a necessity – and one of increasing importance in view of the pressures for micro-flexibility. An active policy for public assistance in such insertion would serve the dual purpose of insulating against micro-flexibility and ensuring favourable terms for mobility. "Globalization-ready" institutions of this nature are arguably those represented in the high social protection/low employment protection countries listed in the lower-left quadrant of table 4.2. These five countries use labour market policies to cushion workers in their transition between jobs and, in so doing, promote the inter-sectoral mobility of workers.

Table 4.2. Employment or employability protection? A typology of OECD countries, late 1990s and early 2000s

	High social protection	Low social protection
High employment protection	Tenure: *2nd longest* LMP spending: *2nd greatest* Job security laws: *2nd strictest* Job security perception: *2nd highest*	Tenure: *longest* LMP spending: *2nd least* Job security laws: *strictest* Job security perception: *lowest*
Countries	France, Germany, Sweden	Japan, Portugal, Greece, Italy, Spain
Low employment protection	Tenure: *2nd shortest* LMP spending: *greatest* Job security laws: *2nd most lenient* Job security perception: *highest*	Tenure: *shortest* LMP spending: *least* Job security laws: *most lenient* Job security perception: *2nd lowest*
Countries	Denmark, Belgium, Netherlands, Finland, Ireland	United States, United Kingdom

Note: Own compilation and assessment based on the data sources below.

Sources: Job tenure data for Europe from Eurostat and for the United States and Japan from national surveys, various years; LMP spending data and strictness of job security laws from OECD, various years; job security perception from International Survey Research database, various years.

The future may well be one in which "protected mobility", backed by public financing, proves to be the most socially and economically efficient path to productivity, competitiveness and decent work.

4.5. Employment tenure in developing countries

The foregoing discussion has focused on industrialized countries. Can the conclusions drawn above also apply to the economic landscapes and labour markets of developing countries? Several stark differences emerge – among them, the relative size of the informal economy and, therefore, the limited reach of formal regulations and institutions. This chapter now reviews the main differences and what these imply for policy.

As noted in table 4.1, one important difference between developed and developing countries is the substantially lower average tenure in the latter. In addition, countries with a high share of long-tenure workers are also those with a low share of workers with less than one year of tenure – and vice versa. Figure 4.13 shows this relationship for several Latin American and European countries, Japan and the United States.

Again, demographic differences no doubt play an important role in explaining tenure differences. But demographics cannot fully account for these differences. For example, table 4.3 compares average tenure by age group of male workers in the private sector in Colombia and the United States in the late 1980s.

Figure 4.13. Distribution of short vs. long tenure in selected European and Latin American countries, Japan and the United States, late 1990s and early 2000s

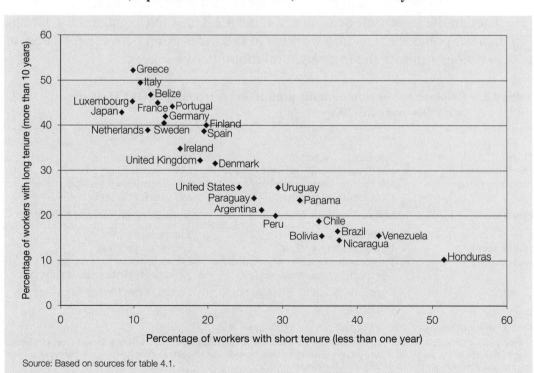

Source: Based on sources for table 4.1.

Table 4.3.   Comparison of average years of tenure, male private-sector workers, Colombia and the United States, selected years

Age group	Colombia 1988	United States 1987
15-20	0.44	0.44
21-30	1.50	2.09
31-50	3.25	4.67
41-50	5.56	9.10
51-59	8.50	13.95

Source: Schaffner, 2001.

Tenure averages are the same in both countries for the 15-20 year old cohort but these averages already begin to diverge at the onset of the early twenties. By the time a private-sector American male worker is in his forties, he has 3.5 more years of tenure than a similarly aged Colombian private-sector male worker; in his fifties, the difference has increased to 5.5 years. Moreover, the study presenting these data finds that a male American worker with the same schooling as a male Colombian worker, performing the same occupation in the same sector in a similarly sized firm, has an 11 per cent greater probability of continued tenure than his Colombian counterpart. For workers with less than one year on the job, the differences in probability of continued tenure are even greater: these workers are over one and a half times more likely to remain in their job in the United States than in Colombia. [34]

In industrialized countries, the close, positive correlation between the stringency of job security and employment tenure was observed. A similar index of job security strictness is available for 12 Latin American countries. Curiously, and although employment protection legislation has often been blamed for impeding job allocation and job creation in Latin America, the positive relationship between job security strictness and tenure characteristic of OECD countries does not prevail in Latin America. As figure 4.14 suggests, the relationship is, if anything, the inverse.

As employment protection legislation is stricter in Latin America than in the OECD countries, its relationship to tenure is not obvious. How then can this anomaly be explained? Perhaps by the fact that most new job creation in Latin America occurs in the informal economy and is untouched by the constraints of labour law, which might well be reflected in the data. It is also the case, of course, that a correlation between job security strictness and tenure needs to rely on compliance with labour law – and compliance is frequently imperfect in developing countries, even in the formal economy. Another possibility is that, however stringent laws are, they may apply only to a specific size-threshold of enterprise. The argument (similarly made in box 4.5 regarding South Asian labour laws) is that a size-threshold criterion provides an incentive for firms to remain artificially small. It is at least true that firm size is smaller in most developing

---

[34] Schaffner, 2001.

Figure 4.14. Job security strictness vs. percentage of workers with long tenure, Latin America, late 1990s

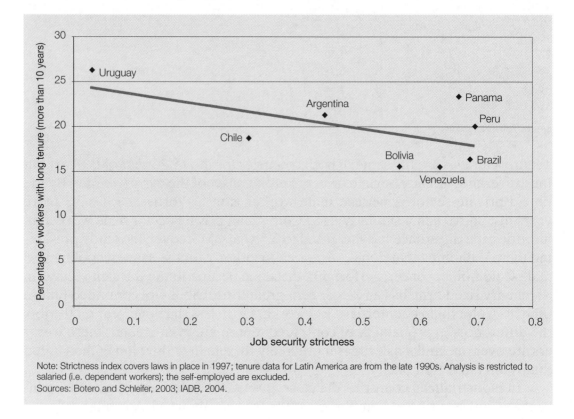

Note: Strictness index covers laws in place in 1997; tenure data for Latin America are from the late 1990s. Analysis is restricted to salaried (i.e. dependent workers); the self-employed are excluded.
Sources: Botero and Schleifer, 2003; IADB, 2004.

countries. A fourth possibility is that the stringency of employment protection applies beyond a certain tenure threshold, thus giving the incentive for a high degree of employment turnover before that threshold is reached. [35]

Of course, a fifth explanation could simply be that labour law is not the impediment to labour mobility that some would claim. Looking at job turnover data, the Inter-American Development Bank finds gross job flows are as high in "rigid" Latin America as they are in "flexible" New Zealand and the United States.

Macroeconomic volatility

Beyond labour law, developing countries are often characterized by other differences with industrialized countries which could explain shorter tenure duration. For example, macroeconomic volatility is greater in developing countries and leads to greater firm death and job loss, lowering average tenure in an economy. As figure 4.15 shows, real annual GDP growth rates in Latin America and the Caribbean region fluctuated wildly during the 1990s, with a regional high of 8.6 per cent growth in 1992 and three years of negative growth in 1990, 1999 and

---

[35] Edwards, 1993; Bronstein, 1998.

Box 4.5.   Towards "protected mobility" in a developing country context: Nepal

Labour law in developing countries often places significant constraints on the ability of employers to dismiss workers for economic reasons. The origins of such stringency are many, but two are particularly significant: in the absence of a social security system offering unemployment insurance, the role of social protection fell to the enterprise; and, as in industrialized countries, stringent employment protection went hand-in-hand with product markets highly sheltered from competition.

The possible consequences of high employment protection are also many. It can be an inducement for capital-intensive production strategies at the expense of much needed employment creation. It can bias economic structure in the direction of small firms, as there is typically an employment threshold at which the law becomes enforceable. Or it can simply lead to widespread non-compliance and thus no employment protection.

In a world of more open economies, laws of all sorts will need to adjust. In the Kingdom of Nepal, the path of adjustment appears increasingly to be based on social dialogue and consensus. The country's employer organization, the Federation of Nepalese Chambers of Commerce and Industry (FNCCI), along with the three trade union federations, General Federation of Nepalese Trade Unions (GEFONT), Nepal Trade Union Congress (NTUC) and the Democratic Confederation of Nepalese Trade Unions (DECONT), reached an agreement in 2004 in which they pledged to "work together and are committed on the following points in order to develop industrial peace and to build cooperative relations between labour and management." Two points are of particular relevance:

- "all employers and business people are committed to maintain minimum labour standards by applying the policy of employment in conditions of decent work"
- "it is necessary to make reforms in the labour laws. Realizing this, taking the seven-point agenda of labour law reform, the process of existing labour law reform is underway".

The seven-point agenda for reform includes: labour flexibility; "exit" or dismissal policy; social security; gender; the informal economy; collective bargaining; and labour administration. If successful, negotiations between the parties will lead to a form of "protected mobility" embedding a quid pro quo in which dismissals on economic grounds become less cumbersome in return for greater social protection through the establishment of a social security system. This is just the path that the parties are following, and it is the same that their counterparts in Sri Lanka followed in 2003.

While the quid pro quo of greater social protection in return for greater micro-flexibility appears logical, it nonetheless poses several challenges. The first of these is inadequate labour demand. Simply put, the chances of finding alternative employment when one loses one's job in an industrialized country are far greater than in developing countries. This, in turn, implies that the income support given to a laid-off worker would have to be of substantial duration, whereas developing countries are not likely to have the fiscal depth to support a substantial degree of social protection. This is no doubt one reason why labour law reform has not proceeded at a rapid pace.

Source: Joint Press Statement by FNCCI and Trade Union Federations, Kathmandu, April 2004.

Figure 4.15. Real annual GDP growth, Latin America and the Caribbean region, 1990-2002

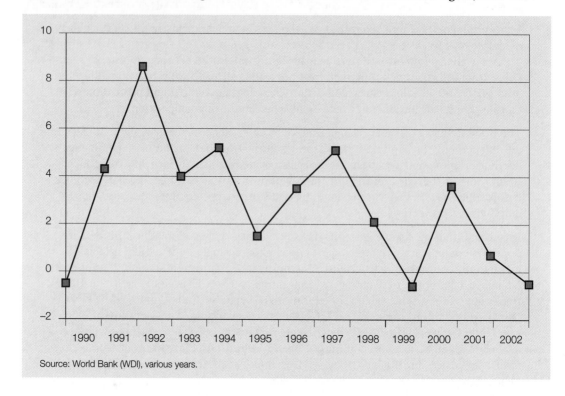

Source: World Bank (WDI), various years.

2002. Overall, average growth for the 12-year period was 2.8 per cent with a standard deviation of 2.6 per cent. For the same period, the average growth rate in the United States was also 2.8 per cent, but with a standard deviation of 1.5 per cent – considerably lower than that of Latin America and the Caribbean region. In the European Union, overall growth was lower, averaging 1.9 per cent, but the standard deviation was a low 1.1 per cent.

Macroeconomic volatility has been shown to negatively affect tenure as it reduces the survival probability of job creation, meaning a greater overall tendency for shorter job tenure.[36] Macroeconomic volatility also discourages mass-production techniques because they require a long-term commitment to fixed capital investments.[37] Such investments also require long-term commitment in human capital: an environment of volatility makes it less likely for firms to establish long-term employment relationships.

Differences in economic structure

In addition to macroeconomic volatility, the instability of employment relationships in Latin America reflects two other important characteristics evident in the

---

[36] Davis et al., 1996, based on an analysis of births/deaths in manufacturing firms in the United States between 1973 and 1988.

[37] Tybout, 2000.

region: the greater percentage of small-sized firms, and the bias toward production activities that can be undertaken with less-tenured workers. There is a concentration of manufacturing activities in less sophisticated products, the consequence of domestic consumption being skewed towards basic goods such as food and beverage, apparel, footwear, furniture and metal products. This has resulted in a bias toward simple manufactured goods that can be efficiently produced in small firms using cottage technologies.[38] Thus, it is possible that the production technologies used in making the same good are different in developing and industrialized countries. While firm exit and turnover are high in cottage production, new firms can enter these sectors more quickly and are able to depend on newer workers to produce these products.

As shown below, one main reason for lower average tenure among salaried workers is the abundance of small firms in developing countries. (See Chapter 5 of the Report for a discussion of small firms and productivity growth.) Small firms exit the market more quickly than larger firms and, with more Latin American workers employed in smaller firms, there is lower average tenure.[39] Table 4.4 illustrates the large variation in employment shares between manufacturing firms, especially in micro-enterprises, in Mexico and in the United States. For example, 13.8 per cent of Mexican workers were employed in the early 1990s compared with just 1.3 per cent of American workers. Table 4.5 gives job rotation rates among manufacturing firms in Argentina during the difficult economic period from 1995 to 2000. In micro-enterprises, defined as employing establishments with fewer than five workers, the job rotation rate was 49.6 per cent – meaning that every year, one-half of micro-enterprise workers changed or lost their jobs. This rotation rate is double the average for the industrial sector, which was nevertheless high for the same period. It also shows that a greater share of workers in small firms contributes to reducing tenure.

The consequences of employment instability

The argument has been made that a substantial degree of employment stability is good for productivity growth. And lower job stability may be one factor that

Table 4.4. Comparison of distribution of employment across manufacturing plants, according to firm size, Mexico and the United States, early 1990s (percentage)

	Firm size by number of employees					
	1-4	5-9	10-19	20-49	50-99	> 99
United States (1992)	1.3	2.6	4.6	10.4	11.6	69.4
Mexico (1993)	13.8	4.5	5.0	8.6	9.0	59.1

Source: Tybout, 2000.

---

[38] Tybout, 2000.

[39] In Japan, for example, employment tenure clearly increases with firm size. Firms with 1-99 employees have an average tenure of 9.6 years; in those with 100-999 employees, average tenure is 11.1 years; but in firms with over 1,000 employees, average tenure is 14.8 years (Auer and Cazes, 2003).

Table 4.5.   Job rotation in manufacturing, according to firm size,[1] Argentina, 1995-2000 (percentage)

Size	Rotation
Micro-enterprises	49.6
Small firms	32.6
Medium firms	24.9
Large firms	16.5
Total	24.5

[1] With the exception of micro-enterprises (defined by the authors as less than 5 workers), firm sizes are categorized according to sales (considered by the authors as more appropriately addressing their concerns on differences in the technology-intensity of production). Small firms are defined as those with five or more workers and sales in Argentine pesos of less than ARS 3 million a year (around US$900,000 at 2004 exchange rates); medium firms with sales between ARS 3-18 million (US$900,000 to US$5.5 million); and large firms with sales above ARS 18 million (US$5.5 million) a year (Castillo et al., 2002).

Source: Castillo et al., 2002.

explains why labour productivity is lower in developing countries than developed countries, even after controlling for physical and human capital.[40] Lower job stability could also result in a comparative disadvantage in endeavouring to develop a production base that relies on the larger, more modern firms, in which longer-term employment relationships are important.[41] Without employment stability, it is more difficult and costly for firms to provide training, as higher turnover may prevent them from reaping the productivity benefits. An empirical analysis of the incidence and outcome of enterprise training among manufacturing firms in Colombia, Indonesia, Malaysia, Mexico and Taiwan (China) found that a sizeable proportion of firms did not provide any training to their workers. Firms in the Latin American region that were more likely to provide training were typically large, employed an educated and skilled workforce and invested in R&D and technology licences (and, for the Asian countries, exported to foreign markets). The study found a significant impact of training on the productivity of skilled workers, but not of unskilled workers.[42]

In industrialized countries, pressure may be mounting for a greater degree of flexibility at the micro-level as globalization heightens product market competition. In many developing countries, the situation is arguably the inverse: excessive flexibility may be a constraint on the development of stable work relations that benefit productivity growth.

4.6.   Concluding remarks

Employment stability makes sense on both the demand and the supply side of the labour market, as it mitigates concerns over job security for the worker and is an inducement to invest in training for both worker and employer. Higher

[40] Hall and Jones, 1999.

[41] Schaffner, 2001.

[42] Ton and Batra, 1995.

productivity is the result. In developing countries, low employment stability and an underinvestment in training appear to go hand in hand.

Nevertheless, it is equally true that excessive barriers to the mobility of capital and labour can constrain productivity growth by impeding the expansion of new, higher value-added sectors. Clearly, the challenge is to find the right balance between enabling the mobility that greater flexibility allows and also ensuring some security. Such a balance is mediated by labour law and labour market institutions in individual economies. It is clear that in a global world of fast-paced economic and technological change and rising economic interdependence, laws and institutions designed for a more sheltered competitive environment are under pressure to adjust.

No single blueprint for change can suit all countries. The appropriate adjustment of laws and institutions is a purely domestic matter. Three conclusions may nonetheless be drawn. First, since national laws and institutions need to strike the right balance between the interests of both the supply and the demand side of the labour market, the shape that such laws and institutions take are most appropriately and effectively addressed by the representatives of supply and demand sides – workers' and employers' organizations. And this is as true for Nepal as it is for the Netherlands. Second, countries are coming to grips with more rapid labour market changes by shifting the balance to active rather than passive labour market policies. Why? Because active policies, when well designed, make the labour market function better than it would in the absence of institutional support and intervention.

This leads to the final point: the simple argument of labour market deregulation as a solution to economic and employment growth has been superseded by a more nuanced view of the role that laws and institutions play in labour market governance. Empirically, this is evident in two observations, the first (and the fundamental theme of this chapter) is that employment stability pays economic dividends and that laws and institutions have a role to play in supporting that stability. The second is that the economies most open to globalization are also those in which spending on labour market policies as a share of GDP is the greatest.

References

Applebaum, E.; Bailey, T.; Berg, P.; Kallenberg, A. (eds.). 2000. *Manufacturing advantage: Why high-performance work systems pay off* (Ithaca, Cornell University Press).

Auer, P. 2000. *Employment revival in Europe: Labour market successes in Austria, Denmark, Ireland and the Netherlands* (Geneva, ILO).

Auer, P.; Cazes, S. (eds.). 2003. *Employment stability in an age of flexibility* (Geneva, ILO).

Auer, P.; Berg, J.; Coulibaly, I. 2004. *Is a more stable workforce good for the economy? Insights into the tenure-productivity-employment relationship* (Geneva, ILO, Employment Strategy Working Paper No 15).

Black S.E.; Lynch, L.M. 2004. Cited in *Economics Letter*, Federal Reserve Bank of San Francisco (http://www.hrbsf.org/publications/economics/letter/2004/el2004-10.html).

Blanchard, O. 2004. *The economic future of Europe* (Cambridge, MA, National Bureau of Economic Research, Working Paper No. 103109), Feb.

Blakemore, A.; Hoffman, D. 1989. "Seniority rules and productivity: An empirical test", *Economica*, Vol. 56, pp. 359-371.

Booth, A.; Francesconi, M.; Zoega, G. 2003. "Unions, work-related training and wages", *Industrial and Labor Relations Review*, Vol. 57, No. 1, pp. 68-91 (Ithaca, NY, Cornell University School of Industrial and Labor Relations).

Botero, J.; Schleif, A. 2003. *The regulation of labor* (Cambridge, MA, National Bureau of Economic Research, Working Paper No. 9756), June.

Bronstein, A. 1998. *Pasado y presente de la legislación laboral en América Latina* (San José, ILO).

Campbell, D. 2001. "Social dialogue and labour market adjustment in East Asia after the crisis", in G. Betcherman and R. Islam (eds.): *East Asian labor markets and the economic crisis: Impacts, responses and lessons* (Washington, DC, International Bank for Reconstruction and Development).

Castillo, V.; Cesa, V.; Fillippo, S.; Rojo-Brievela, S.; Schlesser, D.; Yoguel, G. 2002. *Dinámica del empleo y rotación de empresas: la experiencia en el sector industrial de Argentina desde mediados de los años noventa* (Buenos Aires, CEPAL, Serie Estudios y Perpectivas 9).

Chimerine, L.; Black, T.; Coffey, L. 1999. *Unemployment insurance as an automatic stabilizer: Evidence of effectiveness over three decades* (Washington, DC, US Department of Labor, Occasional Paper 99-8).

Dar, A.; Amirkhalkhali, S. 2003. "On the impact of trade openness on growth: Further evidence from OECD countries", *Applied Economics*, (Coventry, Routledge Press), Vol. 35, No. 16, pp. 1761-1766.

Davis, S., Haltiwanger, J.; Schuh, S. 1996. *Job creation and destruction* (Cambridge, MA, MIT Press).

Edwards, A.C. 1993. *Labour market legislation in Latin America and the Caribbean*, (Washington, DC, World Bank LAC Technical Department Regional Studies Program Report 31).

Economic Policy Institute. 2004. "Jobs shift from higher-paying to lower-paying industries", *Economic Snapshots*, 21 Jan.
(http://www.epinet.org/content.cfm/webfeatures_snapshots_archive_01212004).

European Commission. 2002. *Employment in Europe* (Brussels, EC Directorate-General for Employment and Social Affairs).

Farber, H. 1998. *Mobility and stability: The dynamics of change in labor markets* (Princeton, NJ, Princeton University, Industrial Relations Section, Working Paper No. 400).

Freeman, R. 1980. "The exit-voice tradeoff in the labor market: Unionism, job tenure, quits and separations", *Quarterly Journal of Economics* (Cambridge, MA, MIT Press), Vol. 44, No. 4, pp. 643-673.

Gruber, J. 1997. "The consumption smoothing benefits of unemployment insurance", *American Economic Review* (Nashville, TN, American Economics Association), Vol. 87, No. 1, pp. 192-205.

Hall, R.; Jones, C. 1999. "Why do some countries produce so much more output per worker than others?", *Quarterly Journal of Economics*, (Cambridge, MA, MIT Press), Vol. 114, No. 1, pp. 83-116.

Inter-American Development Bank (IADB). 2004. *Good Jobs Wanted* (Washington, DC).

International Monetary Fund (IMF). 2003. *World Economic Outlook* (Washington, DC).

International Labour Organization (ILO). 1995. *World Employment 1995: An ILO Report* (Geneva).

—. 2003a. *Key Indicators of the Labour Market*, 3rd edition (Geneva).

—. 2003b. *Yearbook of Labour Statistics*, 62nd edition (Geneva).

Ishikawa, J. 2003. *Key features of national social dialogue: A social dialogue resource book* (Geneva, ILO).

Kaldor, N. 1966. *Causes of the slow rate of economic growth of the United Kingdom* (Cambridge, Cambridge University Press, an Inaugural Lecture).

Kramarz, F.; Roux, S. 1999. *Within-firm seniority structure and firm performance*, (London, Centre for Economic Performance, Discussion Paper 420).

Lazear, E. 1979. "Why is there mandatory retirement?", *Journal of Political Economy* (Chicago, IL, University of Chicago), Vol. 87, No. 6, pp. 1261-1284.

Lewis, W.A. 1954. "Economic development with unlimited supplies of labour," *The Manchester School* (Manchester, Victoria University of Manchester), Vol. 22, No. 2, pp. 139-191.

—. 1955. *Theory of economic growth* (London, Allen and Unwin).

Lichtenberg, F. 1981. *Training, tenure and productivity*, (Cambridge, MA, National Bureau of Economic Research, Working Paper No. 671).

Madsen, P. 2003. "Flexicurity through labour market policies and institutions in Denmark", in P. Auer and S. Cazes (eds.): *Employment stability in an age of flexibility* (Geneva, ILO).

McKinsey Global Institute. 1994. *Employment performance* (Washington, DC, McKinsey & Company).

Neumark, D. (ed.). 2000. *On the job: Is long-term employment a thing of the past?* (New York, Russell Sage Foundation).

Nicoletti, G.; Scarpetta, S.; Boyland, O. 2000. *Summary indicators of product market regulation with an extension to employment production legislation*, (Paris, OECD Economics Department Working Papers, No. 226).

Organisation for Economic Co-operation and Development (OECD). 1994. *The OECD Jobs Study* (Paris).

—. 1999. *Employment Outlook* (Paris).

—. 2002. *Employment Outlook* (Paris).

—. 2004. *Employment Outlook* (Paris).

Orszag, P. 2001. *Unemployment insurance as economic stimulus* (Washington, DC, Center on Budget and Policy Priorities, Policy Brief).

Ozaki, M. (ed.). 1999. *Negotiating flexibility: The role of the social partners and the state* (Geneva, ILO), p. 127.

Schaffner, J.A. 2001. "Job stability in developing and developed countries: Evidence from Colombia and the United States", *Economic Development and Cultural Change* (Chicago, IL, University of Chicago Press), Vol. 49, No. 3, pp. 511-536.

Soskice, D. 1990. "Wage determination: The changing role of institutions in advanced industrialized countries", *Oxford Review of Economic Policy*, (Oxford, Oxford University Press) Vol. 6, No. 4, pp. 36-61.

Stephens, Jr., M. 2001. "The long-run consumption effects of earning shocks", *The Review of Economics and Statistics* (Cambridge, MA, MIT Press), Vol. 83, No. 1, pp. 28-36.

Ton, H.; Batra, G. 1995. *Enterprise training in developing countries: Overview of incidence, determinants and productivity outcomes*, (Washington, DC, World Bank, Private Sector Development Department, Occasional Paper No. 9).

Tybout, J. 2000. "Manufacturing firms in developing countries: How well do they do and why?", *Journal of Economic Literature* (Nashville, TN, American Economics Association), Vol. 38, March, pp. 11-44.

US Department of Labor. 1994. *Road to high-performance workplaces: A guide to better jobs and better business results* (Washington, DC, Office of the American Workplace).

Valetta, R. 2000. "Declining job security", in D. Neumark (ed.): *On the job: Is long-term employment a thing of the past?* (New York, Russell Sage Foundation).

Vega-Ruiz, M.L. 2003. *Libertad de asociación, libertad sindical y el reconocimiento efectivo del derecho de negociación colectiva en América Latina* (Geneva, ILO, background paper for IFP/DECLARATION).

Visser, J. 2002. *Union, unionization and collective bargaining trends around the world* (Geneva, ILO, background paper for IFP/DECLARATION), Sep.

Wolter, S. 1998. "The cost of job-insecurity: Results from Switzerland", *International Journal of Manpower* (Bradford, MCB University Press), Vol. 19, No. 6, pp. 396-409.

World Bank. 2002. *World development indicators online* (Washington, DC) (http://derdata.worldbank.org/dataonline/) [accessed Spring 2004].

5. Small-scale activities and the productivity divide [1]

It is widely recognized that small firms greatly predominate over large firms around the world, both in number and the share of the labour force they employ. This is particularly true for developing regions, where besides the share of small firms in the formal economy, the industrial structure is characterized by the high share of self-employed, and of micro- and small firms in the informal economy.

In this context, it is worth remembering that small and medium enterprises (SMEs) [2] have special advantages that give rise to at least four important – if not unique – contributions to economic development. The first and foremost characteristic is that SMEs are said to be creators of *employment opportunities* and therefore hold an important key to employment and poverty reduction. SMEs use relatively less capital to create these jobs compared with those created by larger enterprises. This is a salient feature, especially for developing economies with an abundance of labour and a shortage of capital. Second, SMEs are claimed to be the main *source of economic growth and innovation*. By virtue of their being the source of considerable innovative activity, they are responsible for the development of entrepreneurial talent and export competitiveness. Third, the presence of SMEs in the economy tends to increase competition, which promotes greater economic dynamism. Fourth, SMEs contribute to a *more equitable distribution* of income, not only by providing employment opportunities – especially for poorer people – but also because SMEs tend to be more widely dispersed geographically than larger enterprises, supporting the development and diffusion of entrepreneurial spirit and skills, and thereby helping to reduce economic disparities between urban and rural areas.

Given these considerations, together with the widespread empirical evidence that small-scale economic activities are less productive (especially in the informal economy), the potential and also the limits of small-scale economic activities for raising living standards become clear. The implication here is a potential "productivity" divide between developed and developing countries that is arguably structural in nature. The existence of such a divide is all the more worrying when it is recalled that macroeconomic volatility is greater in developing than in developed countries – and is especially onerous for small firms.

Will competitive markets not automatically ensure that less productive firms are forced out, leaving room for bigger firms with higher productivity but less potential to create employment? Why is it that small firms still dominate the economic structure even in more developed economies? What is their competitive

---

[1] This chapter is based on the work of Vandenberg (2004) and Mazumdar (2004).

[2] SMEs in this chapter will generally regroup micro-firms, small firms, medium firms and those who are self-employed. When necessary, specific distinction will be made.

advantage? Should development strategies ignore small-scale activities in order to raise overall productivity of economies? Does the dominance of small firms hinder or harm poverty reduction? Or is there a way to enhance productivity growth in small firms?

This chapter attempts to answer these questions, first by defining what small-scale enterprises are and describing what their contribution to economic development and employment creation is (section 1). Section 2 presents evidence on the productivity differences between small and large firms. Section 3 explores why small firms, disadvantaged relative to large firms, are not driven from the market. As small firms often provide lower incomes for their employees, section 4 addresses the wage gap and the broader social dimensions of the productivity divide. Section 5 reviews some of the organizational models through which the small-firm productivity disadvantage can be addressed. Section 6 concludes this chapter with a summary of the political implications for development strategies drawn from the present research.

5.1.   A definitional and empirical overview

What are small and medium enterprises?

Small and medium enterprises are a very diverse group, covering a wide range of business activities that include agricultural products for the village, the corner store and shops selling food and drinks, as well as much more sophisticated enterprises selling engineering and computer products for domestic and/or overseas markets. Given this wide range of activities, some SMEs might not be able to provide sufficient income for their owners and employees to overcome poverty. Others may be thriving and providing a decent living standard to their workers and owners. SMEs also function in very diverse markets at all levels – urban, rural, local, national, regional and even international. Because of their diversity, they possess different levels of skills, capital, sophistication and growth orientation.[3]

There is no single definition of an SME. Different indicators are used to define them, such as employee numbers or financial criteria. However, SMEs are generally considered to be private independent firms which employ fewer than a given number of employees. This number varies across countries. The most frequent upper limit designating an SME is 250 employees, as in the European Union. The United States includes firms with fewer than 500 employees. In developing countries, the cut-off point is between 100 and 250 workers. Small enterprises are usually considered to have fewer than 50 employees while micro-enterprises have at most ten or, in some cases, five employees. As will be seen, the definitional variability in employment thresholds is a source of bias when it comes to evaluating the level of productivity.

---

[3] The data presented in this section on SMEs do not usually include the informal economy (see section on the informal economy and small-scale activity).

For example, in terms of financial assets, SMEs in the European Union must have an annual turnover not exceeding €40 million and/or a balance sheet-valuation not exceeding €27 million.[4] Table 5.1 illustrates the variety of definitions that currently exists in selected developing and developed economies.

The empirical evidence on SMEs

In most developing and developed countries, SMEs comprise 90 per cent of all enterprises. For example, according to OECD (2002), SMEs represent between 96 and 99 per cent of the total number of enterprises in most OECD countries. Table 5.2 shows that micro-enterprises (0 to 9 employees) account for 78 per cent of all firms on average, while firms with 0 to 49 employees account for at least 95 per cent of all firms. Only 0.5 per cent of enterprises employ more than 500 workers in the OECD countries.

Why are SMEs important? Their contribution to employment and growth

Microeconomic evidence from individual countries supports the claims that SMEs contribute to socio-economic development through different channels.[5] However, only a few cross-country studies are available on the SME contribution to the economy, because of the absence of comparable international data on SMEs. Here, using data gathered by Ayyagari et al. (2003), an attempt is made to

Table 5.1. Current definitions of manufacturing SMEs in selected economies

Economy	Definition of manufacturing SMEs	
	Criterion	Size
Indonesia	Employment	<100
	Assets	<Rp 10 billion (US$1.4 million)
	Sales	<Rp 50 billion (US$7 billion)
Japan	Employment	<300
	Invested capital	<Y 300 million (US$3 million)
Korea, Republic of	Employment	<300
Malaysia	Invested capital	<MR 2.5 million (US$0.7 million)
Philippines	Employment	< 200
	Assets	<P 60 million (US$1.5 million)
Singapore	Assets	<S$15 million (US$9 million)
Taiwan, China	Employment	<200
	Invested capital	<NT$60 million (US$2 million)
Thailand	Employment	<300
	Assets	<100 million baht (US$2.7 million)
Canada	Employment	<500
	Sales	<C$20 million (US$14 million)
United States	Employment	<500

Source: Hayashi, 2003.

---

[4] OECD, 2002.

[5] See Biggs (2002) for a review of literature on SMEs and their contribution to economic development. See also UNIDO (2001).

Table 5.2. Distribution of enterprises in selected economies (%) according to size-class, 1999 (or nearest available year)

Economy	0-9	10-49	50-99	100-499	500+
United States	56.8	15.8	20.7	5.2	1.5
Norway	63.0	27.6	4.6	3.9	0.8
Germany	67.5	23.7	4.0	4.0	0.8
Spain	68.7	27.1	2.4	1.5	0.2
Austria	69.8	22.4	3.3	3.9	0.6
Denmark	71.4	21.3	3.4	3.3	0.6
United Kingdom	72.0	20.5	3.3	3.5	0.7
Australia	72.6	21.8	2.8	2.2	0.6
Switzerland	79.1	15.5	2.6	2.4	0.3
Portugal	80.6	16.3	2.0	1.1	0.1
New Zealand	81.7	15.0	1.6	1.4	0.3
France	82.4	13.5	2.0	1.8	0.4
Italy	83.7	14.3	1.1	0.8	0.1
Belgium	84.1	12.0	1.9	1.6	0.4
Sweden	84.7	11.4	1.8	1.6	0.4
Finland	85.3	10.7	1.8	1.8	0.4
Czech Republic	88.8	8.1	1.5	1.4	0.3
Mexico	90.3	6.5	1.3	1.5	0.4
Poland	90.3	7.3	1.0	1.2	0.3
Turkey	95.0	3.2	0.8	0.9	0.2
Average	**78.4**	**15.7**	**3.2**	**2.3**	**0.5**

Note: Countries are ranked from lowest to highest in terms of distribution enterprise size.
Source: OECD, 2002.

investigate if SMEs are associated with higher economic growth rates on a cross-country level.[6]

A simple correlation (figure 5.1) shows that the share of employment in SMEs (a cut-off point of less than 250 employees) in total employment is positively associated with higher rates of GDP per capita growth. In other words, countries with a high share of employment in SMEs tend to have higher growth in GDP per capita. For example, a 1 percentage point increase in the share of employment in SMEs in total employment is associated with an increase of .07 percentage points of growth in GDP per capita.[7] However, this analysis using cross-country data is unable to conclude that SMEs exert a causal relationship on economic growth (owing to the many other determinants of economic growth). A note of caution applies here; this relationship may go both ways, because it is affirmed that fast-growing economies also tend to have a vibrant

[6] Data for economic growth (GDP per capita) from World Bank (2004).

[7] The results are similar, even using the official definition of SMEs (SMEOFF) which varies from country to country.

Figure 5.1. Correlation between share of employment in SMEs and GDP growth

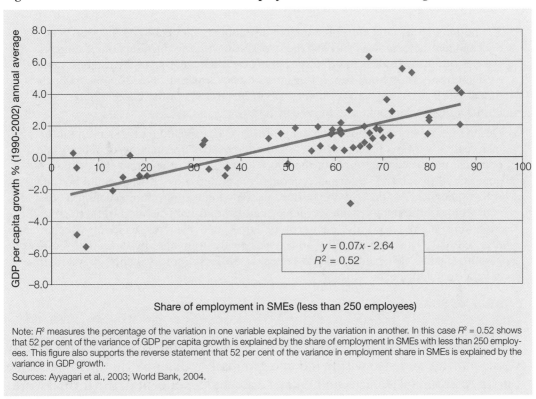

Share of employment in SMEs (less than 250 employees)

Note: R^2 measures the percentage of the variation in one variable explained by the variation in another. In this case $R^2 = 0.52$ shows that 52 per cent of the variance of GDP per capita growth is explained by the share of employment in SMEs with less than 250 employees. This figure also supports the reverse statement that 52 per cent of the variance in employment share in SMEs is explained by the variance in GDP growth.

Sources: Ayyagari et al., 2003; World Bank, 2004.

SME sector. Similar results are also achieved by Beck et al. (2003). However, they were not able to show, at least at the cross-country level, that SMEs reduce poverty. This relationship is one – but not the only – reason why political interest in SMEs has a long tradition (box 5.1).

Employment is widely regarded as one of the most effective ways of overcoming poverty. Therefore, assisting in designing and implementing strategies that promote employment creation can contribute to the objective of poverty alleviation. And the SME contribution to employment creation is considerable. An OECD study[8] affirms that SMEs account for 50 to 60 per cent of total employment in most developing and developed economies – indicating that they are responsible for more employment than the large firms or employment in the public sector and state-owned enterprises. SMEs engaged in manufacturing often account for an even larger share of manufacturing employment, which may rise to as high as 80 per cent, as table 5.3 shows. In developing countries, the role of manufacturing SMEs is even more important, as they are the major sources of employment growth and value added. This applies equally to the transition countries, where large, inefficient state-owned enterprises are giving way to much smaller and more efficient private entities.

[8] OECD, 2002.

Box 5.1.   Origins of policy interest in SMEs

The notion of SME and entrepreneurship development appeared on the growth and development landscape as early as the late 1940s, with the introduction of targeted policies (grants, subsidized credits, special tax treatment, etc.) and the establishment of small business or SME support agencies by governments. For example, publicly funded SME agencies were set up in 1948 in Japan, 1953 in the United States, 1954 in India, 1966 in Tanzania, and in 1976 in Turkey.

Despite a long history of development efforts, SMEs (including those in the informal economy) were perceived as a synthetic construction mainly of "social and political" importance throughout the 1980s and well into the late 1990s. Although domestic SMEs and the informal economy constituted most of what could be (and still are) deemed as "the" private business activity in most developing countries, private sector development strategies advocated for and implemented in these countries were skewed towards the needs of large-scale business, including foreign-invested ones. This type of policy advice was partly motivated by the rather disappointing results achieved through extensive SME support systems operated in developed countries since the 1970s.

Source: OECD, 2004.

The importance of the SME sector in terms of employment varies greatly across countries and also within income groups. For example, in the low-income group in Azerbaijan, Belarus and Ukraine around 5 per cent of the formal workforce is employed in SMEs; this share is more than 70 per cent in Indonesia and Viet Nam. The range is between 4.5 per cent (Belarus) and 86 per cent (Thailand) in the middle-income group and between 20 per cent (Slovenia) and 82 per cent (Portugal) in the high-income group of economies in the world (Ayyagari et al., 2003).

Figure 5.2 shows the SME contribution to total employment and GDP across different income groups. A marked increase is observed in the SME sector's contribution to total employment from the low- to the high-income countries (over 60 per cent). The SME share of GDP follows a similar trend, almost doubling from around 20 per cent of GDP in the low-income countries to over 40 per cent in high-income countries.

These data are somewhat misleading, however, as they exclude the informal agriculture sector and own-account workers in the informal economy – both are substantial in developing countries. When agricultural and own-account workers are included, the overall share of small-scale activity of all types in the economy is greater in developing than in developed countries. The overall share of small-scale activity must therefore integrate the informal economy, as many SMEs in developing countries are operating in the informal economy.

The informal economy and small-scale activity

As stated above, a significant portion of the labour force in low-income countries works for, or owns and manages, micro-enterprises in the informal economy. The

Table 5.3. Distribution of employment in manufacturing (%), according to size-class, selected economies, 1999 (or nearest available year)

Economy	0-9	10-49	50-249	250+
Czech Republic	5.3	16.1	26.8	51.8
Germany	7.4	15.1	23.2	54.5
Denmark	7.8	19.2	26.3	46.6
Sweden	7.9	15.5	21.2	55.5
Belgium	8.1	19.7	20.4	51.7
Norway	9.1	21.1	28.3	41.6
United Kingdom	9.4	17.9	25.7	47.0
Finland	10.3	14.1	20.2	55.4
France	10.3	20.1	22.3	47.3
Korea, Republic of	10.5	29.9	26.4	33.3
Austria	11.0	18.7	27.0	43.3
Japan	11.1	28.3	29.8	30.7
Netherlands	11.7	27.1	28.1	33.1
Italy	12.8	36.3	23.2	27.7
Australia	14.1	20.5	17.8	47.7
Switzerland	15.4	21.3	29.2	34.1
New Zealand	18.3	24.2	22.9	34.7
Spain	18.5	33.5	21.4	26.6
Mexico	18.9	12.0	21.5	47.6
Iceland	20.3	33.5	46.2	10.0
Portugal	27.5	32.4	24.1	16.1
Turkey	34.0	10.5	19.8	35.8

Note: Countries ranked from lowest to highest according to distribution of employment and enterprise size.
Source: OECD, 2002.

informal economy may be defined as all unreported income from the production of goods and services that would generally be taxable if reported to the state authorities.[9] A similar but much broader definition is adopted by the ILO, which refers "to all economic activities by workers and economic units that are – in law or in practice – not covered or insufficiently covered by formal arrangements ... or are operating outside the formal reach of the law".[10] Most SMEs (mainly micro-firms) in developing countries are operating in the informal economy and thus are not recorded in official data. Larger firms find it impossible to operate in the informal economy because of their visibility and size. The SME sector and the informal economy are thus closely linked.

In Africa, for example, the size of the informal economy as a share of GNP is considerable, at around 41 per cent.[11] For Asia, the average size of the informal

[9] Schneider, 2002.

[10] Resolution adopted by the International Labour Conference at its 90th Session, 2002: GB.285/7/2, Resolution concerning decent work and the informal economy, Nov., p. 5. For more details see ILO's website on the informal economy at www.ilo.org/infeco

[11] Schneider, 2002.

Figure 5.2. Contribution of SMEs to employment and GDP, 1990-1999 (average values)

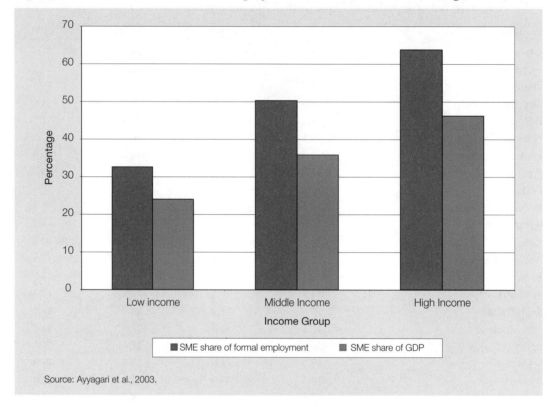

Source: Ayyagari et al., 2003.

economy share is 26 per cent of GNP. However, this figure needs to be seen in perspective since Asia is home to developed economies such as Japan, Singapore, and Taiwan, China. Thailand has the largest informal economy share, at around 53 per cent of GNP, followed by Sri Lanka at 45 per cent and the Philippines at 44 per cent. India has 23 per cent,[12] while China has 20 per cent. At the lower end are Singapore and Japan with shares of 13 and 11 per cent, respectively. In Latin America and the Caribbean, the average size of the informal economy share is 41 per cent of GNP, similar to the figure for Africa. The transition economies have on average a 38 per cent share of GNP, with the highest percentage in Georgia, at around 67 per cent, and the lowest in the Slovak Republic at 19 per cent.

The developed economies of Western Europe have an informal economy ranging from 29 per cent for Greece to 9 per cent for Switzerland. The average size of the informal economy is 18 per cent in these economies. Outside Europe, Canada has an informal economy representing around 16 per cent, followed by Australia with 15 per cent, New Zealand with 13 per cent and the United States

---

[12] These data, however, exclude the agriculture sector, which is largely informal and often at subsistence level in developing countries. To take one example, India's informal economy would employ over 90 per cent of the labour force – if these data were included.

Figure 5.3. Informal economy and levels of development (measured as GDP per capita)

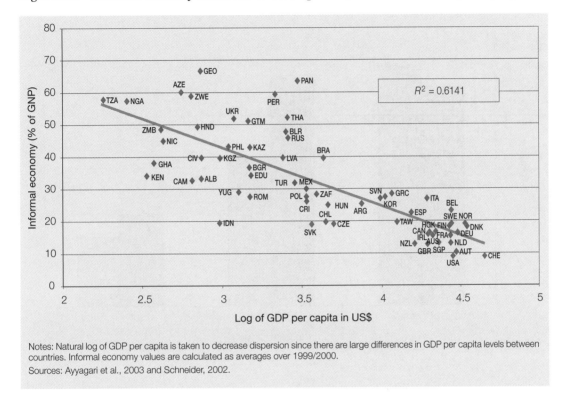

Notes: Natural log of GDP per capita is taken to decrease dispersion since there are large differences in GDP per capita levels between countries. Informal economy values are calculated as averages over 1999/2000.

Sources: Ayyagari et al., 2003 and Schneider, 2002.

at 9 per cent. Figure 5.3 demonstrates that as countries develop (measured by GDP per capita), the size of the informal economy decreases.

Figure 5.4 shows a steady decline in the contribution of the informal economy to GDP, from low- to high-income countries. The informal economy's contribution to *total* employment also shows a general decline from the low- to the high-income group, although it increases slightly in the middle-income group.

Exports by SMEs

SMEs are also an important source of export revenues in some developing countries. Information on the SME shares of manufactured exports in selected East Asian and African developing economies and OECD countries[13] is provided in table 5.4, which clearly demonstrates the export potential of small firms, although it implies that size thresholds may have a role to play in that potential. It should be noted that African countries which define size thresholds at fewer than 50 employees do not compare favourably with those countries whose definitions are based on a higher employment threshold.

---

[13] OECD, 2004.

Figure 5.4.   Informal sector contribution to employment and GDP, 1990-1999 (average values)

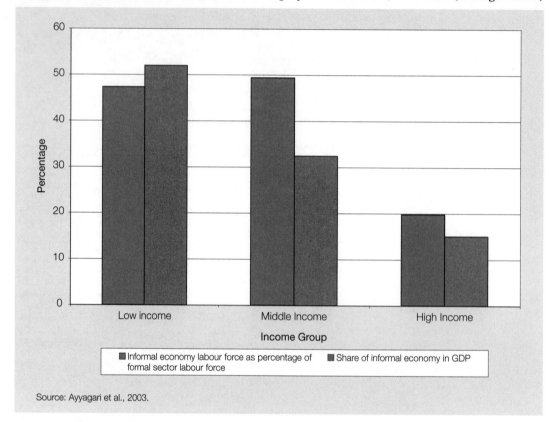

Source: Ayyagari et al., 2003.

5.2.   The productivity divide

A review of the research on small enterprises regarding productivity and employment reveals that productivity tends to rise with enterprise size: small enterprises are typically less productive than large ones. A second characteristic is that wages in small enterprises[14] tend to be lower and workers' rights and conditions tend to be less adequate (i.e. job quality is lower) in such enterprises. Taken together, these characteristics indicate that a significant proportion of the workforce in many economies earn lower wages, with fewer rights, in small, low-productivity establishments.

The bias of "labour productivity" in comparing small and large enterprises

Productivity is a relationship between output and inputs. It rises when an increase in output occurs with a less than proportionate increase in inputs, or when the same output is produced with fewer inputs.

As has been discussed in other chapters of this Report, much of the research on productivity is based on the indicator of labour productivity. This measure is

---

[14] Unless indicated otherwise, the term "small" here groups enterprises normally classified as micro-, small and medium. The actual size of such enterprises varies according to country-specific definitions.

Table 5.4. SME shares of manufactured exports, selected years and economies

Economy	Year	Definition of the SME*	Share of SME manufacturing exports in total manufacturing export (%)
Developing economies			
China	Early 1990s	< 100 employees	40-60
Korea, Republic of	1995	< 300 employees	42.4
Viet Nam	Early 1990s	< 200 employees	20
India	1991/1992	< Rs 30 m investment in plant and machinery	31.5
Singapore	Early 1990s	< 100 employees	16
Malaysia	Early 1990s	< 75 employees	15
Indonesia	Early 1990s	< 100 employees	11
Thailand	Early 1990s	< 100 employees	10
Mauritius	1997	< 50 employees	2.2
Tanzania	2002	< 50 employees	<1.0
Malawi	2003	< 50 employees	<1.0
OECD economies			
Denmark	Early 1990s	< 500 employees	46
France	1994	< 500 employees	28.6
Sweden	Early 1990s	< 200 employees	24.1
Finland	1991	< 500 employees	23.3
Japan	1991	< 300 employees	13.3
United States	1994	< 500 employees	11
Average for 6 OECD economies			**24.4**

*Definition varies according to the official national definition of an SME.
Source: OECD, 2004.

relatively easy to calculate and is practical in the sense that it allows for comparison of trends between countries. It is not always the best measure, however, and while its deficiencies may not pose grave concerns in general cross-country comparisons, they elicit a particular problem in comparing large and small enterprises, as explained below.

Labour productivity is a single-factor measure. It results from a calculation of value added, which is then divided by the amount of labour used.[15] When the number of people employed is taken as denominator, it is called "value added per worker". Despite its name, labour productivity is increased when value added rises through the better utilization and coordination of *all* factors of production. Value added may increase when labour is working smarter, harder, faster or with better skills, but it also increases with the use of more or better machinery, a reduction in the waste of input materials or the introduction of technical innovations. Indeed, any non-labour factor that raises value added will

---

[15] This comprises either the number of people employed or the number of hours worked. The latter would be a more precise measure but again, because of data restrictions, the number of employees is more often used.

raise labour productivity. The term "labour productivity" is therefore correct in that any non-labour change which increases value added makes workers more productive, but is slightly misleading in that it denotes productivity in general and not that which specifically involves workers.

A productivity increase can allow for greater returns to the factors of production. If the increase in labour productivity arises from better trained, better treated or more efficient workers, it can support higher wages. If the increase in labour productivity arises from the use of additional or more productive machinery, however, it will also be reflected as an increase in labour productivity. This implies that enterprises with high capital investment should always have higher labour productivity. Statistics comparing the labour productivity of large firms with that of small firms (which normally exhibit lower capital investment) thus contain a systematic bias.

A second bias exists in the empirical research. Much of the work focuses on data gathered from industrial censuses or surveys of manufacturing firms. Manufacturing – the making of products – is much more affected by economies of scale (the more that is produced, the cheaper it gets) – than service activities. A large proportion of small-enterprise activity takes place in services, notably trading but also food service, repair work and personal services.

And there is a third bias – one that is purely definitional. While the relationship is perhaps not a linear one, productivity levels do seem to correlate with firm size, with employment quantity being the most common measure. If, by definition, a "small" firm is defined as having fewer than 500 employees in one country (United States), and only 50 in another (United Republic of Tanzania), then the productivity gap between large and small firms is likely to be understated in the former and overstated in the latter.

The extent to which these biases affect the data is not known and requires further research. Despite the limitation of "labour productivity" as a measure, much of the available evidence is based on it.

Cross-regional evidence of a size–productivity gap

A positive correlation between enterprise size and labour productivity is evident across the main regions of the developing world – that is, large firms are more productive. Table 5.5 indicates that the productivity of SMEs in the formal economy[16] in ten Latin American economies ranges from one-quarter to three-quarters of that of large enterprises. Over time, the gap has decreased in half the countries surveyed but increased in the other half, suggesting no long-term regional trend.

Data for seven sub-Saharan African countries show similar results in table 5.6, with productivity rising through the five firm-size categories. There are anomalies, though, in Kenya, Côte d'Ivoire and Cameroon, which exhibit lower productivity in the largest size category relative to the second largest size cate-

---

[16] Not including micro-enterprises.

Table 5.5.   Relative productivity: SMEs and large enterprises in Latin American economies, selected years

Economy	Base year	Final year	SME productivity as a percentage of large enterprises	
			Base year	Final year
Argentina	1984	1993	44	57
Brazil	1985	1997	61	77
Chile	1990	1996	41	38
Colombia	1991	1996	48	45
Costa Rica	1990	1996	63	73
Ecuador	1991	1996	44	40
Mexico	1988	1993	48	56
Peru	1992	1994	33	25
Uruguay	1988	1995	53	48
Venezuela	1990	1995	22	25

Note: SMEs are defined according to official national definitions.
Source: Peres and Stumpo, 2000, table 9.

Table 5.6.   Value added per worker index, according to enterprise size, selected African economies, 1990s (250+ worker category=100)

Enterprise size (no. of workers)	Cameroon	Côte d'Ivoire	Ghana	Kenya	Tanzania, United Republic of	Zambia	Zimbabwe
0-9	28	13	22	56	39	38	44
10-49	41	53	35	118	38	67	63
50-99	111	69	33	119	61	65	79
100-249	113	103	72	165	55	71	81
250+	100	100	100	100	100	100	100

Note: Enterprise size based on number of workers.
Source: Mazumdar and Mazaheri, 2001, p. 37.

gory. This is probably due to a large number of relatively unproductive, state-owned firms in this category. Figures for four East Asian countries, including Japan, again show a very consistent pattern of labour productivity rising through ever-larger size categories, as table 5.7 shows.

The data presented above reveal that SMEs are indeed less productive compared to larger firms in most countries of the world. How then do SMEs compete with larger firms and still manage to survive? The following section explores this question.

5.3.   How do small enterprises survive?

Combining the productivity and employment figures, it appears that many workers in the developing (and developed) world are employed by enterprises with relatively lower labour productivity and consequently low incomes. In view of

Table 5.7.   Value added per worker index, according to enterprise size, East Asia, selected years (500+ worker category=100)

Enterprise size (no. of workers)	Rep. of Korea	Japan	Hong Kong, China*	Taiwan, China
5-9	31	32	54*	34
10-49	42	39	61	35
50-99	59	50	66	38
100-199	56	59	71	49
200-499	81	76	82	—
500+	100	100	100	100

Note: Figures are based on an index relative to the labour productivity of the 500+ category.   * = 1-9 workers. Data years as follows: Rep. of Korea (1986), Japan (1987), Hong Kong, China (1982), Taiwan, China (1986).
Source: Mazumdar and Mazaheri, 2001, p. 37.

the productivity gap, the burning question is: How do small firms survive? It is possible that the small enterprises may represent a temporary phenomenon.

Are small firms a transitional phenomenon?

Over time and as countries develop, small firms may be forced from the market by larger firms. For example, Anderson (1982) demonstrated the evolutionary phases of firms: beginning with household and artisan-level firms being replaced by small firms with wage labour, then medium-sized firms taking over and, at a later development stage, large firms becoming dominant. This line of argument was later studied by Little et al. (1987) who confirm the idea of phases of development and the eventual decline of small firms.

This argument is based on two hypotheses known as the "output composition effect" and the "social relations–economies of scale effect".[17] The theory of the output composition effect argues that as income rises, the share of manufacturing output of consumer products (produced by small firms) declines, resulting in the decreasing importance of small firms in terms of employment and output. The second line of argument deals with the notion that as countries develop and their business and financial environment becomes more sophisticated, small-scale family-based firms are gradually squeezed out of the process, since they do not possess the competitive advantage and economies of scale required to survive.

One study shows that as income increases, the share of employment in the SME manufacturing sector increases. This is partly explained by the fact that as countries develop, their capital markets strengthen, which leads to firms being operated more professionally along business lines. In addition, education also plays some role in the supply of skilled labour. In the initial stages of development, foreign investment is more crucial in the manufacturing sector than at later stages.

---

[17] According to Weeks, 2003, p. 340.

Regarding the formal economy, a study of the manufacturing sector in nine developed and developing countries shows a diversity of SME experiences over time.[18] Over periods ranging from 20 to 45 years, small enterprises in five countries captured a greater share of total formal manufacturing employment, as table 5.8 shows. In the four other countries, however, the small-enterprise share declined. The increase of employment in manufacturing was more rapid in the medium-sized firms.

Another study demonstrates that the share of manufacturing employment in SMEs has dropped only marginally in Japan during the long period of post-war industrialization. Between 1955 and 1994, this share declined only 2.5 percentage points to 53.2 per cent.[19]

Similar results are evident for ten Latin American countries in the 1980s and 1990s as table 5.9 shows. With periods ranging from two to 15 years, total employment in the formal SME sector grew in Chile, Columbia, Mexico and Peru, fell in Argentina, Brazil, Costa Rica, Ecuador and Uruguay and was relatively stable in Venuzela (Peres and Stumpo (2000), table 9).

A long-running debate continues in the United States on the employment contribution of small firms. The question is not whether employment in SMEs is declining but whether these firms create more net jobs than large firms. Early studies showed that small firms indeed created more jobs than large firms, thus suggesting that small firms were not being squeezed from the market due to

Table 5.8. **Change in SME share of total manufacturing employment, selected countries, selected periods, 1950s–1990s**

	Period		Small (10-49)[a]		Medium (50-499)[a]	
	Base year	Final year	% in final year[b]	Change from base year (%)	% in final year	Change from base year (%)
Economies with increase in small enterprise share of total employment						
Brazil	1960	1980	24	3.5	55	7.2
France	1962	1990	19	4.3	36	2.8
Hong Kong, China	1951	1996	34	11.5	47	–2
Japan	1967	1990	33	2.4	43	3
United States	1967	1987	15	3.6	47	5.9
Economies with decrease in small enterprise share of total employment						
Colombia	1956	1990	21	–10.5	n/a	n/a
Korea, Republic of	1958	1990	22	–21.5	39	n/a
Pakistan	1954	1988	11	–7.8	33	12.1
South Africa	1950	1988	12	–6.1	48	–4.2

Notes: [a] Number of employees per enterprise; [b] share of total manufacturing employment accounted for by small enterprises in final year.
Source: Weeks, 2002, pp. 13-14.

[18] Weeks, 2002.
[19] Mazumdar, 1998, p. 47.

Table 5.9. Production, employment and productivity in SMEs in the formal economy manufacturing sector, Latin America, 1980s-1990s

Economy	Base year = 100	Comparison year	Change in index value relative to base year		
			Production (Gross output)	Employment	Productivity
Argentina	1984	1993	148	76	195
Brazil	1985	1997	111	86	130
Chile	1990	1996	156	134	116
Colombia	1991	1996	116	111	104
Costa Rica	1990	1996	123	79	155
Ecuador	1991	1996	109	93	117
Mexico	1988	1993	149	117	127
Peru	1992	1994	117	108	108
Uruguay	1988	1995	103	75	137
Venezuela	1990	1995	95	98	96

Source: Peres and Stumpo, 2000, table 9.

economies of scale or other sources of higher productivity.[20] Measuring net job creation accurately is difficult, however, partly because over time the threshold is crossed that distinguishes small firms from large ones. The most refined study of net employment creation, using data from 1973 to 1988, showed no relationship between firm size and net employment growth.[21] While this and other studies revealed that job creation rates are higher in small firms, so too are job destruction rates, an observation that also applies to developing countries.

A study of Taiwan, China concluded that small enterprises exhibiting higher productivity are most likely to achieve net employment gains.[22] On the other hand, evidence for ten Latin American countries is inconclusive, as table 5.9 shows.[23] In general, productivity increases for the formal SME economy as a whole were associated with increased SME employment in some countries and decreased levels in others. In sum, no clear trend emerges at a global level to conclude that increases in SME productivity will lead to higher rates of employment growth. It depends upon what happens to output. There is little evidence, therefore, that the productivity gap will result in the decline of the small-enterprise sector over time. The question thus remains: How is it that small firms are not driven from the market by more productive firms?

Why aren't small firms driven from the market?

The most likely answer is that small enterprises do not compete directly with larger firms. Instead, they find advantageous niches for small firms. Kiosks for food and household goods that bring products closer to consumers are one

---

[20] Birch, 1979 and 1987.

[21] Davis et al., 1996.

[22] Aw and Batra, 2001.

[23] Peres and Stumpo, 2000.

example. Service activities, such as restaurants and vehicle repair shops, are another. In addition, the market may be limited and specialized, with small firms filling specific niches, often in clusters and/or as subcontractors for large enterprises. In these cases, competition takes place with other small, less productive firms. Finally, small and large firms often cater to different segments of the market. Even when they are ostensibly producing the same product, the attributes are most likely to be different: for example, the washing soap or cloth manufactured in small units has less of the luxury elements likely to appeal to high-income consumers.[24]

When small firms do produce goods similar to those made by large firms, they often produce at lower quality levels, thus avoiding direct competition. In poor countries, there are large markets for low-quality but affordable goods purchased by the poorer sections of the community.[25]

The implications of economic "dualism"

As discussed above, many developing countries are characterized by a rather strict cleavage between small, less productive firms and large, more productive ones. This can be taken as evidence of a "dualistic" economy, which is measured not only by differences in enterprise size but, as will be seen, also by differences in livelihoods and standards of living. Such "dualism", moreover, is apparent also in industrialized countries. The classic example is Japan. Its dualistic pattern of industrialization has a long history, whose roots are in the initial conditions of labour abundance during Japan's industrialization (which contributed to labour market segmentation) and the simultaneous development of a complex large industry, of the State and of financial conglomerates that accentuated capital market "dualism" (discussed below).

Some other less developed countries in Asia – India, Indonesia, the Philippines – all share with Japan the dualistic pattern in their modern (formal) manufacturing sector.[26] The productivity difference between the small and the large size-groups of firms is much larger in these Asian countries than in Japan. Thus, while the surplus labour situation in Asian countries causes the dualistic pattern to emerge in a wide variety of Asian economies, Japan had succeeded (by the mid-1980s) in narrowing the gap in productivity between small and large firms that typically characterizes dualistic development. Doubtless there are many explanations for this. An important one is likely to be the growing integration through subcontracting of the small-firm sector with larger firms – an integration that compelled the upgrading of efficiency and quality standards in small firms. This is an issue of policy relevance to which discussion will return.

---

[24] Little et al., 1987.

[25] It is also true that the statistics provided above are very general; many small enterprises (especially but not exclusively in developed countries) will achieve levels approaching those of large firms.

[26] It should be emphasized that the data sets considered here exclude very large household and other parts of the informal sector in establishments employing less than 5 workers.

Asian economies such as those of India, Indonesia, and the Philippines have in common a large labour force in household manufacturing units, which is slowly shifting to the non-household manufacturing sector. The lack of technical dynamism of the small-scale sector reflects its limited upward mobility, leading to the phenomenon of depressed relative labour productivity in small enterprises and the phenomenon of the "missing middle" – or the absence of intermediate-size establishments. All three economies have had their fair share of import-substituting industrialization, characterized by significantly sheltered domestic product markets, which was not particularly conducive to the dynamic growth of SMEs. As far as factor markets are concerned, evidence suggests that industrial and financial policies contributed to there being a marked degree of difference in access to capital: it was available at low cost to large firms, and either not available, or available at high cost, to small firms. The dual consequence of this was, first, to favour the use of capital-intensive techniques in the large-scale sector, and therefore to bias against employment creation there and, second, to curb the growth of small firms.

In short, the stunted growth of dynamism in the small-firm sector is both a reflection and a cause of the failure of greater integration occurring between a relatively unsophisticated small-firm sector and a more dynamic large-firm one. Narrowing the dualistic extremes results, among other things, from greater integration between small and large firms as, again, was likely a factor at work in Japan.

A large difference in levels of productivity and wages between small and large firms implies that the economic distance between the small- and large-firm sectors is wide. Policies designed to shift resources to the SME sector would seem to be called for. But merely increasing employment in the small-scale sector is not enough if wide productivity differentials with large firms persist. In a world of excessive underemployment, employment increase is not only a goal in itself; increasing decent and productive employment is. This would need to be accompanied by measures to reduce the economic distance between large and small firms. And this in turn entails a focus on increasing employment and productivity in SMEs at the same time.

5.4. Social dimensions of the productivity gap

The avoidance of direct competition may answer the productivity–employment question, but it remains true that small firms are producing less value added per worker. This affects the returns that such firms can pay to their owner(s) and their workers. *The concern with small enterprises is not specifically that they exhibit low productivity but that, because of low productivity, the wages they pay to workers and the income they generate for owners may not be sufficient to support a decent standard of living.* Owners and workers may be working but their work may not allow them to exit from poverty.

While low productivity can limit wages and income, it must also be recognized that low wages can limit productivity. This notion, known as the "efficiency wage theory", suggests that raising wages can have an incentive effect on the recruitment and retention of efficient workers and on their motivation within the enterprise. Raising wages to improve productivity will only work up to a certain point, of course, but can be part of a broad strategy to raise productivity. Indeed, different economic theories have demonstrated that wage growth restraint retards labour productivity growth.[27]

The connection between wages/income and poverty is fairly direct. Poverty is partly measured in terms of material well-being, including such physical essentials as adequate food, clothing and shelter and is partly related to essential services such as education, water, sanitation and health care. The ability of a household to provide these essentials is based partly on its capacity to purchase them, partly on its capacity to self-supply them and partly on the receipt of services (at low or no cost) from public agencies. If, as shown above, small-scale activities account for the majority of income-generating possibilities for poor people, then such activities are most important in the struggle against poverty, because they allow the purchase of essentials and a more decent living standard.

Generally, both paid and self-employment will help to reduce the income aspects of poverty if they support:

i)   a move from underemployment and unemployment to employment;

ii)   a rise in the total wages and benefits paid to poor employees (including informal employees and family workers);

iii) a rise in the income from low-paying self-employment (including the movement from underemployment to fuller employment);

iv)   a more general, long-term shift in an economy from lower paid informal, dependent or self-employment to better paid and better protected employment or self-employment.

In addition to insufficient income, poverty is also a condition in which people lack control over their lives and lack security about their future. These issues are closely related to aspects of decent work, notably workers' rights and social dialogue (empowerment issues) and social protection. They can also have an impact on the productivity of enterprises both in the motivation and retention of workers and in the way that work is organized. This point is discussed below.

The wage gap

Because of the differences in labour productivity between small and large firms, wages are also different in these firms.[28] This is unsurprising as low productivity is likely to have an impact on holding wages down and, simultaneously, low wages can limit productivity, as discussed above. In interpreting wage data, it is important to recall that wages will tend to be lower for workers with fewer skills and less experience. Thus, wages may be lower generally in small enterprises if

---

[27] Naastepad and Kleinknecht, 2004.

[28] Mazumdar and Mazaheri, 2001.

they hire less qualified personnel, which owners tend to do. Dualism thus also implies segmentation in access to education and skills. Low wages can be explained wholly or in part, on this basis. Unfortunately, comparisons of wage differences between small and large enterprises do not usually account for differences in skills and experience.

Table 5.10, based on evidence from two Asian and two Latin American countries, confirms the wage gap. On average, wages in small[29] formal manufacturing enterprises are about two-thirds of the level found in large enterprises. Medium firms are closer, at four-fifths. Note that for more developed countries (Hong Kong, China and the Republic of Korea), the gap is narrower than for less developed countries (Brazil and Colombia). In Hong Kong, China wages in medium and large firms are the same. In all cases, the percentage gap between wages is less than the gap in productivity.

A similar wage gap can also be observed in Africa.[30] For example, wages in formal micro-enterprises in Ghana were one-quarter of those paid in large firms. The average monthly wage for micro-firms was slightly above the minimum wage, possibly suggesting that workers from micro-enterprises tend to escape the official poverty line. Similar results are also found in the United Republic of Tanzania.[31]

Given the difference in efficiency and wage levels when small and large firms are working in segmented markets, a reallocation of employment to

Table 5.10. Wage and productivity gaps, according to enterprise size, 1960-1980 and 1970-1989

Economy[a]	Years[b]	SME value added per worker as % of that for large enterprises	SME average wage as % of that for large enterprises
Brazil	1960-80		
Small[c]		56	64
Medium[c]		76	80
Colombia	1970-89		
Small		46	50
Medium		70	71
Hong Kong, China	1977-90		
Small		66	91
Medium		89	100
Korea, Republic of	1970-91		
Small		41	69
Medium		74	81

Notes: [a] No. of total observations for each country: Brazil 270; Colombia 360; Hong Kong, China 195; Rep. of Korea 360. [b] Observations for five years within the time period given in the second column. [c] Small = 10-49 workers, medium = 50-499, large = 500+.

Source: Weeks, 2002, p. 17.

---

[29] Here, small formal enterprises do not include micro-enterprises.

[30] Mazumdar and Mazaheri, 2001.

[31] Goedhuys, 2002.

smaller firms (after markets become more integrated) might imply that SMEs will be forced to upgrade their labour quality. For example, if SMEs participate more extensively in export markets after a change in economic policy, they would need to be more selective in their labour recruitment and more intensive in labour training if they are to attain the quality of product and marketability required by world markets. This would tend to increase the wage level in such firms and reduce the wage difference with respect to large firms.

In order to understand the earnings and wages of small firms, it would be worthwhile to study the nature of small firms in developing countries and, indeed, small-scale activity generally. Very often, firms are of extremely small size in developing countries. These are micro-firms operating in the informal economy each of which has an owner, or a few helpers, who are usually family members.

Micro-entrepreneurs in the informal economy

Most enterprises in developing countries consist of very small, "survivalist" activities, operated mainly by poorer sections of the community. They exist alongside more substantial, competitive small enterprises, which generate greater returns for their owners. These differences will have a great bearing on the extent to which enterprise activities allow their owners to escape from poverty and achieve a decent standard of living.

An estimated 60 per cent of those earning a living in the informal economy are self-employed.[32] Thus the micro-entrepreneur is often the sole person working for the "enterprise".[33] The entrepreneur pays no wages as a result. Any increase in productivity will depend solely on the actions of the entrepreneur (possibly with the aid of family members) and will translate directly into household income. Any financial gain that occurs is shared not with outside workers but with family members. Critical decisions for poor households relate to the division of any gains between consumption, savings and re-investment in the enterprise.

Many micro-entrepreneurs start a micro-enterprise because they cannot find paid work. Being poor, they have very little capital, which forces them to concentrate on activities where investment and working-capital requirements are low.[34] As a result, a large number of poor people are drawn towards similar types of activities. Together, they generate an abundant supply of simple goods and services that keeps competition high and prices, sales and profits low. Nevertheless, many vendors and artisans are underemployed. They remain the whole day at their street stand or in their shops, selling very little but unwilling to produce more because they are already surrounded by unsold finished goods.

---

[32] In some African countries, this figure rises to over 90 per cent (ILO, 2002, p. 20).

[33] Often the owners would not perceive their activities as bona fide "enterprises".

[34] The productivity of the self-employed is affected by the capacity to invest in tools and goods. However, women typically have less access to and control over resources to support their work. Among the informal sector activities of the poor in Dhaka, Bangladesh, for example, women were more likely to be engaged in home-based activities "involving small amounts of capital which generate less earnings" (Salway, et al., 2003). On average, women owned less goods by value and lower valued tools and equipment than men. See also ILO (2004a).

Their poverty trap is reinforced; they lack the capital to engage in more productive, higher-value work and their lack of productive work limits the surplus they can generate to invest in their enterprise. This is one reflection of the poverty trap in developing countries where the effects of poverty then become its causes. The issue here is how to break this cycle of poverty.

As table 5.11 shows, a study of micro- and small enterprises in Kenya found that only 26 per cent of enterprise owners earned an income above the minimum wage.[35] In this situation, the implications for productivity are clear. With no employees or only some family members assisting, there is only a limited basis for increasing productivity through the better management or treatment of the work team. Intra-firm productivity questions relate to the entrepreneur's activities (how efficiently s/he works, how to invest in and manage tools, machinery, inventories, supplies, etc.). Productivity is low – not because work is organized inefficiently, but because there are no incentives and no resources to keep everyone working productively.

In evaluating the productivity of survivalist activities, it is important to recall that this activity may be part of a larger household "multiple livelihood strategy".[36] Such a strategy involves general income from a variety of sources, including: food and cash crop farming, plantation labour, informal enterprise activity, homework/outputting, formal employment in enterprises, and migrant employment in other, richer, countries. A person may derive an income from two or more of these types of employment and family members may contribute income from different types of work activity. Women, because of domestic activities (child-raising, farm work), are more likely than men to take on multiple household activities, although not all may generate income. These roles often include micro-enterprise activity, although women with families are limited in their capacity to engage in such activities on a full-time basis.

Table 5.11. MSE owners earning above the monthly minimum wage, Kenya, 1995

Categories	Percentage of owners earning above minimum wage
All MSEs	26
Gender	
Male-owned	26
Female-owned	23
Education	
Primary or less	24
Some secondary or more	38

Note: MSE = Micro- and small enterprises with 10 workers or less.
Source: Daniels, 1999, p. 61.

---

[35] Daniels, 1999, p. 61.

[36] Bryceson, 2002; Carney, 1998.

Table 5.12. Contribution of MSEs to household income, Kenya, mid-1990s

MSE contribution to household income	% of all MSEs	% of urban MSEs	% of rural MSEs
All or almost all	24	49	15
More than 50%	17	14	18
About 50%	20	15	22
Less than 50%	29	14	34
Negligible amount	10	8	11

Note: MSEs = Micro- and small enterprises with 10 workers or less.
Source: Daniels, 1999, p. 61.

Research on Kenya highlights the existence of these livelihood strategies.[37] Only 24 per cent of micro- and small enterprises, mainly in the informal economy, provide all or almost all of household income, as table 5.12 shows. This aggregate figure hides important differences between urban (49 per cent) and rural (15 per cent) areas, however, as rural landholders have a greater opportunity to rely on food production to support consumption.[38]

For households owning (or renting) land, important decisions about work are made on the basis of productivity and income-earning capacity. If enterprise activities are highly remunerative, then the best use of household labour may be to hire labour for farming and use household labour for non-farm activities. In Honduras, for example, the level of non-farm income contributes significantly to the use of fertilizers on the farms of poor households. This suggests that non-farm employment can raise the productivity of household farming activities and is an example of how farm and non-farm activities impact on each other (see also Chapter 3 of this Report).[39]

Higher incomes for successful entrepreneurs

Many entrepreneurs in the informal, micro-enterprise economy generate a low but decent income, despite evidence of lower productivity. The research to date has tended not to focus on whether enterprise income is above the poverty line but rather on comparisons to a minimum wage (often a proxy for the poverty line) or with formal economy wages.

Research on Peru, for example, has shown that small formal enterprises were between 2.9 and 4.1 times more productive than informal enterprises in the same sectors, as confirmed in table 5.13. However, these differences were not matched by earnings differences of a similar magnitude. Informal entrepreneurs in several sectors earned about nine-tenths of the wages paid to formal-economy employees. In the transport sector, informal operators (notably drivers) earned

---

[37] Daniels, 1999.
[38] This opportunity is not available to the rural landless, of course.
[39] Ruben and van den Berg, 2001.

Table 5.13. Ratios of productivity and income, formal/informal, Peru, mid-1990s

Sector	Labour productivity Formal/informal	Informal income/ Formal wages
Light manufacturing	3.5	0.9
Textiles	3.5	0.9
Construction	2.9	0.9
Transportation	3.3	1.3
Commerce	4.1	0.9
Diverse services	3.6	0.9
Source: Kelley, 1994, p. 1400.		

more than their formal-economy counterparts.[40] Workers may opt for informal activities if micro-enterprise earnings are likely to be higher than wages in the formal economy.

Comparative income data for Mexico indicate that the movement from formal wage employment to informal self-employment results in a 15 per cent *increase* in income.[41] At the same time, the movement from formal wage employment to informal wage employment, in similarly sized enterprises, results in a 12 to 15 per cent income *decrease*. The results depend, in part, on the value of medical and social security provisions that workers receive (and pay for as a deduction from wages) in the formal economy. According to the study, many workers report that the health services are poorly delivered and consequently the health insurance deduction is a loss of income.

The evidence presented in these detailed studies and through the previous discussion regarding survivalist enterprises implies that it may be difficult to generalize about the income earned by SME entrepreneurs. Interventions to help owners lift themselves and their families out of poverty will need to be sensitive to these differences, as policies can easily assist the more successful rather than the poorer entrepreneurs. Box 5.2 explores the question of why SMEs should be subsidized.

Beyond income: The fuller dimension of poverty

While income is an important aspect of poverty, participatory research on the nature of poverty has expanded the frontiers of common understanding. Based on responses from 60,000 poor women and men in 60 countries, the research reveals the importance of political and psychological elements to human well-being.[42] Most notably, these include perceptions of empowerment (control over one's environment) and security (ability to assure one's well-being over time). They are related to physical needs and income, but suggest a longer time frame and the ability and capacity to satisfy one's needs. Such aspects of poverty bear close

---

[40] Kelley, 1994.

[41] Maloney, 1999. The comparison is with net formal sector wages (i.e. after deductions).

[42] Narayan et al., 1999; World Bank, 2000.

Box 5.2.   Do SMEs need to be subsidized?

Reviewing the literature on SME assistance programmes, one can find four economic rationales for subsidies:

- SMEs make special contributions to economic development and poverty alleviation (for example, job creation);
- Market failure creates problems for SMEs in accessing markets and raising technological capabilities;
- Institutional failure raises SME transaction costs, and limits their ability to take advantage of economic opportunities;
- If the two above elements were corrected, firms would need to devise different kinds of strategies, structures, and develop core technical capabilities to respond appropriately to the new market and institutional conditions. This requires considerable costs for the firms.

It is also often asserted that fostering the development of SMEs has beneficial political and equity implications. It is posited that increasing participation of SMEs strengthens dominant values and enhances political stability, thereby promoting economic development and democracy. Moreover, it is stressed that SMEs are owned and run by the poor; hence support for them improves the distribution of income.

In reviewing the rationales for subsidies to promote SME development, one arrives at the general conclusion that a good SME development strategy, first and foremost, is in reality a good "private sector development strategy". However, that being said, there are several areas where a case might be made for selective subsidies.

- First, policy-imposed distortions in some cases may reduce the number of SMEs below efficient levels (i.e. cause extreme size irregularities in the distribution of firms) by imposing fixed costs that bear more heavily on small firms. Removing the policy distortions would be the first order of business in the presence of such problems. However, it is conceivable that a second-best approach, in extreme cases, would involve complementary subsidies to stimulate the formation of more small firms.

- Second, market failure, particularly in the areas of technology transfer, training, and finance often needs to be addressed in developing countries. Interventions to counter such problems, however, would generally be aimed at all firms. But some special size-related issues in these areas also need to be considered. Finance, for example, is a particular case where information and enforcement problems can lead to rationing of small firms from the market. Thus, in addition to programmes to improve financial market development, there may be a need for interventions to assist SMEs in overcoming information and enforcement problems in order to gain greater access to the market. Similar examples apply in the areas of technology transfer and training.

- Third, SMEs need appropriate institutions to prosper. In many developing countries, interventions may be helpful in building up the appropriate *one agency* that deals with small firms. However, as an efficient set of large enterprises is required to develop these appropriate institutional structures for small enterprises, assistance to large enterprises may also be needed to extend their institutional reach to SMEs.

- Fourth, even if policy-makers can effectively intervene with appropriate subsidies to correct market and institutional failure, it is not clear in all countries that SMEs have the prerequisites to respond to the new, subsidy-induced structure of incentives. Often their capabilities are too low, or the learning mechanisms available to upgrade their capabilities too weak to take advantage of incentives. In such cases, interventions should aim to strengthen the existing learning environment and to expand markets for business development services.

Source: Biggs, 2002.

similarity to elements of the ILO's concept of "decent work".[43] Along with the availability of remunerated, productive work, decent work includes rights at work, social dialogue and social protection. Fusing the two approaches provides the following additional poverty elements related to small enterprises and poverty:

i) *Empowerment:* Workers are entitled to freedom of association, collective bargaining and a constructive dialogue with owners and managers on the conditions of work, remuneration and benefits. Empowerment also includes social dialogue at the tripartite level, which allows workers to advocate for better living conditions (health, education, housing, water and sanitation). It also allows the owners/managers of enterprises to dialogue with government on the policy environment.

ii) *Security against income loss:* For workers, security derives in large part from access to social protection against illness, disability, unemployment, old age and the death of a main income earner. For enterprise owners, it also involves freedom from harassment by public officials, the right to hold private property and conduct business, and the right to freedom from expropriation by the State.

For these aspects of poverty, small-enterprise workers and their owners tend to be disadvantaged. The level of unionization is much lower in small enterprises and the rights of workers are often much weaker. This is partly related to the informality of the smallest enterprises, which operate outside of regulation by public authorities. The ILO's efforts to help these operators access the formal economy are aimed at this problem. Small enterprises also lack effective representation vis-à-vis public authorities. In employers' associations and federations, the concerns of small-enterprise members are often overwhelmed by those of larger enterprises. This is changing, however, as many federations have sought to embrace the concerns of small enterprises, and as small enterprises have gradually built themselves representative organizations.

Workers in small enterprises also have less security than those in large enterprises, notably in their access to social protection benefits, such as unemployment insurance, termination payments and health insurance (see, for example, an ILO study on the United Republic of Tanzania).[44]

Such aspects of empowerment and security highlight the lower standards of non-income aspects of poverty. The ILO seeks to raise these standards, where possible, as a contribution to poverty reduction and the promotion of decent work. Like wage increases, non-wage improvements can also contribute to increased productivity. Box 5.3 describes the initiatives to raise productivity taken by the ILO's small enterprises support programme within the SEED (Small Enterprise Development) Unit.

---

[43] ILO, 2000.

[44] Goedhueys, 2002.

Box 5.3. The challenge of raising productivity: ILO/SEED's experiences with job quality

The ILO's small enterprises support programme, IFP/SEED, confronts the productivity challenge by focusing on improvements in work practices – what is referred to as "job quality". It also emphasizes market access in an effort to reduce the problem of underemployment. The overall aim is to create a virtuous cycle in which job quality, along with market access, can raise productivity which can, in turn, result in better wages and income for workers and owners.

By focusing on the work organization aspect of productivity, SEED supports the global productivity movement – a broad approach to increasing productivity which emphasizes the conditions and organization of an enterprise's valuable human resources. It is based on respecting workers' rights, applying international labour standards (including health and safety) and supporting skill training. These changes can reduce work-time loss caused by accidents and injury and can increase the well-being of employees who are better motivated to contribute to enterprise performance. The approach underlines cooperative relations between workers and management, including discussions on the organization of production (such as the quality circle, where workers and managers regularly sit together to discuss how to improve production efficiency and product quality and reduce product defects). Cooperative work practices are designed to empower workers by reducing the distinction between management and labour and allowing the latter to influence production decisions. SEED's contribution to this movement has been to develop curricula for management training and to initiate public awareness campaigns so that the principles of raising productivity through job quality can be transmitted to small enterprises in the developing world.

SEED and productivity

SEED's work has focused on small-business management training. It has recently included social awareness campaigns to reach a large audience regarding the link between job quality/decent work and productivity. Other aspects of SEED's work also contribute to productivity, although not in as direct and focused a manner as the job quality activities. For example, SEED works with governments to create a more conductive policy environment for small enterprises and it works with specific sectoral and business associations to promote decent work and enterprise performance. Its work on market access attempts to increase the demand for goods and services produced or provided by small enterprises in an effort to reduce underemployment or raise the value of output. The full impact of SEED's work on productivity, therefore, is difficult to gauge. Its focus here is on the small-enterprise management training due to its specific goal of increasing productivity and the availability of impact assessments. Assessments are based on specific enterprises and demonstrate the challenge of raising productivity in small enterprises by improvements in job quality.

The ILO has carried out productivity-enhancing programmes in many different sectors in a number of countries. Examples include: improving cleanliness and employee relations in food processing (Ghana); shop-floor conditions and marketing in a brassware cluster (India); drum-making, drumming and driving: a multiple-livelihoods strategy (Trinidad and Tobago); building a kitchen in a small restaurant (Uganda); training workers in paper packaging (Viet Nam). These examples provide

(continued overleaf)

evidence of how the application of job quality can enhance the productivity of small enterprises. Demonstrating the precise impact of small-business management training on productivity is difficult because the training seeks also to support competitiveness and market penetration. While such training does influence the performance of individual enterprises and the lives of their employees, there is a need to expand the impact more broadly across sectors and throughout the economy. SEED's recent work on social awareness, the policy environment, sectoral activities and business associations plays a role. The effects of these activities are part of a wider effort to reinforce the idea that job quality is a key factor for productivity improvement, along with physical capital, skills and technological change.

Source: ILO 2003a.

5.5. Addressing the productivity divide

The heterogeneity of conditions under which small-scale economic activity occurs, from the informal economy street vendor to the dynamic small firm in the formal economy, makes the search for policy prescriptions a complicated one. For example, for many subsistence activities, the basics matter – access to infrastructure, to essential services, to education and health care, to freedom from discrimination – in short, the traditional development agenda. There are, however, other ways in which small firms can address their productivity disadvantage relative to large firms. Here, two organizational models are of particular interest: industrial "clusters" and cooperatives. Both are a means of mitigating the isolation and size disadvantage of the small firm. Both are also a means of generating higher productivity and thus more decent livelihoods.

Encouraging the "collective efficiency" of the small-enterprise sector

It has long been observed that some of the most traditional industries, such as garments, have been able to survive in otherwise high-cost environments (high labour cost and other high production costs), such as northern Italy. How this has occurred is largely a matter of industrial organization associated with the concept of "clustering". Clustering refers to an agglomeration of small firms in physical proximity to one another in the same or related industries. The concept can be thought of as one that balances the competitiveness of the individual firm with cooperation among firms. In turn, this cooperation can be instrumental not only in increasing the efficiency of the individual firm, but also in increasing the "collective efficiency" of the cluster. Clustering is a means of overcoming the competitive disadvantages that confront small firms, acting independently, in relation to larger firms.

Clearly the major disadvantage small enterprises face is that they often lack the potential for economies of scale – that is, the ability to use their existing labour and machinery to respond to increases in demand. Their output thus tends to be small. This, in turn, keeps both productivity and wages low. When groups of firms pool both their inputs (as noted below) as well as share demand in the market, they can achieve economies of scale to the benefit of profits, productivity gains, wage and employment increases.

Clustering can be considered as a means of increasing the productivity and competitiveness of small enterprises (and in so doing reducing the volatility of employment tenure) in two general ways:

1. *increasing the quality and reducing the costs of inputs*: when firms collectively purchase inputs, they typically negotiate a better price, which, in turn, is reflected in lower input costs. There are also advantages in sharing or pooling a number of other business needs. For example, firms could share the cost of training (and, indeed, share the local labour pool), which is a cost-effective way of improving skill levels and disseminating know-how.

2. *increasing the size of the market and reducing the cost of market access*: participation in commercial relations with larger firms is a means of gaining greater market access and thereby increasing output and profits. A common constraint in establishing large firm/small firm linkages is that the small firm lacks the capacity or standards of quality and delivery to service the large firm market. When small firms cooperate to obtain major orders, these constraints can be overcome, and a better price for the firms' products can be negotiated. The latter can occur because small firms acting together have greater "clout" and can also bypass one or several tiers in the value chain.

The foregoing description is necessarily only an outline. There are a host of ancillary advantages when an atomistic or fragmented competitive environment is overcome through clustering, such as access to credit markets on more favourable terms. The advantages, moreover, are not merely economic: they can be part and parcel of a participative local community development strategy.

In discussing clusters, it is appropriate to evoke a concept of "protected stability", since when small firms collaborate, they are better protected against the volatility or instability of markets. Poor groups may also have a particular gender, ethnic or religious composition that restricts access to the means of enhancing their position (see box 5.4). Box 5.5 presents ongoing work conducted by the ILO in assisting a woodworking cluster in Indonesia to meet the challenges of globalization.

The collective advantage of cooperatives

While the concept of clusters does not refer to an ownership structure, the concept of a cooperative does: a cooperative is a firm or a collective of firms, owned by their members, and involved in the production, distribution, or consumption of products. A common feature that cooperatives share with clusters is the organizational concept of overcoming the disadvantages of atomistic competition through a model of inter-firm cooperation.

Box 5.4.   SME clusters: Working to reduce poverty

Clustering – or geographical concentrations of enterprises working in the same industry – can help SMEs compete in local and global markets. Cluster development also helps to reduce poverty, by creating employment, generating income and reducing vulnerability for small producers and poor workers. Two indirect effects on the local economy are creating secondary jobs and attracting service providers.

Numerous examples show small-enterprise clusters in developing countries successfully competing in global markets – from the shoemakers of Brazil's Sinos Valley to the garment producers of Tirippur and Ludhiana in India. Many such clusters began as informal networks in resource-poor regions and at early stages of industrial development. For such communities, clusters offered a gradual and sustained path to industrial growth.

Clustering and poverty: Conceptual links and empirical evidence

Conceptually, clusters and poverty are related in three distinct ways:

- Cluster features: Certain types of clusters can have a more direct impact on poverty. These include rural clusters and, in the urban informal economy, clusters with a preponderance of SMEs, micro-enterprises and homeworkers, clusters in labour-intensive sectors and clusters that employ marginalized and poorer groups of workers, such as women, minority groups, migrants and unskilled labour.

- Cluster processes: Agglomeration economies reduce costs and allow small firms to access markets, thereby raising the capabilities of workers and producers through income and employment. Cluster joint action can take such capabilities further by strengthening the capacity of local firms and reducing their vulnerability to external shocks. The presence of social capital can be critical here, strengthening trust and fostering collaboration. It can also contribute to informal social protection, easing the burden on vulnerable groups.

- Cluster dynamics: Cluster growth produces winners and losers among enterprises and workers, underlining the importance of processes of differentiation. For a poverty reduction agenda, it is critical to note which types of firm (and groups of workers) gain over time and which lose out.

Cluster development provides an important survival and growth opportunity for poor regions in developing countries – from rural artisan clusters that provide critical off-farm incomes to poor households and women workers (Central Java, Indonesia), to urban informal-economy clusters engaged in low-skilled and labour-intensive garment production (Lima, Peru) and vehicle repair (Kumasi, Ghana). Such clusters generate work and incomes for poor, often migrant, households. Moreover, the evidence is clear that producers and workers within clusters fare better in terms of well-being than those in non-clustered settings. In incipient clusters, small producers advance by taking small steps in coordination with others. This allows them not only to survive, but to grow. Local agglomeration economies are salient here, as has been observed in incipient and mature clusters (from rural Indonesia to the urban informal economy of Nairobi, and to the export clusters of Mexico, Brazil, Pakistan and India). Joint action is especially significant, for example, in assisting local producers and workers to confront external shocks. Cooperation through local institutions reduced the vulnerabilities of clustered producers in Sialkot,

Pakistan, and in the Palar Valley, India. Some evidence suggests that social capital in both these areas has strengthened cluster capacities, raising the well-being of local workers and producers. Despite these positive findings, it is also evident that cluster growth trajectories can result in differentiated outcomes. Local linkages often give way to external linkages as outside knowledge and know-how become critical to survival in global markets. Conflicts between the competing interests of large and small firms can become more apparent, with smaller producers often being squeezed. Finally, there are signs that particular categories of workers, especially women and unskilled workers, can lose out as clusters upgrade.

Source: International Development Studies, 2004.

Political thinkers have long suspected that worker ownership has collateral benefits for democracy.[45] Theorists have argued that participative ownership was a training ground for democratic citizenship and citizen involvement. Perhaps the best systematic evidence in support of this claim is a study[46] of three Italian towns with differing amounts of cooperative ownership. The two towns with a higher percentage of cooperative members have lower crime rates, lower rates of domestic violence, more social participation, better developed social networks, and higher trust in authorities. The town with the largest percentage of cooperative members is typically the one with the best of all these outcomes.

The foregoing advantages are not inconsiderable. But does broadened ownership of enterprises by workers, agricultural producers, or small businesses affect enterprise productivity? Do agricultural and small-business cooperatives measure up to conventionally owned firms? A study commissioned by the ILO draws conclusions on this after reviewing literature on farm and small business cooperatives and the relations of these ownership forms to productivity.[47] There are good theoretical arguments for and against a positive relationship between employee ownership and productivity. The results, as in so much of economic theory, appear to depend on the assumptions. But if the theoretical discussion is inconclusive, what does the empirical evidence show?

Most empirical studies (in the developed and developing world) have found that the combination of employee financial ownership together with the ownership right to business information and the right to participate in decision-making, have positive impacts on productivity and other aspects of firm performance. Worker cooperatives provide the full range of such ownership rights.

The cooperative exists for the use of its members. As such, it may act like a conventional company in generating large profits for its owner-members, which it then pays back to them, or it may sell inputs to its members at lower prices and buy outputs from them at higher prices, limiting its net margins or surplus (i.e.

---

[45] Logue and Yates, 2004.
[46] Erdal, 1999.
[47] Logue and Yates, 2001.

Box 5.5. Effects of clustering in the Indonesian woodworking industry

In recent decades, the role of micro-, small and medium enterprises (MSMEs) in employment generation and their important productive capacity has been increasingly recognized by policy-makers throughout the world. However, the potential role of MSMEs is often not fulfilled due to difficulties associated with their size and related difficulties in acquiring resources, maximizing productivity, achieving economies of scale, and gaining a competitive edge to access new market opportunities.

Wood furniture is one of the major manufacturing sub-sectors in Indonesia, contributing 1-1.87 per cent of Indonesian total manufacturing output and adding around 2.7 per cent to the total value of Indonesian exports overall. While these numbers may appear small, they are higher than the share of most other sectors. In 1999, this industry contributed 4.05 per cent to national employment in the manufacturing sector. At the provincial level, the furniture sector is the biggest contributor to the exports from Central Java, with 27 per cent in 2000 and 21.5 per cent in 2001 (according to the Industrial and Trade Office of Central Java), as compared with garments (13 per cent) and textiles (13 per cent).

The geographical distribution of clusters does not come as a surprise. Most are located near the source of raw materials (the Perhutani teak plantations) and have access to roads and ports. Furniture production is primarily a manual process which is labour-intensive. Except in the case of high-volume, mass-produced garden furniture, the process relies on simple technology and artisanal skills. Now, however, times are getting tougher for the industry. Jobs are being lost as the availability of good timber declines and as competition increases from other countries in the region. Globalization is a particular challenge for the independent small firm. For example, from the production perspective, the entry barrier to the woodworking industry is very low. However, the barriers for production firms to enter the export market appear to be significantly higher – investments are steeper, the capabilities needed by management are greater, and it is challenging to establish direct linkages with international buyers, particularly as a first-time exporter.

With the assistance of the ILO, which has undertaken a study of the industry's global value chain, the Central Java timber furniture sector is changing: small and medium enterprises have begun to move away from operating in isolation, by way of linkages with other firms in close geographical proximity – that is, through the establishment of informal clusters. Through greater inter-firm collaboration, small, independent firms can gain greater leverage over global product markets, facilitating their entry into those markets. For example, through clustering, small and medium firms play a more supporting role in the production process, subcontracting to each other so that as a group (or cluster) they can jointly fulfil contract orders. Aside from efficiency gains, such a collaborative approach can pave the way for easier access to new technologies, sharing skills, greater in-house innovative capacity, and new product design capabilities – the results of which are higher value-added activities and a more stable market presence.

Source: ILO, 2004b.

profits) to the minimum necessary for the continuation of the cooperative. When the value added per hour worked in the cooperative is combined with value added by member in farms or enterprises, it may equal or exceed the value added by conventional farms and firms.

The issue is whether productivity is being measured at the level of the individual (cooperative) firm or whether, on the contrary, it is the productivity of the group of firms which is being evaluated. Empirical studies of productivity in individual cooperative firms have found mixed results. Some find that cooperatives have a modest performance edge. Others find that investor-owned firms have a modest performance edge. None takes into consideration, however, the impact of the cooperative on members' productivity.

From the empirical literature, it would seem that farm and business cooperatives have a net positive impact on value added per hour worked when both the individual firm and other member firms of the cooperative are included in the analysis. Indeed, cooperative advocates argue that members join cooperatives precisely for the productivity benefits, so the fact that cooperatives exist establishes that members perceive a benefit. By contrast, conventional economics offers robust analysis of firms only at the individual level, by factoring out externalities like benefits to members in the form of higher prices for their outputs or lower prices for their inputs. Missing in such analyses, therefore, are the *collective* advantages of inter-firm collaboration.

As Chapter 1 of this Report observes, the availability of alternative employment is a factor distinguishing developing from industrial countries. This, in turn, begs the question of how to balance the twin objectives of productivity and employment growth. For people who are largely unemployed, any regular employment makes them more productive than they otherwise were. There is, after all, no productivity in an unemployment line. Since people in developing countries cannot afford to be unemployed, they take up any available job. They are usually underemployed and their working conditions do not fall into the category of "decent employment". [48]

Under these circumstances, the self-help, bootstrap aspect of the cooperative has substantial appeal in developing countries. Cooperatives facilitate people in pooling their greatest asset – their labour – along with small amounts of cash (perhaps all the cash they have), to create a larger enterprise from which they will receive a benefit and return. Under such conditions, the cooperative's members can gain a foothold in the economy, which is another step forward towards economic progress.

As observed above, moreover, there are substantial collateral benefits to cooperatives which may be unrelated to productivity but which are clearly related to the ILO's Global Employment Agenda. [49] If anything, these benefits are likely to be stronger in the developing world and among marginalized

[48] ILO, 2003b.
[49] ibid.

populations in the developed world than in the rich and middle class of the developed countries. They include:

- sufficient economies of scale to make otherwise inefficient small-scale production sufficiently productive in value-added terms to yield higher living standards for the owners and workers of small firms (or small-scale farmers and artisans) and to keep them from joining the ranks of the unemployed;

- the personal and community benefits that accrue from self-organization and bootstrap development – in effect, cooperatives are schools for learning the benefits of collective self-reliance;

- the development of transferable leadership and basic financial skills in poor communities; and

- the likelihood that members of one successful cooperative venture will attempt other cooperative efforts, such as adding a credit union to a successful dairy cooperative, or working with other groups outside the cooperative.

Cooperatives have historically emerged from market failure, from producers' inability to market their crops efficiently, or struggles with monopolistic and exploitative intermediaries. Generally speaking the existence of a cooperative as an alternative mechanism for purchasing and marketing helps to redress those market failures by introducing an element of cooperation and competition, as discussed above. In this way (even for non-member producers), cooperatives increase the efficiency of the market above what it would be in their absence. Last but not least, they increase the income of their members to above what they would earn and own in the absence of cooperatives. Broadening the distribution of income and the ownership of wealth among working men and women improves their life chances and, by improving their economic status, expands their realm of choice and freedom.

5.6. Concluding remarks

Small-scale activities and small firms are important in creating employment and they therefore hold an important key to reducing poverty in developing countries. Despite their handicaps, they are able to survive by operating in different markets as opposed to larger firms. They are clearly instrumental in the reduction of poverty. However, small-scale activities and small firms are less productive compared to larger firms and provide less favourable working conditions to their workers or family members. This productivity–poverty trap limits the potential of increasing the living standards of millions of people.

Because small-scale activities and firms operate in very different environments and settings, one simple policy to shift resources towards small firms will not suffice. Increasing employment will not lead to increasing productivity. These types of activities and firms should be better integrated within the broader economy. What is required is creating decent employment in terms of decent wages, better representation of workers or owners towards public authorities, and better security in terms of social protection and health insurance. This can be achieved by the collective organization of such activities using two avenues.

1.   Clustering – bringing together small firms in a specific physical location and providing them with the necessary infrastructure and services. This in turn will lead to the increase of collective efficiency and thereby overcome the problem of competitive disadvantage.

2.   Promoting cooperatives – which are owned and operated by their members.

Governments should look seriously into the cluster concept in order to provide a conducive environment for small firms to develop through productivity gains. This will lead to better working conditions and reduce poverty by generating employment. The other much older concept of cooperatives should not be overlooked by governments if they want to increase productivity in small firms. These two policy issues are particularly relevant to developing countries.

References

Anderson, D. 1982. "Small industry in developing countries: A discussion of issues", *World Development*, Vol. 10, No. 11, pp. 913-948.

Aw, B.Y.; Batra G. 2001. *Job turnover, firm size and total factor productivity growth: Micro evidence from Taiwan*, Pennsylvania State University, Department of Economics (http://econ.la.psu.edu/Papers/Jobflow.201.pdf).

Ayyagari, M.; Beck, T. 2003. *Small and medium enterprises across the globe: A new database* (Washington, DC, World Bank, World Bank Policy Research Working Paper No. 3127).

Beck, T.; Demirguc-Kunt, A.; Levine R. 2003. *SMEs, growth and poverty: Cross-country evidence* (World Bank, paper prepared for the Conference on Small and Medium Enterprises, 24 October) (http://www.worldbank.org/research/bios/tbeck/sme.pdf).

Biggs, T. 2002. *Is small beautiful and worthy of subsidy? Literature review*, (Washington, DC, World Bank) (http://rru.worldbank.org/Documents/PapersLinks/TylersPaperonSMEs.pdf).

Birch, D. 1979. *The job generation process* (Cambridge MIT Program in Neighbourhood and Regional Change).

—. 1987. *Job creation in America: How our smallest companies put the most people to work* (New York, Free Press).

Bryceson, D. 2002. "Multiple livelihoods in rural Africa: Recasting the terms and conditions of gainful employment", *Journal of Modern African Studies*, Vol. 40, No. 1, pp. 1-28.

Carney, D. (ed.). 1998. *Sustainable rural livelihoods: What contribution can we make?* (London, Department for International Development).

Daniels, L. 1999. "The role of small enterprises in the household and national economy in Kenya: A significant contribution or a last resort", *World Development*, Vol. 27, No. 1, pp. 55-65.

Davis, S.; Haltiwanger, J.; Schuh, S. 1996. *Job creation and destruction* (Cambridge, MA, MIT Press).

Erdal, D. 1999. "Egalitarianism in human evolution", PhD. Thesis, University of St. Andrews, summarized in *Owners at Work,* Vol. 13, No. 2, 2001/2002. A brief summary is available as "People thrive in a social environment characterized by employee ownership" at: http://cog.kent.edu

Goedhuys, M. 2002. *Employment creation and employment quality in African manufacturing firms* (Geneva, ILO, SEED Working Paper No. 26).

Hayashi, M. 2003. *Development of SMEs in the Indonesian economy*, (The Australian National University, Research School of Pacific and Asian Studies, Technical Report Working Papers in Trade and Development No. 2003/01).

Hill, H. 1983. "Choice of technique in the Indonesian weaving industry", *Economic Development and Cultural Change*, Vol. 31, No. 2, pp. 337-353.

International Development Studies (IDS). 2004. *Small firm clusters: Working to reduce poverty*, IDS Policy Briefing, Issue 21.

International Labour Organization (ILO). 2000. *Decent Work* (Geneva).

—. 2002. *Women and men in the informal economy: A statistical picture* (Geneva) (http://www.ilo.org/public/english/employment/infeco/download/menwomen.pdf).

—. 2003a. *Decent employment through small enterprises: A progress report on SEED activities* (Geneva, ILO, Small Enterprise Development).

—. 2003b. *Global Employment Agenda* (Geneva) (http://www.ilo.org/public/english/employment/empframe/practice/index.htm).

—. 2004a. *Global employment trends for women* (Geneva, Employment Strategy Paper No. 8) (http://www.ilo.org/trends).

—. 2004b. *Central Java timber furniture industry: The ILO experience* (Geneva, final report of an ILO/SEED project on the timber industry in Indonesia).

Kelley, B. 1994. "Informal sector and the macroeconomy: A computable general approach for Peru", *World Development*, Vol. 22, No. 9, pp. 1393-1411.

Little, I.M.D.; Page Jr., J.M.; Mazumdar, D. 1987. *Small manufacturing enterprises: A comparative study of India and other economies* (New York, Oxford University Press).

Logue, J.; Yates, J. 2001. *The real world of employee ownership* (Ithaca, NY, Cornell University Press).

—. 2004. "Productivity in cooperatives and worker-owned enterprises: Ownership and participation make a difference!", background paper prepared for the *World Employment Report 2004* (Geneva, ILO); available on the CD-ROM version.

Maloney, W. 1999. "Does informality imply segmentation in urban labour markets? Evidence from sectoral transitions in Mexico", *World Bank Economic Review*, Vol. 13, No. 2, pp. 275-302.

Mazumdar, D. 1998. *Size-structure of manufacturing establishments and the productivity differentials between large and small firms: A comparative study of Asian economies* (University of Toronto, Department of Economics, CIS Working Paper No. 7).

—. 2004. "Employment elasticity in manufacturing", background paper prepared for the *World Employment Report 2004* (Geneva, ILO); available on the CD-ROM version.

Mazumdar, D.; Mazaheri, A. 2001. *The manufacturing sector in sub-Saharan Africa: An analysis based on firm surveys in seven countries*, discussion paper of the World Bank Regional Programme on Enterprise Development.

Naastepad, C.W.M.; Kleinknecht, A. 2004. "The Dutch productivity slowdown: The culprit at last?", *Structural Change and Economic Dynamics*, Vol. 15, No. 2, pp. 137-163.

Narayan, D.; Patel, R.; Schaftt, K.; Rademacher, A.; Koch-Schulte, S. 1999. *Can anyone hear us?* (Washington, DC, World Bank).

Organisation for Economic Co-operation and Development (OECD). 2002. *OECD small and medium enterprise outlook* (Paris).

—. 2004. *Promoting SMEs for development: The enabling environment and trade and investment capacity building*, (Istanbul, background paper for the Second OECD Ministerial Conference on SMEs, 3-5 June).

Peres, W.; Stumpo, G. 2000. "Small and medium-sized manufacturing enterprises in Latin America and the Caribbean under the new economic model", *World Development*, Vol. 28, No. 9, pp. 1643-1655.

Ruben, R.; van den Berg, M. 2001. "Non-farm employment and poverty alleviation of rural farm households in Honduras", *World Development*, Vol. 29, No. 3, pp. 549-560.

Salway, S.; Rahman, R.; Jesmin, S. 2003. "A profile of women's work participation among the urban poor of Dhaka", *World Development*, Vol. 31, No. 5, pp. 881-901.